历代诗词曲英译赏析

Chinese Classical Poems with English Translations & Comments

汉英对照

编译◎刘国善◎王治江◎徐树娟等
校订◎Hon Prof Josephine Bishop

外文出版社
FOREIGN LANGUAGES PRESS

可贵的尝试

刘士聪

百余年来，中外翻译家们出于对中国古典格律诗词的热爱，翻译了包括《诗经》、《楚辞》、唐诗、宋词、元曲等在内的大量作品，为向世界介绍具有悠久传统的中国古典诗词做出了重要贡献；同时，也表现出这些翻译家们在认识到格律诗词英译的艰难时，仍勇敢地接受这一挑战的勇气。

关于诗歌是否可译，历来有不同的认识。有人认为诗歌不可译，美国二十世纪著名诗人罗伯特·弗罗斯特（Robert Frost）说："Poetry is what gets lost in translation."他是说，诗歌一经翻译便丧失了诗意。也有人认为诗歌不但可译，而且可以译得很好。华裔物理学家、诺贝尔奖金获得者杨振宁博士在评论许渊冲的翻译时说："把中国悠久历史上的许多名诗译成英文，译出的诗句富有韵律美和节奏美。"

关于译诗如何翻译才好，历来也有不同主张。有的主张以诗译诗；有的主张也可以以散文译诗；有的主张，原诗既然押韵，译诗也要押韵；吕叔湘认为译诗应以"达意为本，赋形次之"；许渊冲提出"三美"理论；本书译者认为译诗要体现格律，"声趁流波、情遂律动"。总之，如何翻译中国古典诗词，是一个需要继续探索的课题。

序

刘国善、王治江、徐树娟三位先生收集了先秦至唐代的诗歌，唐、五代和两宋的词，以及两宋以来的诗、词和曲，约二百篇，精心将其译成英语。其中有些难度很大，如屈原的《离骚》（节选）、李商隐的《锦瑟》等。这些经典诗作，理解其意尚且不一，翻译起来就更加困难，这是可想而知的。可是译者在准确理解的基础上，运用英诗的韵律和节奏，再现原诗的内蕴和诗意，把诗人的思想和情操表现出来。正如译者所说，"传达情意兼顾韵脚、又遵循Iambics, Trochaics等英诗传统形式"，这是很不容易的。

中国古典格律诗词的修辞非常丰富，翻译过程中修辞格的处理也事关紧要。本书译者对诗词中出现的各种修辞现象都作了相应的考虑，如叠词、反复、排比、对偶、设问等，译文也取得了较好效果。

英译本里加了今译，而且译文很讲究，有的诗味很浓，这不论对外国读者还是对中国读者都十分有必要，为读者理解原诗、批评译文提供了有益的参照。这是此译本的一特色。

不同文化、不同语言之间的翻译之成为可能，一是因为生活在不同文化里的人们有着共同的、或是可以相互理解的思想和感情，二是因为各个文化都能以自己的语言和方式表达这些思想和感情。美国语言学家尤金·奈达(Eugene A. Nida) 说："凡是用一种语言可以表达的内容，用另一种语言也能够表达。"这个说法是成立的。但文化的多元性产生了文学作品形式的多样性。特别是诗歌，一方面特别讲究形式，另一方面在不同文化之间其形式又往往迥异。在内容与形式之间，特别是诗歌的内容与形式之间，翻译时后者更觉困难、更具挑战性。在这方面，中国古典格律诗词的英译尤其如此。

关于汉诗英译的评价，国内译界多有讨论。这对探索汉诗英译的方法，提高汉诗英译的水准，无疑起了积极推动的作用。但有一点不可忽视，即英语读者的反应应予重视，他们是否认可，他们是否欣赏，很重要。因为译诗的主要对象是他们。

多少年来，翻译家们在不断探索如何译诗，取得了可喜的进展和成绩，有的甚至在国际上引起了反响。但也正如本书译者所说，众译家“所要接近或登临的译诗之完美境界，看来仍然只是引导大家奋勇攀援的崇高理想”。

声趁流波 情遂律动

翻译古典诗歌，起码不要误解。王安石《桂枝香》“星河鹭起”可是有鹭腾飞？我们在讲评中点明是鹭洲似起（204页）。通篇难懂之作，我们先行今译，使英译顺理成章。

更高要求是传达韵律。赵元任先生论译诗说“节律跟押韵尤其要紧”（《论翻译中信、达、雅的“信”的幅度》）。为此我们传达情意兼顾韵脚、又遵循Iambics, Trochaics等英诗传统形式，还注意传达原作修辞风格，例如：

1.双叠词——古诗十九首之十“迢迢牵牛星，皎皎河汉女……”六用叠词：

Behold the Cowherd Star so high, high up（抑扬格4音步）
Who's facing the Weaving Maid there fair, fair above.
So slender, slender, her fingers white as snow.
And clicker, clatter, her loom incessant goes…
E'er quiet, across the waters gurgling and dancing,
O longingly, longingly, each at th'other glancing.（37页）

2.三叠词——陆游《钗头凤》“……一怀愁绪，几年离索，错，错，错！”：

Suffusing my heart, my bitter longings thronged;（抑扬格5、3音步）
We parted asunder, thro' lonely years prolonged.

’Tis wrong, ’tis wrong, ’tis wrong!（249页）

3.反复——张养浩《山羊坡·潼关怀古》“兴，百姓苦！亡，百姓苦！”：

Alas, as they rose, all toiling like hell were the folks!（抑扬格、抑抑扬格5音步）

And then as they toppled, suff’ring to death were the folks!（307页）！

4.回还——戴叔伦《转应曲》“……千里万里月明。明月，明月，胡笳一声愁绝。”：

A ... moon is rising brilliant ... A brilliant moon ...（159页）

5.联珠——白居易《上阳白发人》“……一生遂向空房宿。宿空房，秋夜长。夜长无寐天不明。耿耿残灯背壁影，萧萧暗雨打窗声。”英译也用连环与反复：

So at once she was ousted stealthily far away,（抑抑扬格5音步）
And ensconced in such a lonely chamber to stay,
All alone, night in, night out, for the rest of her days.
O nights so long in autumn in the lonely room,
Long nights e’er sleepless; would there be daylight again?
On the wall so faint, faint lit, her shadow loomed.
And pitter-patter tapping the window was th’ rain.（120页）

6.对偶——晏几道《临江仙》词“落花人独立，微雨燕双飞。”：

While lonely I stand ’mid flowers drifting,（抑扬格、抑抑扬格 4 音步）

In pairs the swallows hover, it drizzling.（209页）

7.排比——李煜《乌夜啼》“剪不断，理还乱……”（见186页）

8.设问——马致远《蟾宫曲·叹世》散曲“韩信功兀的般证果？蒯通言哪尽是风魔？成也萧何，败也萧何！”我们也试译成设问形式（译文见303页）

形与神往往浑然一体，缺形似即损神似。倡导神似原则的傅雷也说：“译文须能朗朗上口，求音节和谐；至于节奏与tempo，当然以原作为依归。”（1984商务版《翻译论集》）说的是译散文要讲究“形”之根本的“声”，何况译诗？“声”包括“音美”和第二性的“形美”，“情”包括“意美”或“神韵”。我们追求的是——声情相倚、形神相成；**声趁流波，情遂律动**。趁而且遂，是从外到内化入作品丰韵了吧？传承音律，曲探幽深，就像李白诗云“客心洗流水，余响入霜钟”（《听蜀僧浚弹琴》），常建诗称“曲径通幽处，禅房花木深”（《题破山寺后禅院》）。

法国诗人瓦雷里说，“散文是走路，诗是跳舞”。诗人就像印度大神“湿婆”，在匀称火焰圆环中，以不断的舞蹈、应和着宇宙的韵律与生命的搏动。湿婆三目四臂的舞姿，对应着Apollo七马太阳彩车的巡回。四时不乱，八方不迷。阴阳消长，五行生克。水流荡漾，就连声、光、电子全都依律波动。万象尽逍遥，太和总有序。著译皆丰的卞之琳说：“诗因规律的存在，才成为一种舞蹈，才能获得舞蹈的自由。”

迥异文明背景以相通格律传达，难办啊！连幽情化身的“惊鸿、啼鹃”也是拦路老虎：陆游《沈园》“伤心桥下春波绿，曾是惊鸿照影来”，汤显祖《游园惊梦》“遍青山啼红了杜鹃”。后

例可否作：With cuckoos crying and bleeding, tinted bloody, /Are azaleas abloom across all hillsides so lushy!（315页）。

致力于汉诗翻译的有志之士已相当众多，钱钟书所言“化境”（《林纾的翻译》），即众人所要接近或登临的译诗之完美境界，仍然只是引导大家奋勇攀援的崇高理想。

有人说英美也有“自由诗”，然而，有几篇自由诗像Wordsworth或Longfellow等的名篇那样家喻户晓呢？而李白、杜甫、苏轼、辛弃疾，其名诗名句都可脱口而出。众所熟知的新诗如徐志摩的还是暗含节奏的：

寻梦？ 撑一支 长篙， / 向青草 更青处 漫溯？
满载 一船 星辉， / 在星辉 斑斓里 放歌？
但我 不能 放歌， / 悄悄是 别离的 笙箫。
夏虫也 为我 沉默， / 沉默是 今晚的 康桥！

可见是韵律使诗歌入耳动听。而“叠词”“反复”等辞格，帮助连贯与加强、出神而入化。要让汉诗译品成为英语读者心爱的瑰宝，还应该争取译诗之合律。

深深感谢贾珍霞、王志青、李晓虹、高文艳、曹润宇、陈倩教授，给翻译讲评以宝贵指导；尤其感念恩师熊德兰教授、熊德輗教授：游子面前路迢迢，慈母手中针密密——暂献此编寸草之茸茸，一报师门春晖之煦煦。

编译者

附：

英诗诵读常识之一 ——“抑扬格”常与“抑抑扬格”合用：

Yes! — that was the rea- son (as all men know,

（抑扬格与抑抑扬格交替）

In this king- dom by the sea)

（第二、三音步为抑扬格）

That the wind came out of the cloud by night

（第二、四音步为抑扬格）

Chilling（扬抑）and kill- ing my An- nabel Lee.

(Edgar A. Poc, *Annabel Lee*)

“扬抑格”常与“扬抑抑格”合用；抑抑节拍可含一个音节或三个短促音节：

This is the poem of the air,

(本节开始为规律扬抑抑格）

Slowly in silent syllables re- corded;

(一连-lables re-三轻读音节）

This is the secret of des- pair,

(第二三音步只一个轻读音节）

Long in its cloudy bosom hoarded,

(二三四音步只一个轻读音节）

Now whis- pered and revealed （改抑扬格，一连-pered and re-三轻读音节）

To wood and field.（抑扬格二音步诗行）(Longfellow, *Snow-flakes*)

英诗诵读常识之二 —— 常用的缩略形式、古旧词尾与词形、超常词序：

’d…… had/would	’tween…… between	sick’ning/trav’ler…… 略去非重读的e
’fore…… before	e’er…… ever 略v	comest…… -est 是单数第二人称旧词尾
’gainst…… against	o’er…… over 略v	departeth……-eth 是单数第三人称旧词尾
’mid…… amid	th’east…… the east	doth…… 旧形式相当于 does
’mong…… among	th’west…… the west	thou/thee …… 旧单数主格/宾格/的 you
’neath…… beneath	th’rain…… the rain	thy…… 旧形式单数物主代词your
’pon…… upon	tho’…… though	thine…… 相当于yours 或thy(元音前用thine)
’Tis/’tis……It is/it is	thro’…… through	an islet upon…… 诗中介词可以后置

第一章
先秦、汉、魏、晋、南北朝诗歌

第二章
唐代诗歌

第三章
唐、五代词

第四章
宋代诗词

第五章
元明清诗词曲

第一章

先秦、汉、魏、晋、南北朝诗歌

Chapter 1

Poems Before the Tang Dynasty

关 雎

关关雎鸠，在河之洲。窈窕淑女，君子好逑。
参差荇菜，左右流之。窈窕淑女，寤寐求之。
求之不得，寤寐思服；悠哉悠哉，辗转反侧。
参差荇菜，左右采之；窈窕淑女，琴瑟友之。
参差荇菜，左右芼之；窈窕淑女，钟鼓乐之。

〖今译〗

听着那咕咕而啼的雎鸠，啼唤在河上洲头。
见到那秀美贤慧的姑娘，让人渴慕的佳偶。

参差不齐的荇菜呵，从左边从右边捋在手中。
或是醒来或在梦境，我一心寻觅你采菜的身影。

苦苦寻求，不得相会；清宵枕上，幽梦惊回。
悠悠的神思，神思悠悠；翻过来掉过去，不能入睡。

参差不齐的荇菜呵，从左边从右边摘到手心。
秀美贤慧的姑娘呵，愿弹起瑟、奏起琴，与你相亲。

参差不齐的荇菜呵，从左边从右边采到篮里。
秀美贤慧的姑娘呵，愿敲起钟、打起鼓，与你欢聚。

A *Jujiu* Cooing[1]

On th' islet yonder 'mid running flows, [2] [4音步]
A *jujiu*'s calling, coo-coo, coo!
A graceful maiden comes 'pon the shoal,
And her, a truthful youth does woo.

That water plant named "floating hearts", [3]
Here lush, there sparse, on trailing vines.
That graceful maiden who gathers them,
Both day and night e'er stays in his mind.

He woos, but cannot win her o'er,
In dreams and waking he despairs and sighs.
O longing thoughts, what longing thoughts!
He turns and tosses from side to side.[4]

Here lush, there sparse, the floating hearts,
From th' left, from th' right she picks their leaves.
That graceful gentle maiden he loves,
With lutes and harps he'll have her pleased!

Here lush, there sparse, the floating hearts,
From th' left, from th' right she gathers them afloat.
That graceful gentle maiden he loves,
With bells and drums he welcomes her home!

〖评注〗

(1) 这是《诗经》中第一首。按汉语拼写的 *jujiu* 读如国际音标的['dʒy:dju]（斜体表非英语固有词汇），雎鸠，水禽，鸣声柔美。

(2) 英译最多用抑扬格，对抑扬格四音步诗行，首行注有[4音步]；以下各诗行末所注类同，仅在节律改换或音步增减时，行末改注[扬抑4] [扬抑5] [抑扬6]等。

英诗“轻重相间”的节律主要是：Iambics（抑扬格，轻重音步·—），Trochaics（扬抑格，重轻音步 —·），Anapaestics（抑抑扬格，轻轻重音步），Dactylics（扬抑抑格，重轻轻音步）。

偶有相连的二短音节可读成一个节拍以合音律（参见前言后附注中英诗例句）：

on TH' IS-let YON-der 'mid RUN-ning FLOWS,（-der 'mid二音节读一拍）a JU-jiu's CALL-ing, COO-coo COO! ...（字母全都大写的是重读音节）抑扬格诗句的开头二音节，偶可读成“重轻音步”或两音节双双重读，如二、三节中：BOTH DAY and NIGHT e'er STAYS in his MIND.

O LONG-ing THOUGHTS, what LONG-ing THOUGHTS!

为节律整齐，常有缩略、变序，如 th' islet(the islet), maiden he loves等。

(3) floating hearts（荇菜）因其漂浮心形叶片得名。

(4) tosses and turns, 英语辅音“头韵”；from side to side, 左右来回翻腾。

汉广

南有乔木，不可休思。汉有游女，不可求思。
汉之广矣，不可泳思。江之永矣，不可方思。
翘翘错薪，言刈其楚。之子于归，言秣其马。
汉之广矣，不可泳思。江之永矣，不可方思。
翘翘错薪，言刈其蒌。之子于归，言秣其驹。
汉之广矣，不可泳思。江之永矣，不可方思。

〖今译〗

南山头临风高耸的碧树呵，没有过客能登到它那清荫间歇息。
她便是汉水上自由自在的女神，什么人品才能赢得她的柔情怜惜？
汉江的水面是多么宽广，你再也游不到它的对岸；
长江之流水是多么悠长，你再也绕不到它的水源。

在丛丛错杂的草树中间，要割的只是青青的荆棵；
等到那姑娘成亲过门时，我好来给她喂马、赶车。
汉江的水面是多么宽广，你再也游不到它的对岸；
长江之流水是多么悠长，你再也绕不到它的水源。

在丛丛错杂的草树中间，要割的只是青青的蒌蒿；
等到那姑娘成亲过门时，我好来给她把马驹喂饱。
汉江的水面是多么宽广，你再也游不到它的对岸；
长江之流水是多么悠长，你再也绕不到它的水源。

So Broad is the *Hanjiang*

Atop South Peak a stately arbor stands, [5音步]
With blessed shade no hiker's ever attained. [1]
O'er *Hanjiang* River roams a faerie-like maid,[2]
Whose graces exceed the reach of average swains.
So endless, boundless the *Yangtze*'s waters roll,
Its very source you ne'er can go around.
So amply, broadly the *Hanjiang* spreads its flows,
Its mighty stream you ne'er can swim across.

Among the jumbly, jumbly undergrowth,
The clover alone is sought and mown as forage.
On the day the maid is leaving on her wedding coach,
I'll come to have her horses fitly foddered.[3]
So endless, boundless the *Yangtze*'s waters roll,
Its very source you ne'er can go around.
So amply, broadly the *Hanjiang* spreads its flows,
Its mighty stream you ne'er can swim across.

Among the jumbly, jumbly undergrowth,
The clover sweet is sought and mown as forage.
On the day the maid is leaving on her wedding coach,
I'll come to have her colts decently fodered.
So endless, boundless the *Yangtze*'s waters roll,
Its very source you ne'er can go around.
So amply, broadly the *Hanjiang* spreads its flows,
Its mighty stream you ne'er can swim across.

〖评注〗

(1) 上行arbor（乔木）源出拉丁语，比英语本族词tree要典雅些。stately stands, 辅音头韵。

句中原重读音节即诗行重读处(小写表示轻读)：a-TOP south PEAK a STATE-ly AR-bol STANDS, with BLESS-ed SHADE (that) no HIK-er's E-ver at-TAINED. 少数轻读处两个短促音节读成一拍。

(2) a faerie-like maid, 像仙女似的姑娘。faerie是fairy的变体，诗歌用语。

(3) "之子于归"意指"这姑娘出嫁时"，并非"嫁给我、来我家"。诗经《燕燕》篇写卫君送妹出嫁，说"之子于归，远送于野"；辛弃疾词《贺新郎》写汉女远嫁塞外有"看燕燕，送归妾"句（262页）。因而这是一支单恋之歌，赞美"虽不可得、仍甘奉献"的真情。

蒹葭

蒹葭苍苍，白露为霜。所谓伊人，在水一方。
溯洄从之，道阻且长；溯游从之，宛在水中央。
蒹葭凄凄，白露未晞。所谓伊人，在水之湄。
溯洄从之，道阻且跻；溯游从之，宛在水中坻。
蒹葭采采，白露未已。所谓伊人，在水之涘。
溯洄从之，道阻且右；溯游从之，宛在水中沚。

〖今译〗

郁郁苍苍的芦苇上，冷露凝作薄霜。
心头怀念的人呵，站在前面河岸旁。
逆着水流走去，崎岖的小路弯又长。
顺着河道寻去，她好像围在水中央。

萋萋苍苍的芦苇上，夜露还没吹干。
心头怀念的人呵，站在河岸青草间。
逆着水流走去，那小路坎坷而艰难。
顺着河道寻去，她好像伫立小岛前。

青青葱葱的芦苇上，露珠儿依然亮晶晶。
心头怀念的人呵，恍恍惚惚她岸边的影儿。
逆着水流走去，那小路迂回而难行。
顺着河道寻去，她好像隐在绿洲中。

Reeds Green

Exub'rant, exub'rant — reeds in darkish greens;[1] [5音步]
There shimmers a light frost instead of dewdrops agleam.
My dear beloved, where can you be found?[2]
You're there ahead, to be sure, the waters beyond.[3]

I saunter upstream to look for traces, for her,
Proceeding along the river long and curved.
I saunter downstream looking about for her trace;
Meseems she's 'mid the waters upon the waves.

Profusely, profusely — reeds alongshore green.
And not yet dried are dewdrops clear and serence.
My dear beloved, where do you now hide?
You're there ahead, to be sure, the waters beside.

I saunter upstream to look for traces, for her,
Proceeding along the bank uneven and curved,
I saunter downstream a-searching high and low,
Meseems she's 'mid the waters upon a shoal.

So lush, so lush are reeds by shallows green.
Still sparkling there the dewdrops crystal-clean.
My dear beloved, where's your figure fair?
You're there ahead, to be sure, the waters before.

I saunter upstream to look for traces, for her,
Proceeding along the streamway that winds and turns.
I saunter downstream a-tracking on and on,
Meseems she's 'mid the waters an islet upon.

〖评注〗

(1) exub'rant是exuberant略去一非重读元音的形式，简略可使之合律。

(2) beloved只有用作表语形容词（在 beloved by/of 等结构中）和后位定语时，-ed的e才不发音。它用作前位定语形容词和用作名词时，后缀-ed读作[id]，构成一个音节。

(3) 英诗中介词可以后置，the waters beyond/beside/before和an islet upon 。又如 Walter de la Mare的*Trees*写道：Of all the trees in England/Her sweet three corners in,/Only the Ash, the bonnie Ash/Burns fierce while it is green. 第二行相当于 in her three sweet corners 。

黍离

彼黍离离，彼稷之苗。行迈靡靡，中心摇摇。
知我者谓我心忧，不知我者谓我何求。
悠悠苍天，此何仁哉！

彼黍离离，彼稷之穗。行迈靡靡，中心如醉。
知我者谓我心忧，不知我者谓我何求。
悠悠苍天，此何仁哉！

彼黍离离，彼稷之实。行迈靡靡，中心如噎。
知我者谓我心忧，不知我者谓我何求。
悠悠苍天，此何仁哉！

〖今译〗

经过垅垅黍子，走过行行谷苗。
我两脚沉重，道路迢迢。心中不自禁飘飘摇摇。
知情的人懂得我的哀愁，不知情的却在奇怪：他要把什么寻求？
头顶之上高高的苍天呵，这样的残酷，竟然让我忍受！

黍子吐穗累累，谷穗随风摇荡。
我两脚迟滞，道路长长。心中酒醉般阵阵迷茫。
知情的人懂得我的哀愁，不知情的却在奇怪：他要把什么寻求？
头顶之上高高的苍天呵，这样的残酷，竟然让我忍受！

黍子密密层层，谷子已经黄熟。
我两脚不堪，漫漫长途。心中窒息般阵阵抽搐。
知情的人懂得我的哀愁，不知情的却在奇怪：他要把什么寻求？
头顶之上高高的苍天呵，这样的残酷，竟然让我忍受！

Lush, Lush Millet Seedlings

Midst lush, lush millet seedlings in ranks arrayed, [5音步]
Midst lush, lush sorghum seedlings on parade,
My steps unsteady, staggering, stumbling — astray.
My mind gets wand'ring, wav'ring, on my weary way.[1]

Some friends who know me well enough can see
I'm now in despair, with anguished, burdened heart.
But others knowing not what's amiss with me,[2]
Suspect I'm seeking something near and far.
O Heaven good and gracious above, I ask,
Just why our times must be so ghastly harsh?

Midst lush, lush millet's new ears in ranks arrayed,
Midst lush, lush sorghum's new ears on parade,
My steps unsteady, staggering, stumbling — astray.
My head gets swimming, swirling, on my weary way.

Some friends who know me well enough can see
I'm now in despair, with anguished, burdened heart.
But others knowing not what's amiss with me,
Suspect I'm seeking something near and far.
O Heaven good and gracious above, I ask,
Just why our times must be so ghastly harsh?

Midst lush, lush millet's ripe spikes in ranks arrayed,
Midst lush, lush sorghum's ripe spikes on parade,
My steps unsteady, staggering, stumbling — astray.
My heart gets sickening, sinking, on my weary way.

Some friends who know me well enough can see
I'm now in despair, with anguished, burdened heart.

But others knowing not what's amiss with me,
Suspect I'm seeking something near and far.
O Heaven good and gracious above, I ask,
Just why our times must be so ghastly harsh?[3]

〖评注〗

(1) wandering和wavering有缩略。wand'ring, wav'ring, ... my way，头韵。前有 steps unsteady, staggering, stumbling — astray；后有 despair…distress和swimming, swirling, sickening, sinking 等。

(2) what's amiss with me相当于what's wrong with me.

(3) 诗歌作者是个悲苦的行人，应是人世变迁、故旧失散、颠沛流离、难为生计，使他发出如是哀歌。清学者崔述《考信录》"幽王昏暴，戎狄侵陵；平王播迁，家室飘荡"，无疑是东周早年《黍离》的背景。

黄鸟

交交黄鸟，止于棘。谁从穆公？子车奄息。
维此奄息，百夫之特。临其穴，惴惴其栗。
彼苍者天，歼我良人！如可赎兮，人百其身。

交交黄鸟，止于桑。谁从穆公？子车仲行。
维此仲行，百夫之防。临其穴，惴惴其栗。
彼苍者天，歼我良人！如可赎兮，人百其身。

交交黄鸟，止于楚。谁从穆公？子车鍼虎。
维此鍼虎，百夫之御。临其穴，惴惴其栗。
彼苍者天，歼我良人！如可赎兮，人百其身。

〖评注〗

(1) 春秋时代秦穆公死去时，秦王室以一百七十多人陪葬（in 621 B.C., in the kingdom of *Qin*, 177 people were buried alive with the dead King Mu）,中有子车家的三名男儿，此诗抗议其事。a jujube upon,相当于 upon a jujube.英诗中介词可以置于名词之后。参见10页《蒹葭》评注3 。

(2) a one ...,指特别出众或出奇或可笑的人。

(3) Could he only...相当于If only he could...比较Were he only capable ...= If only he were capable... 本诗英译用扬抑格，即"重轻"音步，译文首行注有[扬抑……]

The Canary

Chirp-chirp, upon a jujube perching the canary says.[1] [扬抑6]
Who is to go with the King, at King Mu's passing away?
Yanxi of Zijus House, beloved Yanxi of ours!
Valiant as Yanxi is, a one for a hundred in fight, [2]
There he's trembling before his pit to be buried alive.
Must our worthies be sacrificed for that deceased?
O Good Heavens above, why so? [扬抑4]
Could he only be redeemed[3],
Willingly hundreds of us would go!

Chirp-chirp, upon a mulberry perching the canary says. [扬抑6]
Who is to go with the King, at King Mu's passing away?
Zhonghang of Zijus House, beloved Zhonghang of ours!
Valiant as Zhonghang is, an equal to a hundred in fight,
There he's trembling before his pit to be buried alive.
Must our worthies be sacrificed for that deceased?
O Good Heavens above, why so? [扬抑4]
Could he only be redeemed,
Willingly hundreds of us would go!

Chirp-chirp, upon a chaste tree perching the canary says. [扬抑6]
Who is to go with the King, at King Mu's passing away?
Qianhu of Zijus House, beloved Qianhu of ours!
Valiant as Qianhu is, a one 'gainst a hundred in fight,
There he's trembling before his pit to be buried alive.
Must our worthies be sacrificed for that deceased?
O Good Heavens above, why so? [扬抑4]
Could he only be redeemed,[3]
Willingly hundreds of us would go!

〖今译〗

落向那酸枣树枝，黄鸟儿喳喳唧唧。
有谁陪着穆公去了？子车家的男儿奄息。
我们这位奄息呵，以一当百的壮士。
身临他的墓穴，却不禁心头战栗。
为什么呵，苍天！大好子弟都要遭难？
要是能把他赎还，以百换一也心甘。

落在那桑树梢上，黄鸟儿唧唧喧嚷。
有谁陪着穆公去了？子车家的男儿仲行。
我们这位仲行呵，以一当百的猛将。
身临他的墓穴，却不禁胆战心慌。
为什么呵，苍天！大好子弟都要遭难？
要是能把他赎还，以百换一也心甘。

落向丛生的荆楚，黄鸟儿唧唧倾诉。
有谁陪着穆公去了？子车家的男儿鍼虎。
我们这位鍼虎呵，以一当百的英雄。
身临他的墓穴，却不禁胆战心惊。
为什么呵，苍天！大好子弟都要遭难？
要是能把他赎还，以百换一也心甘。

湘夫人[1]（节选）

屈原（约公元前340—277）

帝子降兮北渚，目眇眇兮愁予。
袅袅兮秋风，洞庭波兮木叶下。
登白薠兮骋望，与佳期兮夕张。
鸟何萃兮苹中？罾何为兮木上？
沅有茝兮澧有兰，思公子兮不敢言。
荒忽兮远望，观流水兮潺湲。
麋何食兮庭中？蛟何为兮水裔？
朝驰余马兮江皋，夕济兮西澨。
闻佳人兮召予，将腾驾兮偕逝！
……
合百草兮实庭，建芳馨兮庑门？
九嶷缤兮并迎，灵之来兮如云。
捐余袂兮江中，遗余褋兮澧浦。[2]
搴汀洲兮杜若，将以遗兮远者。[3]
时不可兮骤得，聊逍遥兮容与？

〖评注〗

(1) On his way touring the South, King Shun dropped dead from heat and fatigue beside the *Xiang* River under *Jiuyi* Mountains. His wife, daughter of King Yao, came in search of his remains in vain, and drowned herself in the river. Husband and wife became god and goddess of the Xiang River. "帝子""公子"即公主。

(2) 原文"袂"（套袖）"褋"（单衣）重复强调在河岸留下衣物，以便自己各处寻找时，女神来可发现踪迹。另歌《湘君》中有"遗余佩兮澧浦"（把我佩带的首饰留在澧水岸边），那是湘夫人为男神湘君所唱，遗玉佩也为给爱人一点提示。

〖今译〗

帝王的女儿说要降临北湖绿洲上，
为什么我极目远望总不见，使我神伤？
长江头吹下来袅袅不绝的秋风，
洞庭湖波激荡，树叶飘落水乡！
踏上白莎草丛，我在枉然凝神寻觅；
我满心期待着，相约于黄昏的佳期。
但高空的飞鸟，为何聚向水草？
而船头的渔网，为何高挂树梢？

沅水水边丛生白芷，澧水河畔盛开泽兰；
思念君王之女呵，深深思念不好言传。
我心意茫然，向前方望去，只见长河去远，流水漫漫。
山林麋鹿怎么会觅食在庭前？江心蛟龙哪里该匍匐在岸边？
她的踪影，一次次寻找不到，是我错过了她那秀丽的洲岛？

我从清晨纵马驰骋在河湾，到黄昏又徒劳地渡到西岸。
忽然像是佳人把我呼唤，我们将并驾奔腾，同赴乐园！
……
我们会有百种芳草，绿油油满庭院？
我们会有大片鲜花，香喷喷在门前？
九嶷高山的诸神，将一时纷纷出迎，
有如云霞弥漫着，周围处处的山峰。

但遍处见不到她，没有踪迹半点，
我只能留单衣于江滨，愿她发现。
我更从绿洲头采些香草拿在手上，
她从远方一出现就给她佩带身旁。
啊，相会的时刻是多么难得难求！
我只能就这样缓缓地漫游呀漫游？

To the Goddess of the *Xiang* River[1]

The Princess promised she would be here, [抑扬4]
Upon the northern isle she'd appear.
Yet though I strain and strain my eyes,
She's never seen to be drawing nigh!
O why would you, the autumn wind
So steadily stoutly rave and rave?
O'er Lake of *Dongting*'s wavering waves,
The trees are helpless shedding their leaves!

In treading a sedgeland, gazing afar so wild, [5音步]
I'm looking forward to a tryst at twilight mild.
Are my senses reeling: why're skylarks o'er water weeds?
And fishermen's nets festooned atop the trees?

With orchids alongshore the *Lijiang* winds; [4音步]
With angelicas the *Yuanjiang*'s lined.
For absence of my goddess my heart is sore,
Tho' I never dare to speak my thought.

Confusedly o'er the horizon keeping watch, [5音步]
I see but flowing waters twinkling past. ...
What grass do the deer look for within the fence?
And why are the dragons clinging flat to the bank?

From dawn I've been riding the river beside. [4音步]
By dusk I've crossed to the western shore.
But hark, to me my love now calls!
I'll gallop there with her to unite! …
A courtyard teeming with graceful plants?
A doorway perfumed with flowers' scents?
The mountain gods will throng us to greet,
Like clouds will the spirits o'erspread the peaks!

Yet never has my dearest come in sight,
Tho' I've thrown my coat there to catch her eyes.[2]
From th' islet I've plucked some fragrant herbs,
To present to her when at last she appears.
O why so hard just to get together!
Could I but leisurely linger and linger?

山鬼[1]（节选）

屈 原

乘赤豹兮从文狸，辛夷车兮结桂旗。
被石兰兮带杜蘅，折芳馨兮遗所思。
余处幽篁兮终不见天，路险难兮独后来。
表独立兮山之上，云容容兮而在下。
杳冥冥兮羌昼晦，东风飘兮神灵雨。
留灵修兮憺忘归，岁既晏兮孰华予？……
采三秀兮於山间，石磊磊兮葛蔓蔓。
怨公子兮怅忘归，君思我兮不得闲？……
雷填填兮雨冥冥，猿啾啾兮狖夜鸣。
风飒飒兮木萧萧，思公子兮徒离忧！

Fairy of Mount *Wu*[1]

Upon a crimson leopard I ride, [4音步]
My colorful ocelot running beside.
Of magnolia wood is my carriage made;
Osmanthus flowers — my banners gay.
An iris-woven cloak on my back,
And stems of ginger gird my waist.

A sweet bouquet is ready for me
To take thee — the beloved I'm aching to see.
What a shame I'm late for the rendezvous,[2]
In tracing small paths in shady groves!
Alone I stand atop the peak;
Adrift are clouds below my feet.

Then daylight turns so dusky and dark,
And God of Rain starts storms and blasts.
Expecting to see my swain I remain,
Ignoring the torrents having me drenched.
Is it that my youth is fading away,
My looks no longer so fetching and fair?

To gather magic fungi for thee,
All over the mountains I search and seek.
The rocks e'er rugged, rugged I climb;[3]
I stumble o'er crawling, crawling vines.
Still sure thou willst come, I linger alone,
Delaying departure till thou comest anon.
Perchance thou art occupied just the while,
Preparing with me 'fore long to unite?
The storm is raging, thunders roar;

Night falling, monkeys and gibbons growl.
The forest rustles, rustles in gales.
O missing thee I'm sick and dismayed!

〖评注〗

(1)《山鬼》就是巫山神女（炎帝未嫁而卒的女儿瑶姬）所唱深情的恋歌。宋玉所赞美的"旦为行云，暮为行雨；朝朝暮暮，萦绕巫山"就是她的形象。迷濛江峡上下的云雨乃是她的精魂。就是她，曾经帮助苦于洪水的先民劈开大山，让江流在万丈峡谷间奔流而下。也就是她，化身为巫山最高峰，至今伫立在巫峡最险处，指引着来往航船。

灵修，指敬爱的人；留灵修，为等待心上人而逗留。岁既晏，年龄既已老大；华，用作动词，"使开花"，孰华予？谁能使我再像鲜花般娇艳呢？三秀，灵芝（一年开三次花）；於(此处读wū)，於山即巫山。

(2) rendezvous（约会），借自法语，第一和第三个音节都重读。

(3) rugged 词尾元音读成一音节。...ever rugged, rugged, 总那么嶙峋嶙峋的。

〖今译〗

让赤豹为我驾车，让花狸在旁紧跟；
迎春香木的车身，桂花旗飘洒香尘。
我腰束杜蘅草带，身披石兰花巾，
折得芬芳的花束，好送给意中人。
却因所经浓密的竹林，不见天日，
我驰过这险阻的山路，一步来迟。
在高高的山巅，只有我孑然独立。
朦朦的云层，从山腰流过我眼底。

天色阴沉，白昼一变而昏昏迷迷，
东风飘荡，雨神泼开哗哗的骤雨。
为等待良人，茫茫然忘情流连；
是我年齿老大，已失去你爱惜的娇艳？
为了你采摘灵芝，我把巫山走遍，
我不顾这山石磊磊，这青葛盘旋。

恨你不来相见，我怅怅然不知归还；
难道你不得脱身，也还在把我思念？
听雷声又隆隆，看密雨更茫茫；
晚来猿啼呦呦，寒夜狖鸣凄怆。
狂风呼啦啦吹，林间萧萧喧响；
我满心悲伤呵，枉然把你盼望！

离骚（节选）

屈 原

汨余若将不及兮，恐岁月之不吾与；
朝搴阰之木兰兮，夕揽州之宿莽。
日月忽其不淹兮，春与秋其代序；
惟草木之零落兮，恐美人之迟暮！
……
长太息以掩涕兮，哀民生之多艰；
余虽好修姱以鞿羁兮，謇朝谇而夕替。
既替余以蕙纕兮，又申之以揽茝。
亦余心之所善兮，虽九死其犹未悔。

〖今译〗

我犹如紧随着飞逝的时光奔跑，
惟恐这如水的流年会把我丢掉。
我清晨来攀折青山头木兰的枝条，
到傍晚又采摘沙洲边经冬的香草。
匆匆而去的太阳、月亮！哪个肯停一停脚步？
刚刚还是明媚的春光，忽换作秋色凄楚。
试想那苍苍翠翠的草木呵，竟然会如此衰败凋枯，
你一腔美好心愿不得眷顾，恐将流落于途穷日暮！
……
我哀哭，这人生的苦难与劳瘁，
我长叹不已，擦不完我的泪水。
虽为一身尽善尽美，惹来羁绊自受牵累，
竟然早晨才进直言，晚上我便横遭斥退。
既为了佩戴蕙草招致贬损，我偏又采来白芷佩在胸襟，
只管把神圣意愿铭刻在心，虽然九死一生也永无悔恨。

Lamentations Over Estrangement (Excerpts)

I hurry along for fear I'll be left behind, [5音步]
As swiftly run the flows and fly the years.
At dawn I pluck magnolia on hillsides high,
At dusk, on islets, weathered fragrant herbs.[1]

O neither Sun nor Moon in the sky will be staying awhile; [6音步]
And springs and autumns pass in haste, as seasons will.
With grass and leaves so luxuriant withering all too soon,
I suffer worries: my Beauty to gloomy age be doomed!...[2]

Repeatedly drying tears, with long, long sighs, [5音步]
I'm grieved by life's entrapping troubles and trials.
So anxious to keep my garments neat, from stains,
I cannot help being held in tight, tight reins.[3]
Yet should the earnest advice I advanced in the morn,
Apart from my post by twilight have got me torn!

Although on account of orchid sweet being sent away, [6音步]
I'd readily wear, moreo'er, an angelica bouquet.[4]
For the sake of my heart's devotion alone, O just for that
I'd die a dozen deaths, with no remorse or regret!

〖评注〗

(1) 第一、三行-hind和high“半谐音”(元音后辅音不同)；二、四行years和herbs押近似韵。

(2) my Beauty…be doomed,虚拟语气，相当于should my Beauty …be doomed.

By “my Beauty（or the Beauty）” the poet-patriot hinted at that sincerity and faithfulness of his own, at that noble devotion he himself embodied, or sometimes at himself — he who later drowned himself when word came that his country, Kingdom *Chu*, was conquered by *Qin* troops and the capital *Yin*(郢) burnt down by thc invaders. 原文“美人”在此指贤良，尤指诗人自己。《哀郢》有“美超远而逾迈”(忠正之士超脱恶俗，愈加遭到疏远贬逐)，《离骚》后更有“众女嫉余之娥眉兮”，娥眉也指对民族的忠贞。gloomy, doomed，行内韵；下有entrapping troubles and trials, 辅音头韵。

(3) 重读音节后接实词时，也一重一轻，叠词亦然。如本节long, long sighs 和 tight, tight reins.

又如：O my Love's like a red, red rose/That's newly sprung in June. (Robert Burns *A Red, Red Rose*)

O pale, pale now those rosy lips,/I oft have kissed so fondly! (*Highland Mary*)

下行，情态动词should可因强调而重读。morn即morning的原词；一些古旧词语常用于诗歌中。

(4) I'd readily是I would readily之略；-o'er 是-over之略,本行读法是I' d (轻读) REA-dily WEAR, more-O'ER, an an-GE-li-CA bou-QUET。其中angelica第二、四音节都重读 。

垓下歌

项羽（公元前232—202）

力拔山兮气盖世，时不利兮骓不逝！
骓不逝兮可奈何，虞兮虞兮奈若何？

〖今译〗

空有拔山大力、盖世豪情，
时运不利，乌骓马再也无力驰驱！
乌骓马无力驰驱，我能把它怎的？
虞姬呀，虞姬，让我如何来守护你？

〖评注〗

(1) Should…be…! “一旦竟然遭到……”为虚拟语气条件从句。秦灭后，项羽号称楚霸王。“垓下”是楚汉两家争夺末了楚残兵被困处（公元前二百多年秦朝被起义军灭亡后），随军爱姬虞姬在此自尽，项羽暂时突围（项羽本名项籍）。

In the year 202 BC Liu Bang and Xiang Ji, at the head of 2 opposing forces, were contending for control of the empire. The result was a debacle for Xiang, who found himself and his remnant army tightly encircled at a place called *Gaixia*. In an extemporaneous song he expressed his worries for the safety of Lady Yu, his favorite consort, who by now had dissolved in tears. Lady Yu, for fear that she might prove a burden to her husband in the attempt to break through, ended her life with a sword.

Xiang fought through until he arrived at the *Wujiang* River, still pursued by the enemy. A boatman offered to ferry him to the east side of the river. That reminded him of his start with 8,000 young men of the East Region;

The Last Song at *Gaixia*

E'en mountains I could, if I would, just pluck, [4音步]
The world was shadowed entire by my might.
Should one be forsaken once by luck,[1]
One's battle steed would fail to fight!
O what's to be done with my steed now spent?[2]
With thee, my fair, for thyself to be spared?

now with all of them lost, how could he face the elders of his homeland? He committed suicide by the side of the river.

(2) spent"被折腾得筋疲力尽的" 是过去分词表被动。What is to be done (by me)? "我可能做什么（有何办法）？" What am I to do? 表"我该做什么，有何事可干"。

(3) 虞姬《和霸王歌》(*In Reply to Hegemon King's Last Song*)："汉军已略地，四面楚歌声。大王意气尽，贱妾何聊生？"

Our foe, the Liu Bang horde, the battle has gained,
Now seizing our land, thy once reputed domain.
E'en *Chu* folk songs are sung round the camps besieged,
Our juniors drafted and driven as the victors please.
Despite thy dauntless will, thou expect'st the worst;
How can I cling to life, if thine be cursed?

大风歌

刘邦（公元前256?—195）

大风起兮云飞扬，
威加海内兮归故乡！
安得猛士兮守四方？

〖评注〗

(1) It was the year 202 BC when Liu Bang unified the whole country. Han Xin, Liu's highest general, was made Duke of Qi, then re-created Duke of Chu, governor of part of the southeastern territory. Not unexpectedly, Liu Bang, now the First Emperor of the Han Dynasty, became more and more suspicious of his leading generals. Han Xin was presently demoted to bearing the empty title of the Marquis of Huaiyin without any manor to his name. They said rumors were flying regarding his disloyalty. He was ordered to stay idly in the capital, Chang'an.

Han Xin was passing each of his days on tenterhooks when one old general garrisoning *Yangxia*(in *Henan* Province now) rebelled. The Emperor personally led an army to suppress the rebellion. While the operation was nearly but not quite at an end, that wicked wife of his, the iron-handed Empress Lu Zhi, with the secret collaboration of the Prime Minister Xiao He, hoaxed Han Xin into believing that he was "invited to attend the celebration of the victory over the rebels". Xiao He, in order to be of more service to the court and preserve his own position, called at Han Xin's residence and brought Han Xin into the Palace himself. The politically heedless Han Xin was thus entrapped, and was immediately murdered in a bell-chamber without rhyme or reason. It wasn't a lawful or formal execution. "Now the hound is to be boiled! How I repent not listening to Kuai Tong, resulting in my ignominious death at the hands of a woman!" Kuai Tong, Han Xin's counselor, had once warned Han Xin of the danger of his being envied and killed by Liu Bang, and pointed out the way to save himself, i.e., to break away from Liu and set up his own Empire.

Ode to the Rising Gale

There rises a heartening gale, and clouds are driven apart. [6音步]
Now Lord within Four Seas, I'm again at my dear old hearth.
O where to get the brave — my broad, broad borders to guard?[1]

Actually Empress Lu was acting with the Emperor's consent. A few years later, all former meritorious generals were butchered by Liu Bang or his wife.

刘邦消灭了项羽的军队，登上皇位（史称汉高祖），庆功封赏。他提出丞相萧何建了首功，武将中颇有不以为然者，冲锋陷阵、出生入死，不更有功吗？于是刘邦拿打猎作比方："追杀兽兔者，狗也；而发踪指示兽处者，人也。今诸君徒能得走兽耳，功狗也。至于萧何，发踪指示，功人也。"不久，他因多疑，逐一惩办主要武将。在其纵容下，由曾封楚王降为淮阴侯的韩信，被他的妻子吕后诱杀。曾封梁王的彭越，随之受诬陷为刘邦处死。

刘邦返乡宴请父老、高唱《大风歌》"安得猛士兮守四方？"后，又杀了从早就是自己贴身卫士的樊哙，连宰相萧何，也因建议允许农民耕种皇家猎场空地，一度下狱。后来清代诗人黄任，在通往彭城的路上，想起这古都附近有刘邦的家乡沛县，而且被封为楚王的韩信之封地也就在这一带，慨叹韩信、彭越等"功狗"下场，写了《彭城道中》(*On My Way to Pengcheng*)："天子依然归故乡，大风歌罢转苍茫。当时何不怜功狗，留取韩、彭守四方？"

A sovereign, too, will visit his native home;
The Song of the Gale he sings, as if helplessly though.
O shouldn't you have had pity on "hounds" of old?
And spared their lives for them the borders to patrol?

(The term "hounds" means the generals whom were referred to as meritorious hounds by the emperor. He referred to his prime minister Xiao He as the meritorious hunter.)

秋风辞

刘 彻[1]

秋风起兮白云飞，草木黄落兮雁南归。
兰有秀兮菊有芳，怀佳人兮不能忘。
泛楼船兮济汾河，横中流兮扬素波。
箫鼓鸣兮发棹歌，欢乐极兮哀情多。
少壮几时兮奈老何？

〖评注〗

(1) 刘彻即汉武帝（公元前156-87）。他建乐府、采民歌。广为传诵的《上邪》(*By Heaven*) 即一汉乐府民歌："上邪！吾欲与君相知，长命无绝衰。山无陵、江水为竭，冬雷震震、夏雨雪，天地合，乃敢与君绝！"

By Heaven! I pledge by Heaven High —
I'll ever remain beloved of thine,
While thou for ever mine,
Till mountain peaks should crumble ,
And rivers all run dry,
In winter thunders rumble,
In summer snow flakes fly,
In the sky be jumbled up the Earth and the Sun —
O not until that day be our union undone!

(2) 读作 OR-chids BLOOM, chry-SAN-the-MUMS give Forth their SCENT。

(3) keep time to, 应和……的节奏。

(4) unbid 或 unbidden(未经邀请的)，状语修饰 come to all。上行swift 也是状语。

Ode to the Autumn Wind

Autumn wind arises, flying are white, white clouds. [扬抑6]
Grass and trees turn yellow, wild geese sweeping south.
Orchids bloom; chrysanthemums give forth their scent, [2]
Pining for my Fair, O her, I ne'er can forget.

Barge-pavilions cross the *Fenhe* River, [5音步]
Midway breaking snow-white ripples risen,
Flutes and drums keep time to rowers' songs.[3]
Reveling and feasting prelude sadness long
— How the youthful years are fleeting swift!
Why must old age come to all unbid?[4]

行行重行行

古诗十九首之一

行行重行行，与君生别离。
相去万余里，各在天一涯。
道路阻且长，会面安可知?
胡马依北风，越鸟巢南枝。
相去日以远，衣带日以缓。
浮云蔽白日，游子不顾返。
思君令人老，岁月忽已晚。
弃捐勿复道，努力加餐饭!

Trudging On and On

E'er on and on you're trudging your way, [抑扬4]
Being torn away by force from me.
A myriad miles extend between,
We're each beyond the horizon unseen.
E'er arduous and tortuous, your way you toil,
To get together we've scarce chance at all.
The Northern horse is attached to the vast,[1]
While a Southern bird belongs in her nest.

Still farther and farther you travel away;
I'm wasting thinner from day to day.[2]
Bedimmed the sun by clouds so dark,
The tramp is kept afar from his hearth.
O missing you renders me old and gray,
So quietly and swiftly advancing my age.
Deserted, not any more I'll whine;
Just pray you to pluck up your heart to survive!

〖评注〗

(1) the vast：旷野，广漠（北国特有的风光）。

(2) 原诗"衣带日以缓"，表明人消瘦了。柳永《凤栖梧》词"衣带渐宽终不悔，为伊消得人憔悴"。下句，浮云蔽白日，喻恶势力一时埋没了公理，李白《登金陵凤凰台》"凤凰台上凤凰游，凤去台空江自流；吴宫花草埋幽径，晋代衣冠成古丘。三山半落青山外，二水中分白鹭洲；总为浮云能蔽日，长安不见使人愁"。

迢迢牵牛星

古诗十九首之十

迢迢牵牛星，皎皎河汉女。
纤纤擢素手，扎扎弄机杼。
终日不成章，泣涕零如雨。
河汉清且浅，相去复几许？
盈盈一水间，脉脉不得语。

〖今译〗

高高的牵牛星，他在银河彼岸守望；
莹莹的织女星，你只在银河这一旁！
你舒展又娇柔、又白净的双手，
在织机上织绢，扎扎不住地忙。

一天也织不成，一块花纹图样；
泪水就像雨水，洒在那丝线上。

那银河之水，应是又清又浅，
同心的二人，相距能有多远？
单单隔一道、清浅的天河啊，
只脉脉相望，不得促膝倾谈。

Cowherd Star So High High Up

Behold the Cowherd Star so high, high up,[5音步]
Who's facing the Weaving Maid there fair, fair above.
So slender, slender, her fingers white as snow.
And clicker, clatter, her loom incessant goes.[1]

Her pattern not yet done when a day's gone by.
Her tears get pourings like raindrops down the sky.
The Milky River severs her from him,[2]
Although so limpid, shallow and wadable it seems.
E'er quiet, across the waters gurgling and dancing,
O longingly, longingly, each at th' other glancing.

〖评注〗

(1) 诗歌中可用形容词代替副词作状语，这incessant相当于incessantly。

(2) 英语的"银河"是Milky Way，按西方神话，那是天后 Juno 的乳汁喷射而成的。但我国说法，天河是王母娘娘用发簪划出、阻挡牛郎的。这首诗中把它作为一条河，英译变通为 Milky River, 不难理解（如说 Silver River 就费解些）。

The Milky River, a river separating the Cowherd from his love.

The Milky Way is called "Milky River" in China. The river is said to have been "drawn" by the Supreme Goddess with her hairpin to interrupt the chase of the Cowherd after his wife. The weaver-wife was by birth a granddaughter of the Ethereal Emperor. Her former home was in the Heaven. Once she felt bored by her work, she peeped down on earth. She happened to see the young cowherd and took a fancy to him. One afternoon the girl and her sisters came down to bathe in a river. The ox, a divine being, told the youth to steal the red dress of the weaver-girl. When all the other sisters had left for home on high above, the girl with her dress lost was left below looking for it, crying helplessly. The Cowherd came out from hiding. With the ox acted as their go-between, the two became husband and wife. They lived happily for several years during which time a son and a daughter were born.

But soon the disappearance of the girl from the heavenly palace was discovered by the Ethereal Emperor. He located her and ordered her, under pain of her family's destruction, to return right away to her loom. For the life of her dear ones, she had to comply and started to fly back. The Cowherd found his wife gone, and carrying his wailing children in baskets on back of the ox, hastened to race after her.

Then there came the Supreme Goddess. She had her hairpin in hand and made a stroke with it in the air. A whitish or "Milky" river made up of tiny

shimmering stars appeared before the runners. The river flows blocked the husband's way ahead. From then on The Cowherd Star(Vega) and The Weaver Star(Altair) have been separated on opposite banks. On very clear nights you can see two small stars under the big bright Cowherd, and those are none other than his son and daughter. The husband's eyes are fixed on his wife, and the children's on their mother across the Milky River.

It's only years and years later that the authorities' anger abates a little. They give the couple permission to meet merely once a year on the 7th evening of the 7th month (of the lunar calendar), when thousands upon thousands of magpies gather and hover over the Milky River. Ever since the bird-bridge facilitates the unique yearly rendezvous for the wife and her man with their children from opposite banks.

饮马长城窟行[1]

汉乐府民歌

青青河畔草，绵绵思远道。
远道不可思，宿昔梦见之。
梦见在我旁，忽觉在他乡。
他乡各异县，辗转不可见。
枯桑知天风，海水知天寒。
入门各自媚，谁肯相为言?
客从远方来，遗我双鲤鱼。
呼儿烹鲤鱼，中有尺素书。
长跪读素书，书中竟何如?
上言加餐饭，下言常相忆。

〖评注〗

(1)《饮马长城窟行》是乐府歌曲名。最早其词应述远戍长城之苦。此诗只是借用旧题。旧题新咏仍入乐可唱；但久后使用旧题、句读有变不再入乐的诗，习惯上还称乐府诗歌（除风格可模仿民歌外实已同于文人诗作)。这种诗题（即原歌曲名）不必译出。可用诗歌开头词语为题。

(2) parts 相当于places。

(3) a pair of wood-cut carps 指上下文点明的 message case 或 fish-case(for a letter to be carried therein) 。据说游鱼能传递书信，古时人们便把书信装在刻成一双鲤鱼形状的木盒中，使其安全传送。

(4) (You) Be blessed ...，第二人称祈使句："愿你们得到（老天的）祝福。"

Our River Banks

Our river banks abound in green, green grass. [5音步]
The grass extends my longings fond, fond afar.
'Tis hard to imagine farther, farther parts.[2]
In dream I met my man on his rugged path.

I dreamt we both were looking face to face;
I woke to find him myriad miles away.
Away you roam through many a village and town,
From place to place, enduring ups and downs.

A mulberry tree, though with'ring, feels the gale;
Sea waters, free from freezing, know the chill.
When men get home, each couple prattling in delight.
Whoever cares about my wanderer's plight?

Then suddenly comes a stranger with a message case —
Into a pair of wood-cut carps, it's shaped.[3]
I call my boy to open the fish-case quick,
And inside a letter is found, a piece of silk.

I kneel to read the letter written thereon.
O what contains the letter for which I've longed?
It starts: "Be blessed you all remaining there".[4]
And ends, "I'll think of you for e'er and e'er".

孔雀东南飞[1]

汉乐府民歌

孔雀东南飞，五里一徘徊。
“十三能织素，十四学裁衣；
十五弹箜篌，十六诵诗书；
十七为君妇，心中常苦悲。
鸡鸣入机织，夜夜不得息。
三日断五匹，大人故嫌迟。”
……
府吏得闻之，堂上启阿母：
“结发同枕席，黄泉共为友。
……
今若遣此妇，终老不复娶！”
阿母得闻之，槌床便大怒。
……
新妇谓府吏：“感君区区怀！
君既若见录，不久望君来。
君当做磐石，妾当做蒲苇；
蒲苇韧如丝，磐石无转移。”
……
阿兄得闻之，怅然心中烦：
“先嫁得府吏，后嫁得郎君。
……

〖评注〗

(1)原《古诗为焦仲卿妻作》，后人改以首句为题。

不嫁义郎体，其往欲何云？”

……

其日牛马嘶，新妇入青庐。
奄奄黄昏后，寂寂人定初：
“我命绝今日，魂去尸长留。”
揽裙脱丝履，举身赴清池。
府吏闻此事，心知长别离。
徘徊庭树下，自挂东南枝。

……

东西植松柏，左右种梧桐；
枝枝相覆盖，叶叶相交通。
中有双飞鸟，其名谓鸳鸯；
仰头相向鸣，夜夜达五更；
行人驻足听，寡妇起彷徨！

Peacocks Southeast Travelling

A pair of peacocks a-flight to the southeast travelling. [5音步]
At every couple of leagues they look back faltering.
"Beginning working on looms at thirteen of age,
I learned at fourteen clothes to cut and make.
At fifteen played I music on *Konghou* chords;
At sixteen recited our classical poems and prose.

While sev'nteen cherished wife of yours I became,
Yet since, my heart's been ofttimes saddened and shamed.
I rose to weave from dawn as crowed the roosters;
Till deepest night my hands were seldom rested.
While ev'ry three days done were five whole rolls,
Our Mother displeased would call me stupid and slow."

The husband soon about the matter learned.
When home, decided and daring, to Mother he turned:
"Our bridal pillow and mat I've shared with her,
We'll be hand in hand on leaving for Nether World!
Should Mother actually part my Lanzhi from me,
I'd never remarry, this you might believe!"
Beside herself with rage at his talking confronting words,
His mother banged the stool and madly cursed ...
Lanzhi replied to her man where the main road forked:
"I can't but be deeply grateful for kindness of yours.
If really resolved you're to keep me partner for life,
Come swift to fetch me ere I face more strife.
I wish your stand to be fixed as a rock immense,
And mine resistant as a vine unharmed if bent.
You see the vine is tough as silken braids,
A massive rock is ne'er to be turned away." ...

But there was Lanzhi's elder brother, the host,
With a mind more worldly than theirs, his temper he lost:
"Your former man a clerk so humble and low.
This noble youth is far more promising, you know.
If we're not to get united with his noble house,
Wherever you'll proceed from such a footing as ours?"…

What noises from oxen, horses and carts for the day!
Lanzhi was brought along in bridal array.
Then gloomy, gloomy dusk was followed by night;
Guests gone, so quiet, quiet came the awaited time.
"Right now," she said to herself. "My life is ending.
My corpse may stay, but my soul to the heavens is wending!"
She doffed her silken shoes, tucked up her dress,
And leaped into the clear pond's very depth.

Her loving husband presently got the news.
He knew 'twas time for him to pass o'er too.
He paced and paced a garden tree about;
Thereupon he hanged himself on a southeast bough.
… To east and west were grown cypresses and pines.
On the right and left were Chinese planes aligned.
All branches and branches embracing overhead,
One leaf caressing another closely attached.

'Mid foliage show themselves a pair of birds.
They're known as "Eternal-Lovers", unique on earth.
They each to the other continue crooning and crooning,
Thro' night and night till the following day is dawning.
The passers-by are stopped, enchanted on hearing,
And widows awakened, aroused and lost in yearnings!

短歌行

曹操（155–220）

对酒当歌，人生几何？
譬如朝露，去日苦多。
慨当以慷，忧思难忘。
何以解忧？唯有杜康！
青青子衿，悠悠我心。
但为君故，沉吟至今。
呦呦鹿鸣，食野之苹。
我有佳宾，鼓瑟吹笙。
明明如月，何时可掇？
忧从中来，不可断绝。
越陌度阡，枉用相存。
契阔谈宴，心怀旧恩。
月明星稀，乌鹊南飞。
绕树三匝，何枝可依？
山不厌高，水不厌深。
周公吐哺，天下归心。

A Short Song

With wine just out of flavorful cask, [4音步]
O why should we not sing our songs!
As morning dew will never last,
So worldly days for us aren't long!

My heart is laden heavy with dole.
Altogether helpless do I pine.[1]
And none can rid me of my woe,
Except for Dukang, Father of Wine.

So blue, so blue's thy scholar's robe;
How eager, eager for thee I've longed![2]
Since countless uneasy years ago,
For thee I've sung these yearning songs.

The deer each softly calling to th' other,
While gaily grazing upon the plain.
My honored guests are coming hither.
Let lutes and lyres now sound the strains!

My ideal is like the moon that's shining,
But when will it be finally attained?
My worry within continues rising.
There seemeth to it yet ne'er an end.[3]

O all the paths criss-crossing thou trudged!
So kind thy presence from afar 'fore us.
On meeting after parting for years,
Friendship is treasured ever so dear.

How splendid is the moon, and sparse the stars!
The magpies completing their southward flight
Are circling repeatedly o'er the larch —
On which of the branches are they to alight?

With rock 'pon rock, the mountain reacheth its height; [5音步]
From dribbles, from trickles, the ocean gaineth its depth.
Duke Zhou so sincere with every one of his guests,
By him attracted from all o'er the world were the wise.[4]

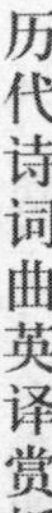

〖评注〗

(1) 相当于 I do pine altogether helplessly. 诗中可用形容词代替副词，修饰动词。

Cao Cao (155-220), the author of this poem, was the prime minister of the *Han* Dynasty's last emperor Xian Di. Before he took office, the uprising of the Yellow Turbans had shaken the sovereign power, and great confusion had been reigning in China, with local governors fighting for control of vast territories. Through innumerable hard battles, all the warlords in the North were wiped out one by one by Cao Cao, the greatest strategist of the day. But he failed to conquer the forces of Sun Quan occupying the Southeast and those of Liu Bei, who established themselves in the Southwest. Then began the historical period of "Three Kingdoms". As is stated in the poem, Cao Cao was all the time care-laden — in deep concern about the unification of the country, his ideal for life. He knew that wise and knowledgeable advisors were needed in large numbers to help him attain his goal. So he went out of his way to enlist the services of the learned and talented. In Stanza 3, the blue robe is a symbol of the scholar. In the 7th stanza, magpies choosing a branch to alight on hints at the choice of masters the virtuous scholars were to serve.

(2) 诗歌中形容词常用来代替副词，longed eager 相当于 longed eagerly 。

(3) seemeth 末 -eth 是古动词现在时单数第三人称词尾，诗歌中常借用，以求典雅；相当于现代所用-es/-s。

(4) 原诗中，握发、吐哺，指周公常“一浴三握发、一饭三吐哺”的故事。为及时接待来访，洗一次澡，三次握出头发所沾的水，出来会客；吃一顿饭，三次吐掉未嚼烂的食物，郑重迎宾。

燕歌行

曹丕（187–226）

秋风萧瑟天气凉，草木摇落露为霜。
群燕辞归鹄南翔，念君客游思断肠。
慊慊思归恋故乡，君何淹留寄他方？
贱妾茕茕守空房，忧来思君不敢忘。
不觉泪下沾衣裳。
援琴鸣弦发清商，短歌微吟不能长。
明月皎皎照我床，星汉西流夜未央。
牵牛织女遥相望，尔独何辜限河梁？

〖略译〗

我双手捧来瑶琴，
奏起凄清的商音。
只短短几句低唱，
我已受不住乐曲的悲凉。
皎皎的月光照在我床前，
星河西泻，秋夜还没有过半。
牛郎织女呵，相互望眼欲穿，
你俩有什么过错，被隔在天河两岸？

〖评注〗

(1)《燕歌行》为乐府歌曲名，燕（yān），今河北省北部。

(2) trees a-shedding leaves 正在飘落黄叶的树木。原为介词、本义 on 的前缀 a-在诗歌和谚语中，可加动名词前来调节韵律。如英语谚语 Who goes a-borrowing, goes a-sorrowing.（总是借钱，总是心烦。）

Night Longings[1]

A rustling, rustling autumn breeze is blowing the country bleak, [7音步]
With dew replaced by frost, and shivering trees a-shedding leaves.[2]
Along with wild geese, swallows are leaving for warmer latitudes.
E'er since you left I've always remained at a loss, in solitude.
On roaming afar, one's apt to yearn so fondly, fondly for home.
O why must you be delayed behind so long in places remote?

While lonely, lonely, I keep to the vacant chamber, the vacant yard,
Through dreary days, I only cherish dearer your name in my heart,
Unaware of my dress being wetted by tears, unbidden, futile and fast.
I take my lute; there rings some tender, trilling tune on its strings.
But merely short songs — how could a wretch like me the long ones sing?

Now moonbeams brilliant, brilliant flood my bed and chamber wide,
The River of Stars is flowing west, in deepest quiet of the night.
Behold, the Cowherd and Weaver Stars are each at the other glancing.
But does the couple deserve to be parted by the Milky River gleaming?[3]

---

(3) About "the Milky River" severing the Cowherd and his wife Weaver, see p.38《迢迢牵牛星》, Note 2.

the River of Stars 或者 the Milky River 是"银河"一词在相关上下文中的英译，兼顾了其在中国民间故事中的形象。该英语词本是 the Milky Way（由罗马神话中的"天后"Juno 之奶汁喷洒而成）。

原诗"发清商"：古代音律有宫、商、角、变、徵（zhǐ）、羽、变宫七声。商音悲凉，故称为清商。据战国时的《列子》说，郑国的师文跟师襄学琴，三年不成，继续苦练，终于得法，一次试奏，正当春日，但师文叩动商弦，凉风忽至，草木结实。

野田黄雀行

曹植（192–232）

高树多悲风，海水扬其波。
利剑不在掌，交友何须多？
不见篱间雀，见鹞自投罗？
罗家见雀喜，少年见雀悲。
拔剑削罗网，黄雀得飞飞。
飞飞摩苍天，来下谢少年。

The Lark Snared[1]

The tallest tree sustains the bitterest winds, [5音步]
The highest seas are troubled in wildest storms.
The mighty sword being not in hands of yours.[2]
In vain you cherish dear your many friends.

Behold the lark o'er the fence escaping from hawks:
It tumbled headlong into the readied net.[3]
The cold-blooded catcher was glad to get it caught;
The cordial lad was sad to see it snared.

The lad with a dagger cut the net knots loose;
The victim struggled and out of the meshes flew.
In clouds it soared then came below to alight
To thank the lad who gave it another life.

〖评注〗

(1) 曹植《野田黄雀行》(The Lark Snared) 反映着他自己和他的友人常受迫害的危险处境。

(2) 比起 in your hands 来，in hands of yours 语气更强。“利剑不在掌，交友何须多？”表明，这篇《野田黄雀行》是曹植为朋友受害而写的：

曹操的长子曹昂早亡，而四子曹植最富才华，吟诗作赋，挥笔而就，人称“天下才共一石，曹植独占八斗”。魏王曹操原偏爱他，想立为王太子，后因曹植率真不羁，而次子曹丕曲意逢迎，后来还是曹丕被立为王太子，继魏王位。不久，曹丕迫使汉献帝把皇帝宝座“禅让”给自己后，立即借故杀了曹植好友丁仪等文人，把几个兄弟分封各地，永远不许来往。派去的“监国使者”第二年就控告曹植“饮酒悖慢”，威吓使者。多亏母后讲情，曹植才没有被杀，而是被贬低爵位，改封贫乏地区。

(3) 本行读作 it TUMB-bled HEAD-long IN-to the READ-ied NET.

介词属虚词，但有时在英诗中偶可赶上重读。如 REAP-ing and SING-ing BY her-SELF (Wordsworth, *The Reaper*)。又如本书12页英译正文第二行读作：mid LUSH, lush Sor-ghum SEED-lings ON dis-PLAY.

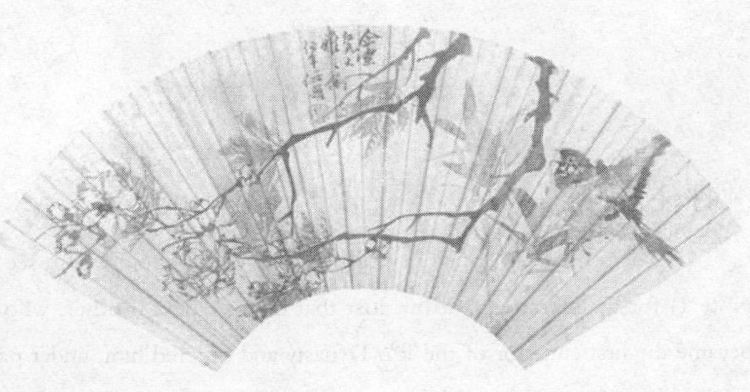

七步诗

曹植

煮豆燃豆萁，豆在釜中泣。
本是同根生，相煎何太急？

Poem Composed Within Seven Paces' Time[1]

O beans should be boiled on a beanstalk fire! [4音步]
From the pot a plaintive voice out shoots:
Why do you burn with seething ire,
As indeed we sprang from the selfsame roots?"

〖评注〗

(1) The poet won the favor of his father Cao Cao(about whom see p.49, Note 1) for his literary talent but lost that of his eldest brother, who later became the first emperor of the *Wei* Dynasty and ordered him, under pain of death, to compose a poem within the time of taking 7 paces.

饮酒（之五）

陶渊明(365—427)

结庐在人境，而无车马喧。
问君何能尔，心远地自偏。
采菊东篱下，悠然见南山。
山气日夕佳，飞鸟相与还。
此中有真意，欲辩已忘言。

Written Over a Cup of Wine

I've built my cottage where people come and go, [5音步]
Yet never hear I clamor of horses and hoofs.
If asked "O why is this so", I'd readily say,
"Secluded heart secures secluded site."
While chrysanthemums I pluck by the eastern hedge,
The scene of the southern hills presents itself[1].
The hillside views get charming towards the night,
One bird inviting another on homeward flight.
O aren't there some enlightenment and truths profound?
For which my words would not clearly account.

〖评注〗

(1)鲁迅评陶: "除论客所佩服的'悠然见南山'之外，也还有'刑天舞干戚'之类的'金刚怒目'式，在证明着他并非整天整夜地飘飘然。"（《"题未定"草》）

陶诗《读山海经》("*Thoughts on Reading 'Mountains and Seas*'"），表现他"金刚怒目"的本色："精卫衔微木，将以填沧海。刑天舞干戚，猛志固常在。同物既无虑，化去不复悔。徒设在昔心，良晨讵可待？"《山海经》讲炎帝的幼女精卫溺死于东海，化作"精卫鸟",不停衔来西山木石，要把东海填平；巨兽"刑天"与天帝争权，被砍掉了头,"以乳为目，以脐为口，操干戚而舞",仍在挥动盾牌和战斧；死去等同于异物也不怕；但美梦难成啊！

Jingwei the Bird with pebbles or twigs in bill,
Aims the boundless open ocean to fill.
Xingtian, beheaded, axe and shield still wielding,
Dauntless is he, to tyranny never yielding.
No regrets for forbidding transformation,
Never distressed for former existence's cessation.
Yet in vain they uphold their spirit of yore —
What time is the day to come they languish for?

杂诗（之一）

陶渊明

人生无根蒂，飘如陌上尘。
分散随风转，此已非常身。
落地为兄弟，何必骨肉亲？
得欢当作乐，斗酒聚比邻。
盛年不复来，一日难再晨。
及时当勉励，岁月不待人。

Miscellaneous Poems (The First)

Not a fig's firm base, nor a banyan's roots [4音步]
On poor frail humans are ever bestowed.
Like dust or high or low being blown,
By winds, we're scattered, about let go.[1]
And teased-tossed, ne'er the master of our own!

Once down into the world, being born, with a cry,
Is each a brother or sister to others.
Though we're not of common father and mother,[2]
Your kindness does more than kinship's ties.
O joys to be sought, if right is the while.
For neighbors to meet just out with your wine![3]

It comes to you but once, the prime of life; [5音步]
In a day a second morn is not to find.
Encourage one another before it's late,
Since time and tide for none will ever wait.

〖评注〗

(1) about let go 为 being let go about之略，相当于being made to go about。两个短语 being blown like …, being let go…，修饰 we're scattered。下有省略 And teased-tossed, (we're) never the master of our own.

(2) 读作 though we're NOT of COM-mon FA-ther and MO-ther 。其中的 of common … mother 相当于 born of …"是某某所生"。并列的 father and mother 前可不用冠词。

(3) Out with your ...，惯用语，相当于Quickly take out your ...

敕勒歌

北朝民歌

敕勒川，阴山下。
天似穹庐，笼盖四野。
天苍苍，野茫茫，
风吹草低见牛羊。

〖今译〗

敕勒人的平川呵，绵亘在阴山之旁。
碧天像圆顶毡帐，笼罩着旷野四方。
苍苍的无际碧空，茫茫的无边草场。
清风吹动了草浪，浪谷里望见牛羊。

Steppe of Us Tiele Tribes

This stretching Steppe of ours, of the Tiele tribes',[1] [5音步]
'Neath the Shady Mountains, bordering the mountainsides.[2]
The firmament spread around like a tent with its dome
To over-roof the vast expanse that we roam.
O azure, azure the skies. [3音步]
Immense, immense the Steppes.
Where grass is battered low by the breeze, [4音步]
There're seen our grazing cattle and sheep.

〖评注〗

(1) 敕勒部族，又名“铁勒”族，为避免音译成 Chile（智利），可译作 Tiele。

(2)《敕勒歌》本是北方鲜卑族民歌。在南北朝（420-589）时期的北方，鲜卑语和汉语通用。鲜卑军队的“敕勒人”大将斛律金，曾在东魏丞相高欢的应和下，在军营中高唱译成汉语的鲜卑歌曲《敕勒歌》。这支歌，鲜明生动地描绘了塞上原野牛羊成群、草场繁荣的和美画面。金末诗人元好问是鲜卑族分支拓跋氏的后代，他慨叹先人多少慷慨曲调没有流传下来，只是这首天然绝唱，传唱不衰：“慷慨歌谣绝不传，穹庐一曲本天然。中州万古英雄气，也到阴山敕勒川！”（《论诗绝句》之七）

川，指平原，如说“平川广野”。敕勒人，原生活在北海之滨（今俄罗斯西伯利亚贝加尔湖畔），南北朝时，归附强大的北魏，定居阴山山麓，把漠南一带开发得牧草丰美、牛羊肥壮。

第二章

唐代诗歌

Chapter 2

Poems of the Tang Dynasty

送杜少府之任蜀州

王勃（650—676）

城阙辅三秦，风烟望五津。
与君离别意，同是宦游人。
海内存知己，天涯若比邻；
无为在歧路，儿女共沾巾。

〖今译〗

这里京城外，有三秦富庶田园作为依傍；
那边风烟间，是五座繁忙渡口隐隐相望。
你我同为官员，听凭调遣四方，
即将分手一别，各自寄身他乡。
四海之内、既有自己的知音，
远隔天外，也如同近在比邻。
又何必在分道扬镳的大路口，
像痴儿女，让手帕沾满泪痕？

Farewell to Mr Du Off to *Sichuan*

Here're Palaces guarded by three of th' Empire's thriftiest lands;[6音步]
There hazes obscuring five of the busiest ferries in *Chuan*.[1]
For us to bid each other farewell, this is the day,
As both are officials oft-transferred from place to place.
So long as bosom friends we remain in our heart of hearts,[2]
We'll feel like closest neighbors despite the distance apart.
Then shed not silly tears as youngsters always do.[3]
Going different ways, you and I should say inspiring adieus.[4]

〖评注〗

(1) *Chuan*(川) is the short for Sichuan，territory of the ancient State *Shu*.（"川"是古蜀地四川的简称）。

(2) So long as，只要；引导条件从句 we remain bosom friends…（为保持轻重相间可倒装）

(3) 代替 Do not shed, 说 Shed not, 是诗句中常用形式。

(4) adieu, 原为法语"再见"，相当于 good-bye，高雅英语中常常借用。复数 adieus 或 adieux。

春江花月夜（节选）

张若虚（生卒年代不详）

春江潮水连海平，海上明月共潮生。
滟滟随波千万里，何处春江无月明？
江流宛转绕芳甸，月照花林皆似霰。
空里流霜不觉飞，汀上白沙看不见……

人生代代无穷已，江月年年望相似。
不知江月待何人，但见长江送流水……
可怜楼上月徘徊，应照离人妆镜台。

玉户帘中卷不去，捣衣砧上拂还来……
昨夜闲潭梦落花，可怜春半未还家。
江水流春去欲尽，江天落月复西斜。
斜月沉沉藏海雾，碣石潇湘无限路。
不知乘月几人归，落月摇情满江树。

〖评注〗

(1) th'是the的缩略，用于元音或 r 等字母开头的词前。

(2) thine upstairs chamber over 相当于 over your upstairs chamber。元音前用 thine以代替 thy 。诗歌中介词可以后置。

(3) hammering block（砧）, a big stone on which coarse cotton stuff is hammered (beaten) with clubs to be made flexible before making clothes.

(4) frontiers 指"碣石"。碣石山在今河北昌黎县，是南临渤海东接山海关的古战场。曹操远征乌桓时过此作《步出夏门行·观沧海》："东临碣石，以观沧海。"诗中以碣石代表关塞迢迢的北疆。

潇湘：潇水与湘江在今湖南零陵县西汇合，湖南南部常称潇湘。诗中以潇湘泛指江河漫漫的南国。

Spring Riverside with Moonlit Blossoms (Excerpts)

The vernal river rises high as the high-tide seas. [6音步]
Above the seas the moon soars up with brilliant beams.
She follows th' ripples shimm'ring, shimm'ring for myriads of miles.[1]
Whatever shores are not immersed in her lucid lights?

The river winds about the fragrant shores abloom,
With moonlit flowers, purely white, like patterns of snows.
'Tis not perceived, the hoary frost o'er flowers flying;
Distinguished not are sands on islets as white and shining...

For ages and ages human offsprings come and go.
From year to year the moon's unchanged, not growing old.
Who knows for whom above the river she lingers long?
We see but the River Great is surging on and on...

O sadly hovers the moon thine upstairs chamber o'er,[2]
Before thy dressing glass alone thou sitting forlorn.
Up rolled the window screen, the moonbeams aren't gathered in.
Tho' swept is the hammering block, the light thereon remains...[3]

I dreamed of blossoms falling 'pon the somber pond last night;
How sad I can't return with the prime of the year gone by!
The flows the last few spring days carrying away in haste,
Across the river is the moon declining desolate.

The moon declining sinks 'neath mists on seas remote,
And seems the farther and harder from frontiers journeying home.[4]
Are any of your men returning with moonlight showing their path?
O'er riverside trees its gleams revealing hurts on your hearts.

登鹳雀楼

王之焕（688—742）

白日依山尽，黄河入海流。
欲穷千里目，更上一层楼。

〖评注〗

(1) 把 You climb again upon an upper storey. 改成这样的倒装句，强调了“更高一层”。

鹳雀楼，在唐代河中府（今山西省永济县蒲州镇），楼高三层，原南北朝时筑于蒲州西南黄河河道中的一高岗上，因常有鹳鸟（与鹤相似）飞落其上，名为鹳雀楼。北宋沈括《梦溪笔谈》记其“前瞻中条，下瞰大河”。后来楼被河水冲毁，楼匾移到蒲州城西南角楼，以存旧迹。蒲州城东南靠中条山，西面俯瞰黄河（黄河经此南流转东）。

诗中“山”指黄河西岸、太阳落处即鹳雀楼对岸的远山。“欲穷千里目”，穷，表示“穷尽”，“使（目力）……达极点”。

关于五绝之最，历来诗歌评论家多推王之涣的《登鹳雀楼》。清朝朱之荆增补的《增订唐诗摘抄》称其：“两对工整，却又流动，五言绝句，允推此为第一首。”清李瑛辑《诗法易简录》说：“不言楼之如何高，而楼之高已极尽形容。且于写景之外，更有未写之景在。此种格力，尤臻绝顶。”

不过，也还有人推崇戴叔伦的《三闾庙》（104页），清代施补华撰《岘庸说诗》论《三闾庙》道：“并不用意，而言外自有悲凉慷慨之气。五言中此格最高。”

On Top of Stork Tower

The blazing sun behind the mountains goes; [5音步]
The Yellow River toward the oceans flows.
To view the most beyond a thousand miles,
Upon an upper storey again you climb.[1]

凉州词

王之涣

黄河远上白云间，一片孤城万仞山。
羌笛何须怨杨柳？春风不度玉门关。

〖评注〗

(1) *"Willow"* here is the title of a flute tune。《杨柳》指《折杨柳》乐曲。末行 Jade-Pass's 中's 可读作[iz]，也可不发音。

据说，唐玄宗开元年间，诗人高适(700?-765)、王昌龄(698-757?)、王之涣(688-742)常有交往。一次三人又上旗亭（酒楼）聚会。恰逢一队乐工和四个歌女登楼演唱，三诗人就相约，听听歌女唱不唱三人的诗，唱谁的次数较多。

乐工坐好后，一个歌女开始唱了："寒雨连江夜入吴，平明送客楚山孤；洛阳亲友如相问，一片冰心在玉壶。" 这是王昌龄的《芙蓉楼送辛渐》（芙蓉楼在润州，今江苏镇江；一颗透亮的心如玉壶冰晶，毫无功名富贵的杂念）。轮到第二个歌女，她唱道:"开箧泪沾臆，见君前日书；夜台今寂寞，犹是子云居。" 这是高适的《哭单父梁九少府》（单父，地名，今山东单县；梁九少府，即兄弟排行第九的梁少府；夜台，坟墓；子云居：西汉杰出的文学家和哲学家扬雄，字子云，子云住处，喻指贤士之家。）王昌龄和高适二人相视而笑。接着第三个歌女唱来："奉帚平明金殿开，暂将团扇共徘徊；玉容不及寒鸦色，犹带昭阳日影来。" 这又是王昌龄的《长信宫怨》（奉帚，

Beyond the Jade Pass

The Yellow River rises remote in clouds all dim, [6音步]
Alone a castle's perched 'mid soaring peaks so grim.
O why *Qiangs*' flutes o'er "*Willows*" sad will wail away?[1]
Our Spring has never ventured west of Jade-Pass's way.

恭恭敬敬地拿起扫帚打扫宫苑，指班婕妤到长信宫照料太后，关于班婕妤及其诗见160页评注；昭阳，受汉成帝专宠的赵飞燕所居宫殿）；王昌龄好不得意，瞥了王之涣一眼。王之涣低声说："别急，最后这位最端庄、最秀丽的歌女，该唱我的诗了。如若不然，我甘败下风。"那最末上前的歌女开口了，声调特别深切动人："黄河远上白云间，一片孤城万仞山；羌笛何须怨杨柳？春风不度玉门关。"正是王之涣的名作《凉州词》。

从军行

王昌龄（698—757?）

琵琶起舞换新声，总是关山离别情。
缭乱边愁听不尽，高高秋月下长城。

〖评注〗

(1) dark and dejected, decline, 头韵。find（感受动词）the moon decline（不带to）。

“琵琶”本作“批把”（外来语），推手前曰批，引手却曰把。宜译 *pipa* 。

(2) 夏完淳《即事》(*Situation as It Stands*) 也写从军，却不止军中思乡，而且惨遭溃败：“战苦难酬国，仇深敢忆家？一身存汉腊，满目尽胡沙。落月翻旗影，清霜冷剑花。六军浑散尽，半夜起悲笳。”关于他的事迹，见 322页《卜算子》。

In bloody battles bleeding our bravest men,
Unable our imperiled nation to recompense.
Profound and bitter hatred torturing my soul,
How dare I indulge myself in yearning for home?
I set my mind on holding dear at heart

In the Army

For the dance the *pipa* strikes a tune quite new. [5音步]
Yet why's it retuning to parting complaints of old?
By passes and mountains distanced from home remote,
You're always hearing upsetting border drones.
The autumn moon from high above you find
Upon the Great Wall, dark and dejected, decline.[1]

Our long-established faith in our sacred land.
Yet meeting my eyes in every corner and part
Dust storms from the North of savages, clouds of sands.
In dull and gloomy glimmers of the setting moon
So dim are the wavering flags of marching troops.
At dawn such frost is formed severe and gray,
As to lend our swords a glimmer so gelid and pale.
Alas, while whole battalions fighting their way
Through thick and thin being scattered all apart,
In the quiet of night, to the sleepless fighters' dismay,
Heart-rending bugle's notes keep sounding afar.

出塞

王昌龄

秦时明月汉时关，万里长征人未还。
但使龙城飞将在，不教胡马度阴山。

〖评注〗

(1) 重读后自然轻读。如首行：the MOON from QIN'S years SHINES yet O'ER the PASSES from GREAT Han's（轻读）DAYS 。介词可逢重音，如 O'ER(over) 。

(2) swoop，"飞扑下来"、"突然袭击"。General Lee the Swooper，飞扑而来般奔袭入侵者的"飞将军"李广 。英语绰号通常放在原来的称呼之后，如古马其顿建立横跨欧亚非"亚历山大帝国"的 Alexander the Great，原法国诺曼底公爵、征服英国而自立为英王的 William the Conqueror 。

西汉李广任平卢 (今河北卢龙，又名龙城) 节度使，匈奴人称他为"大汉飞将军"，为之不敢侵犯边境（西汉Great *Han*，疆域比秦时更广）。

李广克己爱兵，"乏绝之处，士卒不尽饮，广不近水；士卒不尽食，广不尝食"。但他没口才，少说话，总受不到封赏。后卫皇后之

On the Frontier

The moon from *Qin*'s years shines yet o'er the passes from Great *Han*'s days.[1] [7音步]
Our men can't return from fighting tens of thousands of *li* away.
Were General Lee the Swooper of Dragon Fort in garrison there,[2]
No Tartar horsemen to steal across the *Yinshan* range would dare!

弟"大将军"卫青伐匈奴，李广虽已年老，仍坚请汉武帝让自己担任前锋。卫青从俘虏口中查知匈奴单于所在，为使其亲信公孙敖立功受赏，他半途中改任公孙为主力前锋，强令李广绕行东道。李广找不到向导，迷路误了会师的日期。陈子昂《感遇》第三十四："何知七十战，白首未封侯。"王维《老将行》："卫青不败由天幸，李广无功缘数奇（命数特别糟糕）。"随后高适写有《燕歌行》："相看白刃血纷纷，死节从来岂顾勋？君不见沙场征战苦，至今犹忆李将军！"他写此诗的时代，唐玄宗信任的是李林甫、安禄山之流，他们失地丧师，编造边功。"边庭流血成海水……新鬼烦怨旧鬼哭！"（杜甫《兵车行》）有识之士，却是报国无门。

黄鹤楼

崔颢（700—754）

昔人已乘黄鹤去，此地空余黄鹤楼。
黄鹤一去不复返，白云千载空悠悠。
晴川历历汉阳树，芳草萋萋鹦鹉洲。
日暮乡关何处是？烟波江上使人愁！

〖评注〗

(1) Once (it has) gone, the yellow crane is never coming back 前面的 once 为连词。

黄鹤楼在今武汉市长江南岸武昌临江的蛇山山头，传说古时道人费祎修炼成仙，从这里乘黄鹤飞升。The Yellow Crane Tower, situated on the lofty southern bank of the *Yangtze* River, is said to be the spot where an ancient sage, Fei Wei, on becoming an immortal, flew away on back of a yellow crane.

南宋严羽著《沧浪诗话》称："唐人七言律诗，当以崔颢《黄鹤楼》为第一。"明朝高棅编《唐诗品汇》记述："李白登黄鹤楼，道'眼前有景吟不得，崔颢题诗在上头'，至金陵乃作《凤凰台》以拟之。今观二诗，真敌手也。"清谭宗编《近体秋阳》也指《黄鹤楼》说："此与太白《凤凰台》篇，当同冠七言。"不过，明朝胡应麟曾在《诗薮》中说，杜甫《登高》（见94页）是"古今七言律诗第一"。

清朝高士奇辑、何焯评论的《唐三体诗评》提到《黄鹤楼》说："此篇体势，可与老杜《登岳阳楼》匹敌。"杜甫五律《登岳阳楼》（见96页）被众多评家誉为五言律诗之最。如《唐诗品汇》称："气压百代，为五言雄浑之绝。"南宋刘克庄所著《后村诗话》说："岳阳城赋咏多矣，须推此篇独步。非孟浩然之辈所及也。"

李白《登金陵凤凰台》，见35页评注2 。

Yellow Crane Tower

Astride the yellow crane the ancient sage was gone. [6音步]
What use a tower after its name to be left hereupon?
Once gone, the yellow crane is never coming back.[1]
Alone there cloudlets white forever waft and waft.
'Tis fine — across the river, trees serene are seen.
Upstream on Parrot Islet, grass looks gracefully green.
With twilight dimming, where to discern my home afar?
By mist enveloped the waves, and heavily laden my heart.

相思

王维（701–761）

红豆生南国，春来发几枝？
愿君多采撷，此物最相思。

〖评注〗

(1) 明代医学家李时珍《本草纲目》记述，“相思子”即红豆。传说春秋时代吴国某人从军远征，多年没有音讯，其妻思念而死。不久她的坟上，长起一棵高有丈余的奇树，条条柔枝、对对叶片，都伸向丈夫前去的东南边疆。这树称作“相思树”，所结荚果晶莹光泽，红如珊瑚，就是相思子或红豆。实际红豆树不耐湿冷，只生于江南温暖又较干燥的地方，是近乎珍稀的树种。成熟的红豆可以长久贮存，豆皮坚韧饱满，色彩浓艳不变。有人收藏红豆，颇多几百上千年的珍品。

感叹句前what引导前置宾语，二行相当于The shrub… shoots out such prosperous sprouts …。本行读作 the SHRUB that BEARS red BEANS shoots OUT! 重读音节后的音节自然轻读。

(2) 副词 though 不表“虽然”而表“不过”（你会因而染上相思）。 it 指上句 (you) gather the beans。“此物最相思”，并非意指红豆能够害相思病，而是说，晶莹相思子，必不可免引起人们对坚贞情爱、远方亲人的反想与眷恋。

王安石子王雱《秋波媚》（全文及英译见 206、207页）写道：

“……而今往事难记省，归梦绕秦楼。相思只在，丁香枝上，豆蔻梢头。”

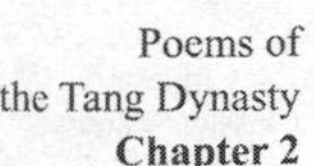

Lovesick Beans

What prosperous sprouts in Spring of the South [4音步]
The shrub that bears red beans shoots out![1]
As many as possible — gather the beans!
You'd then be lovesick, though, it means.[2]

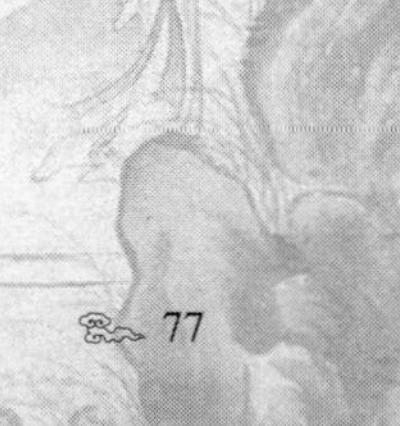

渭城曲

王 维

渭城朝雨浥轻尘，客舍青青柳色新。
劝君更进一杯酒，西出阳关无故人。

〖评注〗

(1) ere，诗歌用语，相当于before (you go far)。下行 thro' 是through之略。

关于七绝之最，七嘴八舌，莫衷一是。南宋刘辰翁《王孟诗评》论王维《渭城曲》道："更万首绝句，亦无复近，古今第一矣。"明代敖英辑评的《唐诗绝句类选》说："'秦时明月'一首，汤用修、李于鳞谓为唐诗第一，愚谓（我说）王之涣《凉州词》神骨声调当为伯仲（伯仲之间即不分上下）。"清朝沈德潜编《唐诗别裁》记载："（清）王渔阳（王士祯号渔阳山人）则云：必求压卷，王维之"渭城"、李白之"朝辞白帝"、王昌龄之"奉帚平明"、王之涣之"黄河远上"其庶几乎（或许便是吧）！而终唐之世。绝句亦无出四章之右者矣（没有胜过这四首的）。

清代黄生辑评的《唐诗摘抄》道："先点别景，次写别情。唐人绝句大多如此。毕竟以此为第一。古人神境，未易到也。"清钱良择所辑《唐音审体》说："刘梦得（刘禹锡字）诗云'更为殷勤唱渭城'。白居易诗云'听唱阳关第四声'。相传其调最高，倚歌（伴奏）者笛为之

Farewell Outside *Wei* City

All o'er the dust on roads from *Wei,* [4音步]
So softly drifting is the morning rain,
The taverns washed now fresh in shade
Of willows sprouting lively green.
My Lord, I pray, another toast
Do drink with me ere far you go;[1]
You travelling west thro' *Yangguan* Pass,
This meeting of old chaps will long be your last.

裂”（第四声，指在唱过原诗扩展而成的《阳关三叠》之后，再唱原诗。所谓“三叠”，是后人扩展文字）。清徐增撰《而庵说唐诗》称：“此诗之妙只是一个真字。真则能动人。后维偶于路旁，闻人唱诗，为之落泪。”渭城，在唐都城长安（今西安市）西北渭水北岸，为秦代都城咸阳旧址（今陕西省咸阳市东北十公里处），汉武帝时改称渭城。从长安送客西行，多到此折柳赠别，摆酒饯行。送客东去则送到灞桥，参见153页《忆秦娥》评注1。

春思

李 白（701—762）

燕草如碧丝，秦桑低绿枝。
当君怀归日，是妾断肠时。
春风不相识，何事入罗帏？

〖评注〗

(1) 读作：that SPRING breeze to ME is a STRAN-ger AN-y-HOW 。

(2) What are you about? 你要干什么？”似 What are you up to? 你在搞什么？

丈夫在“燕草如碧丝”的边疆，说明诗歌写的是妇女怀念征人。李白另有《子夜歌·秋》(*Autumn Night Song*)，同是闺房幽怨主题：“长安一片月，万户捣衣声。秋风吹不尽，总是玉关情。何日平胡虏？良人罢远征。”

Steeped in mellow moonlight the Capital *Chang'an* the whole,
Myriads of households are beating cloth for fighters' clothes.
Cares for frontier warfare pervading, zephyrs fleeting,
Fighting for *Yumen* Pass is upsetting homefolks' feelings.
When would foes barbarian thither be vanquished at last?
Never again are our goodmen to combat away so far!

比李白大12岁的孟浩然，写《春晓》(*Spring Morning*) 也以设问结尾：“春眠不觉晓，处处闻啼鸟。夜来风雨声，花落知多少？”

Unaware of it dawning, I wake into daylight of spring ,
All around are heard now birds to chatter and sing.

Spring Thoughts

As grass in the North grows green like silk, so fresh, [5音步]
In the South here mulberry trees are bending their heads.
You wonder when you'll make your homeward way,
While my heart, alas, my heart for reunion aches!
That spring breeze to me is "a stranger", anyhow —[1]
'Tis parting the screen of my bed, but what's it about?[2]

In my ears it's the midnight showers that still resound —
What a lot, I guess, of flowers are downed to the ground!

孟浩然隐居田园，一度写《临洞庭上张丞相》求仕未遂。该诗有"气蒸云梦泽，波撼岳阳城"名句；但同杜甫"吴楚东南坼，乾坤日夜浮"（96页）不可同日而语。

长干行

李　白

妾发初覆额，折花门前剧。
郎骑竹马来，绕床弄青梅。
同居长干里，两小无嫌猜。
十四为君妇，羞颜未尝开。
低头向暗壁，千唤不一回。
十五始展眉，愿同尘与灰。
常存报柱信，岂上望夫台?
十六君远行：瞿塘滟滪堆，
五月不可触，猿声天上哀。
门前旧行迹，一一生绿苔。
苔深不能扫，落叶秋风早。
八月蝴蝶来，双飞西园草。
感此伤妾心，坐愁红颜老。
早晚下三巴，预将书报家。
相迎不道远，直至长风沙。

Wife Left Home at Riverside Street

A fringe of hair began my forehead covering; [5音步]
Before the gate in sport I was flowers plucking.
A hobbyhorse was to bring you up to the scene.
Round wellhead railings we'd play with plums still green.
Being neighbors living close on Riverside Street,
We two so intimate, and yet so naive.[1]

At fourteen so girlish a bride of yours I became,
Still hardly able to bare my bashful face.
I'd turn to the shady wall and lower my head;
Though called a thousand times I'd ne'er look back.
At fifteen then being able to unknit my brows;
To be yours till turned to dust and ashes I vowed,
Being ready to keep my faith at the cost of my life,
But not Awaiting-Husband Terrace to climb.[2]

At sixteen I saw you off on a journey unsafe,
Thro' *Qutang* Gorge o'er Rapids with ghastly reeves,
Where boats oft wrecked in May with floods so high,
Where monkeys wail from peaks in gloomy skies.
Your footprints have long been worn away 'fore the gate,
Replaced by patches of moss, the path bedimmed.
The moss becomes too thick to be swept away;
In early autumn winds, are leaves adrift.

September brings the yellow butt'rflies flutt'ring,
In pairs across the Western Garden's grass.
The sight cannot but cause to ache my heart —
Alone I stay, my rosy cheeks now fading.
Some day you'll leave the Highlands downstream for home,
Forget you not beforehand to let me know.
I'll come to meet you, minding not fatigue,
O e'en halfway to get to Long Winds Beach.

〖评注〗

(1) intimate，第一和第三个音节都要重读。原文"绕床"的"床"字指井栏。古乐府《淮南王篇》"后园凿井银作床"（参见《辞海》），因而"绕床"译作 Round wellhead railings。

(2) 接上而略 But not (being ready) to climb (the) Awaiting-Husband Terrace, 不料要登"望夫台"。

中唐王建（760?-830?）作有短诗《望夫石》(Woman Turning into a Statue)：

"望夫处，江悠悠。化作石，不回头。江边日日风和雨，行人归来石应语！"

She stood awaiting her man for long and long,
Above the river rushing on and on,
Until a statue of stone she became at last,
O never looking about, eyes straining afar.
From day to day in winds and rains e'er raging,
The statue's to cry aloud, her man returning![3]

(3) 比较 (When) Her man (is) returning, the statue, (standing) in winds and rains (that are) ever raging ... , is going to cry aloud. 如说 is going to cry aloud（预计），不如 is to cry aloud（固定安排）语气更强。

闻王昌龄左迁龙标遥有此寄

李 白

杨花落尽子规啼，闻道龙标过五溪。
我寄愁心与明月，随君直到夜郎西。

〖今译〗

当柳绵飘落净尽，枝头杜鹃，哀哀啼唤，
听说你被贬龙标，正在渡过、“五溪蛮”那五条溪涧。
我把这忧伤思念之心，付与天外的明月高悬，
让月光与心愿陪伴你，一直西上夜郎的荒山。

To Wang Changling on His Banishment to Longbiao

As willow-down's all gone and cuckoos out with disturbing cries,[1] [7音步]
I hear of thy fording five streams trudging for *Longbiao* on tribesmen's heights.[2]
I entrust to the bright and lofty moon my sorrow-laden heart,
For it to accompany thee to the west of *Yelang*, thy lonely part.

〖评注〗

(1) 句有省略 ... is all gone and ... (are) out ...。down, 茸毛，从开过的杨树花或柳树花(catkin)上飘飞下来的毛茸茸的轻絮。汉语“杨花”和“柳絮”通用，是杨树或柳树花已开罢、很快结出的带茸毛的种子。晚唐郑谷七绝《淮上与友人别》“扬子江头杨柳春， 杨花愁煞渡江人。”子规即杜鹃，传说中蜀王杜宇魂灵所化，逢春哀啼。

(2) tribesmen's heights，少数民族居住的山区。比较今译中的“五溪蛮”，东汉、唐、宋时，居住湘西一代的少数民族，与今苗、瑶、侗族有渊源关系。

王昌龄比李白约大三岁。李白一度进京求仕、失望而去，王昌龄早已进士及第。但没等到李白经道士吴筠荐举、应诏入宫，年约四十的王昌龄就被贬为龙标（今湖南靠近西南边境的黔阳县）尉。李白闻讯，寄诗致意，有“我寄愁心与明月，随君直到夜郎西”之句。夜郎，本为古代西南山区少数民族聚居地的名称。《汉书》记载，夜郎国人不知中原比夜郎大小，遂有“夜郎自大”一语。唐时曾在今湖南、贵州边界设夜郎县（今湖南芷江西南），李白诗中以夜郎指王昌龄被贬往的边远地区（可谓湘西夜郎）。后来，李白从皇宫被“赐金放归”；他因安史乱起，曾应唐肃宗李亨弟永王李璘之聘、参加其欲讨安禄山的部队，被判“附逆”死罪，改贬夜郎；那是今贵州北部的正安、桐梓县一带（遵义以北）更远的一个同名的地方（可谓黔山夜郎），也是少数民族聚居区。

早发白帝城

李 白

朝辞白帝彩云间，千里江陵一日还。
两岸猿声啼不住，轻舟已过万重山。

Leaving White Dragon City at Dawn[1]

I said good-bye at dawn to the lofty City 'mid rosy clouds, [7音步]
And doing a thousand *li* a day, I'm back in *Jiangling* now.
On either bank the monkeys keeping hailing with ceaseless shrieks,
'Fore torrents the boat has left behind some myriads of ranges and peaks.

〖评注〗

(1) 李白58岁时，险些被处死，改流放夜郎。在去夜郎的艰辛行程中，忽然传来朝廷为荒年“大赦”的命令，他免罪东还，顺流而下，即将同老妻幼子团聚，安享天伦之乐，与知心诗友会合，共图国家中兴。宛如霪雨乍晴，顿使绝处逢生；真是喜从天降，令人心驰神往。就是在这样的欢欣鼓舞、热情洋溢之中，他写下了一气呵成、千古传颂的七言绝句《早发白帝城》。

月夜

杜甫（712—770）

今夜鄜州月，闺中只独看。
遥怜小儿女，未解忆长安。
香雾云鬟湿，清辉玉臂寒。
何时倚虚幌，双照泪痕干？

〖今译〗

今晚在鄜州小县，凄寂闺房窗前，
只有你静夜不眠，独自望月怀远。
我在遥遥京城总把幼小儿女挂牵，
可怜他们还不懂得惦记我在长安。
眼角湿润漫及眉端，将你香鬟轻沾；
月色临照如玉手臂，应觉夜深凄寒。
什么时候我们能够同倚家中的床幔，
让明月照见两个人终于把泪痕擦干？

On a Moonlit Night

In *Fuzhou,* the small town, lying in bed in your room, [5音步]
You're watching all alone the rising moon.
Afar, I feel for babies, beside their mother,
Not knowing of Capital, nor of detention of Father.[1]
Your balmy curls bedewed with moisture from th' eyes;
And graceful arms now chilled in watery light.
What day the moon could light us side by side,
On the curtain of the bed our tearstains barely dried?

〖评注〗

(1) 上行 babies (beside their mother) 接此行的后位定语 not knowing of (the) Capital, nor of (the) detention of Father. 杜甫写此诗时，正被扣留在沦陷的京都。

安禄山进逼、玄宗出逃之后，杜甫要去为在宁武即位的唐肃宗效力，但半路上遭叛军俘虏，押到长安。因他还是无名小辈，未受重视。当时在京的朝臣王维就被安禄山勒令出任原职。王维服药声嘶，假装哑巴，被软禁。诗友裴迪偷偷去看他，告诉他，安禄山强迫梨园子弟奏乐、多人落泪难从而被杀。王维口占《菩提寺私成口号》："万户伤心生野烟，百僚何日更朝天？秋槐落叶空宫里，凝碧池头奏管弦！"

叛军进长安后，匪首安禄山就要享受皇帝的宴乐。他命令在凝碧池前摆酒，乐队高奏。称病不来的乐师雷海清，也被押了上前。演奏起来，乐队中多人悲不自禁，声调错乱。叛匪大怒，凡是流出眼泪的，全都拉出杀头。雷海清一跃而起，摔碎心爱的琴，边哭边骂。安禄山令人把他一刀刀凌迟了。

王维那诗辗转相传，继玄宗为帝的肃宗也听说了。京城收复后，奖赏功臣、惩治降官。王维就因装病一番和小诗一首，得免处分。

秋兴（之一）

杜 甫

玉露凋伤枫树林，巫山巫峡气萧森。
江间波浪兼天涌，塞上风云接地阴。
从菊两开他日泪，孤舟一系故园心。
寒衣处处催刀尺，白帝城高急暮砧。

〖今译〗

晶莹的冷露，打残了江上的枫林，
巫山巫峡间，弥漫着愁惨的烟云。
河谷中江水奔腾，狂流激浪连天翻滚；
边关上风云低沉，天色山影一片阴森。
丛丛的秋菊已两度开放，年年招惹迷惘的泪眼；
孤零零小船还碇泊未行，单单把归心牵向家园。
寒风扑上山川，到处催动刀尺把寒衣裁剪；
高高白帝城头，急急的砧声一直响彻夜晚。

Autumn Thoughts

All maples in the woods dejected with crystal drops of dew, [6音步]
Depressing and desolate loom Mount *Wu* and the Gorge below.[1]
The billows in torrents surge as high as if shooting at skies;
And clouds on winds bedim the horizon, the borders wild.
Already twice seen blooming, chysanth'mums 'fore tearful eyes,[2]
A lonely boat's still mooring — yearning for home poor souls![3]
As winter garments are pressed to be presently sent by post,
O'er the perching City cloth-beat sounds in haste at night.

〖评注〗

(1) 读作 de-PRESS-ing and DE-solate LOOM mount WU and the GORGE be-LOW。

(2) chrysanthemums 有略：al-REA-dy TWICE seen BLOOM-ing chry-SANTH-mums 'fore TEAR-ful EYES。 相当于 Chrysanthemums seen blooming already twice before...，过去分词独立结构作状语，修饰下句子主体。原诗“他日”指往昔或以前平素（不同于现在常表的“以后”之意）。

(3) 后半行相当于 (though) poor souls (are) yearning for home，省略成现在分词独立结构。

咏怀古迹（之三）

杜甫

群山万壑赴荆门，生长明妃尚有村。
一去紫台连朔漠，独留青冢向黄昏。
画图省识春风面？环珮空归月夜魂。
千载琵琶作胡语，分明怨恨曲中论。

〖今译〗

千万条清泉，来自千万重翠岗，汇成那荆江浩荡，
大江岸旁是昭君出生成长的地方：那秀丽的村庄。
永别了，紫禁宫苑的楼台，胡骑已驰进黄沙莽莽；
你只把一座常青的高冢，留作黄昏时滋润的光芒。

可曾从画工笔下识得你的仪容？你和美有如春风；
只落得深夜月明、空有幽魂归来，响着环珮叮咚。
千秋万世，人们听那琵琶弦中，依然是胡语呢哝，
弦语虽然难解，却分明是当年说不尽的怨恨重重。

On Historic Sites

All are drawing to the Gorge, the myriad ranges and dales; [扬抑6]
There was Zhaojun born and nurtured, the palace maid.[1]
Out of the Purple City you went on deserts wild,
Merely a Green Tomb is left, at dusk to shimmer mild.[2]

Did the portrait bring them forth, your graces spring-like?[3]
Vainly returns your spirit, pendants tinkling in moonlight.
Thousands of years the *pipa* singing in Tartars' tongue,
Plainly bitter complaint and resentment sounds the tone.[4]

〖评注〗

(1) “明妃”即王昭君，本名王嫱（字昭君），西晋时为避司马昭（晋开国皇帝司马炎之父）讳，改其名叫“明君”或明妃。“紫台”指皇家宫苑楼台；也称紫宫、紫禁宫、禁城或禁苑。唐贾至《早朝大明宫》：“银烛朝天紫陌长，禁城春色晓苍苍。” 开头 There 重读，“就是在那里……”。参见202页评注。

(2) at dusk to shimmer mild 相当于 to shimmer mildly at dusk。英诗中常用形容词代替副词。关于青冢，见102页评注。

(3) 传说汉元帝让画工毛延寿为众宫人画像，将按肖像选召。众女为求美画而向毛延寿行贿，但昭君不屑于此。她的肖像不佳，人也未得理睬。匈奴单于求亲，元帝传令寻求志愿出塞之女，昭君宁愿去国，以免终身埋没。她临行时，元帝才惊见昭君之容貌。后毛延寿被杀。“画图省识春风面？”是反问，强调画像误导。省(xǐng)识，即认识或察看。 bring them forth 相当于 make them seen/known（使对方看到…），them 指代下面点明的 your graces 你的优雅。

(4) sounds，联系动词，常与形容词或名词表语连用；the tone sounds ... , 这曲调听起来是…… 。

登高

杜甫

风急天高猿啸哀，渚清沙白鸟飞回。
无边落木萧萧下，不尽长江滚滚来。
万里悲秋常作客，百年多病独登台。
艰难苦恨繁霜鬓，潦倒新停浊酒杯。

〖评注〗

(1) 头韵wild, wind; skies, scaring。行内韵 wild, high, skies, cries；limpid shallows, pallid sands 。

(2) ailments，尤指连绵不断的病痛。heights，复数形式，表示“高地”“高台”。

(3) wear and tear (worn and torn 二过去分词)，惯用语。前第三行 thick and fast 也是惯用语。杜甫留蜀 6 年，763年正月，叛军首领史朝义兵败自缢（先前安禄山被其子安庆绪暗杀，安庆绪被叛军将领史思明杀死，史思明又被其子部将所杀），杜甫于这年春天闻讯写了《闻官军收河南河北》：“剑外忽传收蓟北，初闻涕泪沾衣裳。却看妻子愁何在？漫卷诗书喜若狂。白日放歌须纵酒，青春作伴好还乡。即从巴峡穿巫峡，便下襄阳向洛阳。”他满想立刻回到东京洛

Ascending the Heights

Wild's the wind, and high the skies, and scaring cries of apes. [扬抑7]
Limpid the shallows, pallid the sands, there hovering birds astray.[1]
Thick and fast, unending tumbling about are leaves in flakes.
Rolling, roaring, endless pouring down the River Great.
Homeland thousands of miles away, a stranger with autumn gloomed,
Nearly a lifetime's ailments through, I climb the heights alone.[2]
Worn and torn by worries, my hair as hoary as frost I find.[3]
Downcast, dismayed, I've got to keep apart from my cup of wine!

阳旧居，但是紧接着吐蕃、回纥入侵，藩镇割据逞凶，使他久未成行。765年，严武病故，杜甫受排挤辞官，才不得不离开成都，顺岷江而南、入长江而东，准备绕道返回洛阳家园；却因中原烽火此伏彼起，途中屡屡停滞。夔州（今奉节）迟疑两年还多；再登舟到江陵（今江陵）、岳州（今岳阳）、潭州与衡州（今长沙与衡阳）；他始终无地容身，小舟漂泊于长江湘江上。不仅耳半聋、齿零落，右臂偏枯，疟疾和肺病也一再发作。

杜甫从夔州白帝山城远望荆门，写下《咏怀古迹》（之三），追念明妃，更在为正直士子深深埋没而悲愤诉说。《秋兴》八首是夔州第一个秋天的怀乡之作。夔州又一个凉秋到来，他写下尤其凄惨、对景伤怀的这首《登高》。

登岳阳楼

杜 甫

昔闻洞庭水，今上岳阳楼。
吴楚东南坼，乾坤日夜浮。
亲朋无一字，老病有孤舟。
戎马关山北，凭轩涕泗流！

〖今译〗

以前总听说洞庭湖浩瀚的奇景，
今天得登上岳阳楼最高的楼层。
吴疆楚土从此处向东南陡然断裂，
太阳月亮漂浮水上形成日日夜夜。

亲戚朋友啊，各在异乡何处，没有音信半点；
衰老病痛中，我能凭靠什么，除此孤舟水面？
战祸绵延，战马嘶鸣，北望关山间阴阴惨惨；
楼窗人寂，楼外风紧，泪水禁不住洒落涟涟！

Ascending *Yueyang* Tower

So long and well I've known of *Dongting* Lake, [抑扬5]
Which now on *Yueyang* Tower for myself I see:
From Central Plains here split the South and the East;
The Universe, Sun and Moon, seem afloat on the waves.[1]
No word e'er comes from former friends and kin;[2]
Both aged and ailing, a lonely boat I'm in.
Invading tribesmens' horses our homeland trampling,
Afar I gaze while tears down cheeks are streaming.

〖评注〗

(1) 原文"乾坤"在《周易》中指"阳""阴"，引申为"天地"、"日月"、"男女"、"万物"（见《辞海》）。这里取其形象，用于"日夜浮"，则突出指示"日""月"，宇宙首先呈现的景观。

(2) word from 是"来自……的信息"， 这里 word 属于不可数名词。e'er 为 ever之略。kin 集合名词。

《登岳阳楼》作于768年冬；一年多后，诗人衣食无继、医药无缘，病逝于湘水舟中。

枫桥夜泊

张继（生卒年代不详）

月落乌啼霜满天，江枫渔火对愁眠。
姑苏城外寒山寺，夜半钟声到客船。

〖评注〗

(1) 有人怀疑，当年的寺庙偏偏会夜半敲打大钟吗？事实是肯定的，尤其是山中的庙宇，有诗文记载可予以证明。唐朝皇甫冉诗就写过："秋深临水月，夜半隔山钟"。

残月和霜天，是"冷色"；枫叶和渔火，却是"暖色"。乌啼和寺钟是"低响"，夜江和寒山却是"沉寂"。声色交织当中，暗暗积淀的总是羁旅的哀愁。

历来多把这首小诗，和晚唐张祜的《题金陵渡》(*Written on the Wall of Jinling Ferry-House*)相类比："金陵津渡小山楼，一宿行人自可愁；潮落夜江斜月里，两三星火是瓜州。"

'Pon the hill-foot turret at the *Jinling* ferry-head,
How lonely is the traveler staying for the night!
On the ebb is the darkish river; in the west the moon retreats;
There *Guazhou* is, where shimmering sparkes in twos and threes.

两首绝句，把南京东北的"瓜州渡口"和顺流稍前的"姑苏枫桥"，永远留作了中华古代文明的迷人胜地。南京古称金陵；瓜州在长江北岸，南对镇江，北邻扬州。从镇江东南行不远，就是太湖和姑苏（今苏州）了。

Mooring at Maple Bridge for the Night

Upon the river a sallow moon sets low. [5音步]
Frost fills the sky; the cold wrings plaints from crows.
'Fore the maples' loom and the fishing torches' glow,
In bed yet sleepless, I'm steeped in gathering gloom.
On outskirts of *Gusu* is the Temple of Chilly Hill.
The boat resounds with their tolling midnight's bell.[1]

寒食

韩翃（生卒年代不详）

春城无处不飞花，寒食东风御柳斜。
日暮汉宫传蜡烛，轻烟散入五侯家。

〖评注〗

(1) flowers and catkins 是上行 fly “使飞”的宾语。原文的“斜”读 xia，与“花、家”押韵 。

(2) the Day 指标题所点明的 Cold Food Day，纪念春秋时期晋国大臣介子推的寒食节：在护送晋文公国外流亡期间，介子推是特别劳苦功高的。但文公终于归国成为国君、并大赏功臣时，他拒绝文公的封赏，逃进山林。文公派人搜寻，无法找到，就令人放火来烧树林，想迫使他出来，他却宁死不肯露面，竟被烧焦在密林里。清明前三天是他殉难之日，晋文公为此让整个晋国年年在此时期禁火三日，大家都熄灭炉灶，不点火做饭，只吃凉的东西。这一做法以后成了中国的传统节日“寒食节”。本诗后两句描写纪念日终了的晚上，人们重新燃起火种并互相传递时、宫中以蜡烛向贵族人家传送新火的情景。

韩翃为“大历（代宗年号）十才子”之一，颇有诗名，他的《寒食》广为传诵。他进士及第，但很久不得可心官职。一天深夜，有人猛敲韩翃家门，高喊：“皇帝任命你为郎中，给皇帝起草诏书！”韩翃难以相信突如其来的消息，来人说：“德宗皇帝要找秘书，而宰相所荐都不称心，便自己提出韩翃；经宰相查找，韩翃有二，一是江淮刺史，一是你；请示时，皇帝说用作《寒食》‘日暮汉宫传蜡烛’的韩翃，还有错吗？”可见唐代是上上下下全都喜爱吟诵诗歌啊！

Cold Food Day

All o'er the capital, Spring is flying at will [扬抑5]
Flowers and catkins of hers e'er far and wide.[1]
Palace willow twigs are drifting aslant,
Greeting the Day, in an easterly wind alert.[2]
Now at nightfall, candles are passed about,
Emperor's court throughout, within then without.
Silver smoke from tapers is seen extending
Into the neighboring noted nobles' dwellings.

征人怨

柳中庸（生卒年代不详）

岁岁金河复玉关，朝朝马策与刀环。
三春白雪归青冢，万里黄河绕黑山。

〖评注〗

(1) 相当于 It's beyond Jade Pass ... (that) we'll go. 诗歌中介词可后置。

(2) 相当于 or to wield spears and swords in close combats（短兵相接近战中……）。spear, sword 头韵；下面有 snows, serve, springtime, soil 和 remote, run, Range。

(3) The palace maid Wang Zhaojun(Lady Ming) of the *Han* Dynasty was married to a Tartar King. She spent her life helping maintain peace across the border regions. After her death, it is said, her tomb remained the only evergreen spot across the vast deserts over which roamed the tribespeople. See p.202, Note 1.

玉门关简称玉关，在黄河上游东面；金河据某些资料，在今呼和浩特市南；青冢即王昭君墓在呼和浩特南郊，据说荒漠中那高墓常年草木滋润（见93、202页）；黑山有多处，呼和浩特北面的杀虎山亦

Soldiers' Complaint

O year 'pon year, for sure we only know [抑扬5]
It's Jade Pass or Golden Rapids beyond we'll go.[1]
Then day in day out, whether our horses we whip,
Or spears and swords in combat close we wield.[2]
All melted winter snows just serve to moist
Thro springtime a green, green tomb 'mid the desert soil.[3]
Why'd you, that Yellow River, while running on,
Keep winding and winding the Darkish Range along ?

称黑山。该诗把玉门、长城和三千多里以外河套东北的金河、青冢联在一起，说黑山像黄河一样绵延远去，都不是实指，而是喻指。说的是，日复一日、年复一年，遥山远水、荒凉边塞，士兵的困苦可想而知。

“岁”对“朝”，“金”对“玉”，“马策”对“刀环”，再加平仄相应，韵脚回环，使委婉情意，更加荡气回肠。翻译中，应该是尽量使用头韵、尾韵、反复、对称等等传达手法。

三闾庙

戴叔伦（732—789）

沅湘流不尽，屈子怨何深？
日暮秋风起，萧萧枫树林！

〖评注〗

(1) Qu Yuan had served his homeland the *Chu* Kingdom as a political advisor and the administrator of the 3 royal families'affairs (三闾大夫) , before he was exiled to the South of the *Yangtze* River. So the temple to Qu Yuan is called in Chinese "三闾庙". See p.25, *Lamentations Over Estrangement.*

清代施补华撰《岘庸说诗》论《三闾庙》道:"并不用意，而言外自有悲凉慷慨之气。五言中此格最高。"

三闾，三姓人家；三闾庙，即屈原祠；屈原曾任"三闾大夫"，掌管楚国昭、屈、景三姓贵族子弟的教育。屈子，即屈原。据传，湖北汨罗屈子祠原有对联："何处招魂？香草还生三户地；当年呵壁，湘流应识《九歌》心。"

呵壁，对着墙壁呵斥。东汉王逸为解释屈原《天问》所作《天问序》写道："屈原放逐，忧心愁悴，彷徨山泽，经历陵陆，嗟嚎昊昊，仰天叹息。见楚有先王之庙及公卿祠堂，图画天地山川神灵，琦玮谲诡，及古贤圣怪物行事……因书其壁，呵而问之，以泄愤懑，舒泻愁思。"《天问》意即质问苍天，屈原所作《九歌》之一 。

The Temple to Qu Yuan[1]

The rivers *Yuan* and *Xiang* keep rushing on their ways. [6音步]
Injustice the patriot suffered will never be washed away!
Thro' maple woods that've heard him on departing his
prayers say,
At twilight tears a gale, and groan and moan the trees.

和梧叶诗

顾况（725—814）

愁对莺啼柳絮飞，上阳宫女断肠时。
君恩不闭东流水，叶上题诗知给谁？

〖评注〗

(1) 关于“上阳宫”见119页《上阳白发人》的评注。

willow fluff a-flying，飞舞着的柳絮。a- 常加于名词或动名词，构成表语形容词，作表语或后位定语。参见 50页《燕歌行》评注2。

(2) Isn't it kind of...(not) to... ? 趋于肯定的疑问句，相应肯定句句型是 It is very kind of the emperor to do something. 或 It is very kind of him not to do something. 但这首诗中，是反衬与嘲讽。

(3) 梧桐因类似原产欧洲的 plane tree（悬铃木，法国梧桐），多译作Chinese plane，简称plane。这首诗是对中唐时上阳宫女“梧叶诗”的答复。据传，从洛阳上阳宫外流水中拾得梧叶诗的青年书生，把该诗交给自己的老师、著名诗人顾况。顾况为之写此《和梧叶诗》。原《梧叶诗》(*Poem on a Plain Leaf*) 是：“一入深宫里，年年不见春。聊题一片叶，寄与有情人。”（下边英文解说的中间四行即其英译）

As the title of this poem has made clear, it is a reply to another poem, and about that poem there goes a strange story. It was in the middle of the Tang Dynasty. A young scholar was taking a walk along the brook streaming down through *Shangyang* Palace. The Palace was situated in *Luoyang* City, hundreds of miles from the Capital *Chan'an*, and was lived in by pretty maids who had been chosen from all over the country as possible imperial concubines but had never had a chance to come in sight of the Emperor. The youth noticed a plane leaf afloat on the flow and picked it up. On that leaf he found to his surprise these lines：

In Reply to a Poem on a Plane Leaf

Upset by warblers warbling and willow fluff a-flying,[1] [6音步]
You maid confined, your youthful days away you're sighing.
Yet isn't it kind of His Majesty — ne'er to block this brook?[2]
The leaf with your verse may reach one taking pity on you![3]

E'er since I was caged herein, in palaces deep,
O no more spring days' scenes for me to see.
Here written on a leaf to be sent out adrift are my lines —
Just who would by chance receive it and feel for the confined?

He took the leaf to his teacher, the famous poet Gu Kuang. Having read the curious lines-on-leaf, Gu wrote his "*In Reply to a Poem on a Plane Leaf*"(the poem above the notes). A copy of Gu's lines was made on another plane leaf that was dropped into the brook somewhere upstream, above the Palace. To the greater astonishment of all, just the next day another poem-on-leaf was discovered and brought back to Gu Kuang. That reads as follows（the next poem, included in Note 4: *Once More Written on a Plane Leaf*）.

(4) 令人惊奇的是，顾况的答诗从上游投入溪流的次日，有人在下游再次发现另一梧叶，题有《又题洛院梧叶》（*Once More Written on a Plane Leaf*上阳宫佚名宫女作）："一叶题诗出禁城，谁人酬和独含情。自嗟不及波中叶，荡漾乘春取次行。"

One leaf was out of the palace deep with my lines.
Now who's so kindly written his poem in reply?
What a shame I'm not as lucky as leaves on the flow,
As those that're drifting away for a springtime stroll!

红叶诗

韩 氏

流水何太急，深宫尽日闲。
殷勤谢红叶，好去到人间！

〖评注〗

(1) steal by,（时间等）悄悄地溜过去。

(2) 传说此诗作者韩氏原为唐朝长安宫女，她把题诗的红叶投入御沟后，正好有个读书人于佑，在宫外闲逛，欣赏秋景，赏玩霜叶。他恰巧望见水面漂来那又红又大的叶片。怎么叶上还似乎有字？他赶快用树枝拨它过来，发现了那首小诗。他听说过顾况和梧叶诗的故事，便也另寻红叶，题写两句，转到御沟上游，送诗叶下水。叶上写道：“曾闻叶上题红怨，叶上题诗寄阿谁？”（《红叶联句》）

于佑考进士，多年没有考取。为了谋生，在一个大宦官韩泳的亲戚家里教孩子们读书。韩泳和于佑渐渐熟悉后，赶上皇帝要放一批宫女嫁人，就对于佑说：“你虽然没有取得功名，但也不应该耽误成家。现在皇上恩典，准许三千宫女出宫。有个和我同姓的女子人品很好，我来给你作个媒，好吗？”

于佑同意，便和那宫女结了婚。一天，新婚的妻子给丈夫收拾书箱，突然见到夹在书中题有小诗的红叶，又惊又喜。原来她就是写诗的韩氏。她问明于佑得叶情况后说，自己投诗御沟后也曾从御沟里拾回一叶，上面有诗二句。她取出那片红叶给于佑看时，于佑认出，正是自己所题。韩氏随即告诉丈夫，她还为得此诗叶写了另一首诗《惊

Written on a Red Leaf

What haste you're in, O drifts in imperial garden's stream, [6音步]
While idle days steal by, deep palaces staying still,![1]
I entrust to a red, red drifting leaf my longings shy,
In quest of someone's pity in human world alive.[2]

得红叶联句，更使望空兴叹》，说着拿诗给于佑看：

“独步天沟岸，临流得叶时；此情谁会得，肠断一联诗。”

不久，韩泳请于佑夫妻吃饭，对二人说：“你俩该感谢我，促成这段姻缘。”韩氏答道：“当然要感激大人，然而更要感谢老天的美意。”随即把两片诗叶拿给韩泳看，韩泳连连惊叹：“这真是天赐良缘！天赐良缘！”就此，韩氏又提笔写下一首新诗《红叶缘》（*The Red Leaf as Match-Maker*）：“一联佳句随流水，十载幽思满素怀。今日却成鸾凤友，方知红叶是良媒。”

With flows adrift were red leaves of autumn bleak;
For years my heart was filled with yearnings unrevealed.
At length we're granted conjugal blessings divine,
Our thanks to the leaves — our miraculous go-between !

历代深宫中关闭的宫女能以千、万计吗？其中碰上奇迹、似此结缘的真曾有过？而像白居易所写“上阳白发人”的又有多少呢？

夜上受降城闻笛

李 益（748—827）

回乐烽前沙似雪，受降城外月如霜。
不知何处吹芦管，一夜征人尽望乡。

〖评注〗

(1) 单纯陈述不如一问一答意味浓烈：O no one knows whencc(from where) there waft the plaintive notes of a flute. — Whence …? O no one knows!

受降城：唐初，太宗击败来犯的突厥军，亲临灵州（今宁夏灵武）受降。后突厥仍常侵扰，朔方道大总管张仁愿在黄河上游（今宁夏、内蒙交界处）筑三座受降城，借以防御。本诗所写一城在灵州回乐县（今灵武县西）。

回乐烽，指回乐受降城烽火台，beacon tower 。

与此诗有些相似,李白《春夜洛城闻笛》(*Flute Tune heard in Luoyang*)，也是一首七言绝句："谁家玉笛暗飞声？ 散入春风满洛城。此夜曲中闻折柳，何人不起故园情？"

Whose window is it from, this doleful, doleful tone of a flute?
All over *Luoyang* City the spring breeze gets it diffused.
On hearing *Plucking Willow Twigs* the farewell strain,
Whoever could tonight from thoughts of homeland refrain?

《折柳》即《折杨柳》乐曲，王之涣《凉州词》（68页）："羌笛何须怨《杨柳》？"所指也是那支乐曲。

李白诗《听黄鹤楼中吹笛》："一因迁客去长沙，西望长安不见家；黄鹤楼中吹玉笛，江城五月《落梅花》。"五月并非梅花凋落之季节，梅花是早春很早就开花的。那《落梅花》实际就是听到笛子吹奏的《梅花落》曲调。

On Hearing a Flute at Night from the Gate-Tower of *Shouxiang* City

Beyond the beacon towers spreading sands like snows; [6音步]
Before the City walls the moonlight shines like frost.
Whence waft those plaintive notes of a flute? O no one knows![1]
All night, bewildered, our warriors seeking dreams of home.

游子吟

孟 郊（751—814）

慈母手中线，游子身上衣。
临行密密缝，意恐迟迟归。
谁言寸草心，报得三春晖？

Chant of the Rover

In loving Mother's hand a thread keeps shuttling, [5音步]
To mend a travelling suit for thee who'rt parting.
O why doth she with stitches small, small sew?
For fear be thou away so long, long on th' rove![1]
Say not a petty grass-blade grateful, can possibly repay[2] [6音步]
Spring sunshine's nursing unfailing — throughout its suckling days!

〖评注〗

(1) on the rove=roving on and on; 上who'rt（旧形式） = who is。

(2) 抑扬格诗句，偶有开头音步二音节，同属重读的，如 SAY NOT a PET-ty GRASS-blade, GRATE-ful, can POS-sibly re-PAY。下面末行开头，Spring Sun- 也双双重读。原文“三春”指孟春、仲春、季春，各约一个月（另有三夏、三秋、三冬的说法）。

酬乐天扬州初逢席上见赠

刘禹锡（772—842）

巴山楚水凄凉地，二十三年弃置身。
怀旧空吟闻笛赋，到乡翻似烂柯人。
沉舟侧畔千帆过，病树前头万木春。
今日听君歌一曲，暂凭杯酒长精神。

Responding to Bai's Poem on First Meeting

Up heights I tramp — the wildest West, [4音步]
Down streams and swamps — I find no cheers,
Being e'er an exile given to unrest,
Thro' all these score and three long years.

While missing friends of old I cite,
Though helpless, lines from "*Saddening Flute*";
Perchance my axe has decayed with time?
I getting home know not who's who.[1]

Alone the shipwreck's stranded waste,
With endless sails by passing swift.[2]
Around a tree pest-stricken in gloom,
All buds of spring will be forth abloom.

Had not I heard this chant of thine,
Away my heart would be pining in vain,[3]
From both thine hands, a glass of wine,
My spirits stirring up again.[4]

〖评注〗

(1)《闻笛赋》原名《思旧赋》，魏晋间向秀所作。向秀的好友嵇康被阴谋篡夺魏政权的司马昭诬陷斩首后，向秀路过嵇康故居，听到吹笛，作此赋悼念亡友。刘禹锡因参与改革；故旧死难，自己两次被贬长达23年，旅途遇见白居易，说自己怀念旧友的心情和向秀相仿。

"烂柯人"指传说中的东晋樵夫王质，他入山打柴，见两个少年在下棋，把斧子放下，看了一会儿。少年催他回家时，他的斧柄已经成了朽木，到家发现亲人都已去世，人说他离开已逾百年。这两行也可译作 Have centuries glided past so swift? On getting home I don't know who's who.

Like Rip Van Winkle in *Sketch Book* by the American writer Washington Irving (1783-1859), a wood-cutter, Wang Zhi, in the Chinese story, had a similar adventure. He saw two boys playing chess in some mountainside woods, and watched the game for a while. When he was about to leave for home, urged by one of the youngsters, he was surprised to find the shaft of his axe decayed. On getting home, none of his family members were there. People asked him what time it was when he went out to cut wood. It turned out that over a hundred years had passed since his going up the mountain.

(2) by passing swift 读作"轻-重-轻-重 "；如用swiftly passing by 则是"重-轻-重-轻-重"。

(3) 相当于 If I had not heard ..., my heart would be pining away ...；away 有"一直……下去"之意。

(4) h 前的 thine 相当于 your：... a glass of wine, from both your hands, stirring up my spirits again.

乌衣巷

刘禹锡

朱雀桥边野草花，乌衣巷口夕阳斜。
旧时王谢堂前燕，飞入寻常百姓家。

Black Dress Lane[1]

Beside the Red Bird Bridge grow rampant flowers wild.[2] [6音步]
The entrance to Black Dress Lane at sunset is tinted mild.
The swallows that used to nest 'neath eaves of the great and honored
Are nowadays seen to fly into humble peoples' quarters.

〖评注〗

(1) 豪奢、权势犹如过眼云烟。旧京建康（古金陵，现南京）秦淮河上有"朱雀桥"，桥头曾由东晋丞相谢安饰以一双朱红铜雀。南岸是起初东吴乌衣部队的营地，后来"乌衣巷"权贵汹汹、冠盖如云。曾几何时，这里已尽是野花杂草、俗子凡夫。

东晋初建时期，王导（276-339）作了丞相，其堂兄王敦（266-324）任大将军，二人掌握军政大权；王敦一度因晋元帝抑制王氏势力而攻占京城建康、杀死元帝谋臣。东晋后期谢安（320-385）作丞相；其弟谢石、其侄谢玄奉谢安之命迎击北方"前秦"南下的大军，取得淝水之战辉煌胜利；但是谢石搜刮民财、贪得无厌。王、谢指六朝第二个朝代东晋的这两大家族，译诗以 the great and honored 代表二者。

(2) 重读音节后轻读(bird, grow)：be-SIDE the RED bird BRIDGE grow RAM-pant FLOW-ers WILD.

(3) 刘禹锡金陵怀古绝句与《乌衣巷》齐名的有《石头城》(*Stone City*)："山围故国周遭在，潮打空城寂寞回；淮水东边旧时月，夜深还过女墙来。"淮水，指秦淮河，六朝歌舞胜地；女墙，城墙上边呈凹凸状的短墙。英译如下：

Grave hills remain surrounding the site the monarchs left.
Quiet tides at the wall of the forsaken capital flow and ebb.
To the east of the *Huai*, the moon that their merry-making has seen[4],
As of yore, now rises o'er battlements in nights serene.

(4) The ancient capital *Nanjing* has the great *Yangtze* River passing on the North, and its tributary the *Qinhuai* (or simply the *Huai*) flowing through the city.

古原草

白居易（772—846）

离离原上草，一岁一枯荣。
野火烧不尽，春风吹又生。
远芳侵古道，晴翠接荒城。
又送王孙去，萋萋满别情。

Grasses on an Ancient Plain

Lushy, lushy, grow the grasses o'er the plain; [杨抑6]
Yearly, yearly, they wither yet to thrive again.
Hard as heath fires ever attempt to burn them out, [1]
Vernal breezes wafting, back they're all about.

Stretching the green afar, o'ergrowing ancient roads;
Th' emerald shining brightly, reaches lonely abodes.
Friends are seeing the wanderer off on his way once more.
There the country is filled with our endless parting remorse.

〖评注〗

(1) 所强调Hard后的as相当于though：Though heath fires forever attempt hard to burn them out, ...

白居易这首诗原题《赋得古原草送别》。“赋得”是唐代科举考试诗题前面通用的两个字；而此诗是白居易 16 岁时首次到京城长安、谒见“著作郎”顾况时，呈阅的习作之一。顾况曾玩笑地议论其名“居易”。说长安米贵，居京实在不易，后读这首五绝立刻补充说：“道得个语，居即易矣！”

王孙，原指王侯的子孙，此处作为对名门子弟或体面男子的称呼。

汉朝开国大将韩信当年贫困，在河边钓鱼不得，饿得躺在地上。漂洗新纱的妇女中，一位慈祥“漂母”怜悯他，给他拿饭吃，多日不断。他说：“吾必有以重报母。”漂母生气地驳斥道：“大丈夫不能自食，吾哀王孙而进食，岂望报乎？”后来，韩信封为楚王，找到仍然健在的老太太，礼毕奉上千金，酬谢赐饭之恩。

王维《送别》：“山中相送罢，日暮倚柴扉；明年春草绿，王孙归不归？”

萋萋，碧草繁茂的样子；西汉淮南王刘安《招隐士》“王孙游兮不归，春草生兮萋萋”（西汉刘向编《楚辞》）。

上阳白发人（节选）

白居易

上阳人，上阳人，红颜暗老白发新。
绿衣监使守宫门，一闭上阳多少春？
玄宗末岁初选入，入时十六今六十。
同时采择百余人，零落年深残此身。
忆昔吞悲别亲族，扶入车中不教哭。
皆云入内便承恩，脸似芙蓉胸似玉。
未容君王得见面，已被杨妃遥侧目。
妒令潜配上阳宫，一生遂向空房宿。
宿空房，秋夜长。夜长无寐天不明。
耿耿残灯背壁影，萧萧暗雨打窗声。
春日迟，日迟独坐天难暮。
宫莺百啭愁厌闻，梁燕双栖老休妒。
莺归燕去常悄然，春往秋来不记年。
唯向深宫望明月，东西四五百回圆。
……

A Shut-in Old Maid at *Shangyang* Palace

With one in Shangyang, with her, what a piteous plight! [抑扬5]
In vain her rosy cheeks fade pale from bright;
Her black hair turning grey, and newly white.
The palace gate being guarded by wardens in green,
On its shutting all her springs were locked therein.

She came along in late years of Xuanzong's reign;
Her sixty-years of age was then sixteen.
Although arrived together scores and scores,
Now all, except for her, remain no more.

While long ago she was parted from dearest folks,
"No more of your tears, O no," on the coach she was told.
"She's certain to win the Emperor's heart in a day,"
There everybody took it for granted and sure —[1]
"Because like a water-lily abloom is her face;
Her neck and breast as fair as white jade pure!"

But ere she had chance to be within His Majesty's sight,
She was spied by Guifei the Consort's jealous eyes.
So at once she was ousted stealthily far away,
And ensconced in such a lonely chamber to stay,
All alone, night in, night out, for the rest of her days.[2]

O nights so long in autumn in the lonely room,
Long nights e'er sleepless; would there be daylight again?[3]
On the wall so faint, faint lit, her shadow loomed.[4]
And pitter-patter tapping the window was th' rain.

And then came spring with lonesome longer days.
Spring days grew longer and longer; she sat there still,
Ne'er time for the dusk to creep on her window-sill.[5]

The warblers warbled away; she was utterly bored.
The swallows on beams in pairs were envied no more.

Those birds would be gone for days of solitary sighs;
Unnumbered were Springs and Autumns coming and going,
But for Moon being seen in the deepest of palaces moving
From east to west at its full for hundreds of times ...

〖评注〗

(1) 读作：there E-very-BO-dy TOOK it for GRANT-ed and SURE。

(2) 上行 lonely，本行 All alone，下行有 lonely；本行 night in, night out，下面 O nights so long … Long nights；一起传达原文的连绵"遂向空房宿。宿空房。秋夜长，夜长无寐"等。

(3) Long nights ever sleepless 同位语修饰上一行的 nights。

(4) On the wall so faint(ly) faint(ly) lit 状语修饰 her shadow loomed。

(5) Never time for the dusk to creep on..., 相当于 It would never be time for the dusk to creep on ...

上阳宫，本是东都洛阳皇帝的行宫。白居易原诗前有小序："天宝五载(746)以后，杨贵妃专宠，后宫之人无复进幸矣。六宫有美色者，辄置别所，上阳是其一也。贞元（785年为贞元元年）间尚存焉。"

即经四代皇帝，四五十年后，还保留着这囚禁美女的"别宫"。晚唐诗人章碣以上阳宫人口气写绝句《东都望幸》："懒修珠翠上高台，眉月连娟恨不开。纵使东巡也无益，君王自领美人来。"皇帝各处巡游，自带专宠。上阳宫女，盼望皇帝从长安过来，也是空盼一场。

章碣此诗实际是在讽刺科举私弊，不过，空等怜惜的弱女子和妄求赏识的读书人，自怜自误是一模一样的。

离思

元稹(779—831)

曾经沧海难为水，除却巫山不是云；
取次花丛懒回顾，半缘修道半缘君。

〖今译〗

既曾行经沧海，何方还会有那般水域？
除非深入巫山，别处哪里见如彼云霓？
任随千花万朵一丛丛过我面前，何曾看上一眼？
说是为清心安神，还是为对你刻骨铭心的思念！

In Memory of the Departed

Once having known the open seas wild surging, [5音步]
Just nothing of waters elsewhere would one be seeking.
O nowhere is seen a cloud of genuine appeal,
Except for that o'er Mount *Wu* drifting with ease.
Now none of the flourishing flowers draws from me my regard [6音步]
An ascetic I've turned, enshrining your memory at heart.[1]

〖评注〗

(1) memory 第一、三音节都重读。原文"取次"，任随哪个。黄庭坚《次韵裴仲谋同年》"烟沙篁竹江南岸，输与鸬鹚取次眠"。在本诗中该词的这一转义，不同于在107页附诗《又题洛院梧叶》中的"取次"所表本义"挨次"。参见《辞海》。

元稹的原配妻子，中年而逝，他的悼亡诗歌，还有著名的《遣悲怀》(*Venting My Grief*)："昔日戏言身后事，今朝都到眼前来。衣裳已施行看尽，针线犹存未忍开。尚想旧情怜婢仆，也曾因梦送钱财。诚知此恨人人有，贫贱夫妻百事哀。"

One day we said in jest: "Imagine one of us departs?"
But now before my eyes the scene has really come to pass.
As handouts, clothes of yours have almost all been given away.
Your needles and threads in the packet I cannot bear to open and see.
Rememb'ring your kindness to maids and servants, to do the same I try.
And dreaming of you, our needy folks I aid from time to time.
I know there's no escaping for every couple the parting of death.
Yet I, having long, long gone thro trials with you, I'm the saddest wretch.

金缕衣

杜秋娘（生卒年代不详）

劝君莫惜金缕衣，劝君惜取少年时。
花开堪折直须折，莫待无花空折枝！

〖评注〗

(1) 杜秋是中唐杰出歌女，“娘”是附加称呼。有人说此诗是镇海节度使李锜所作（杜秋是他家侍妾），可能因设想杜秋娘不如其主人高雅。实际上杜秋多才多艺，当时就以唱此诗闻名，清代蘅塘退士所编《唐诗三百首》认为她即作者。后李锜谋反，杜秋入宫，曾任穆宗幼子漳王的傅母（女教师）。

(2) 据说此诗是杜秋为赠别所爱的书生虞仲父而作的，后来虞仲父在京城被宦官禁军打死。

杜秋博览诗书，多才多艺，因父早亡，自幼饱受摧残，抱恨终身。她15岁被迫为镇海节度使李锜之妾。李锜谋反，事败被杀，杜秋娘受累俘入唐宫；在宫中为偏妃，当傅母，经四代皇帝，近30个春秋，终以被诬附逆，放逐还乡。

杜秋娘把穆宗幼子“漳王”从10岁抚养教育至21岁时，宦官诬告宰相宋申锡谋立漳王为帝。唐文宗听任宦官囚禁漳王、拷打宋申锡与杜秋娘，三人险被处斩。众臣说所告可疑，文宗才只把幼弟削王为“公”，宋申锡被贬，殁于异乡；杜秋娘时已48岁，被逐出皇宫，远返京口（今镇江），隐姓埋名，贫困致死。

晚唐诗人杜牧，京兆万年（今陕西西安）人，曾注孙子兵法，

Golden Brocade[1]

Prize not your golden-thread brocade; [4音步]
Prize but your golden youthful days!
Pick flowers the while they're blooming fair.
And tarry not till sprigs are bare.

有兴邦壮志，因无所用，蔑视权贵，但对备受蹂躏的歌女艺妓十分同情。杜秋娘被逐还乡二年后，杜牧31岁，因公过京口，寻访杜秋娘，写了《杜秋诗》：“……吴江落日渡，灞岸杨柳垂；四朝三十载，似梦复疑非。归来四邻改，茂苑草菲菲，清血洒不尽，仰天知问谁？”

金铜仙人辞汉歌

李贺（790—816）

茂陵刘郎秋风客，夜闻马嘶晓无迹。
画栏桂树悬秋香，三十六宫土花碧。
魏官牵车指千里，东关酸风射眸子。
空将汉月出宫门，忆君清泪如铅水。
衰兰送客咸阳道，天若有情天亦老。
携盘独出月荒凉，渭城已远波声小。

〖今译〗

安居于在茂陵墓中的刘郎，吟诵过《秋风歌》的汉帝，
可是又来看望我这故友？夜里听你马嘶，清晨不见踪迹。
画栏跟前，桂树挂满繁花，飘送着秋天的馥郁。
旧王朝三十六处宫苑，已布满苍苔，片片碧绿。
魏皇派官员拆我露台，驾好车要载我迁移千里；
一出东关便凄风凌厉，刺眼疾风让我痛彻眼底。
枉然让汉代留下的月亮相照，永远从故宫离去，
回想你武帝的恩遇，我潸然泪下，像铅水滴滴。
这咸阳古道上，送我远行的，只几朵幽兰低迷；
苍天呵，它若知情知意，也会为世事衰老悲戚。
带着捧露铜盘，孤零零上路，荒凉月影斜落天际。
渭城呵，汉宫！渐行渐远，渭水波声已不很清晰。

〖评注〗

(1) Zephyr's Song 即 Ode to the Autumn Wind。见32页《秋风辞》。
(2) disc，（承露）盘；所接露水，据说和玉屑饮用，长生不老。

中唐时期，藩镇割据、烽火迭起，李贺忧心忡忡，渴望为国效力。但是他父亲的名字“晋肃”与“进士”的前一个字同音。嫉妒李贺的

The Bronze Statue Taking His Leave

From your mausoleum, you Emperor-Poet of Zephyr's song. [6音步]
Your horse, heard neighing deep in the night, by dawn is gone.[1]
'Mid the painted galleries lingers the scent of osmanthus abloom,
O'er dozens of vacant palaces moss grows green in gloom.

Another dynasty's envoy's ordered to cart me afar,
At the East Gate bitter blasts are stinging my eyeballs smart.
No one but the moon from the Great *Han's* days is seeing me off,
With you at heart, dear Lord, my leaden tears down fall!

Then withering orchids watch me take to the ancient road.
Should Heaven be conscious, it too would be getting sick and old.
The farther I go, alone with the disc, the fainter the moon,[2]
The town out of sight, the waves of the *Wei* out of hearing soon.

人便散布流言，说他不能考取进士，那将违犯"家讳"。倾轧偏颇的科举考试中，李贺遭到强烈排挤。报国无门，后来只短期担任过九品卑微官职，因体衰多病，不得不含恨离京，返回昌谷（今河南宜阳西）故乡。李贺回乡仅三年，便在愁苦中病故，刚刚27岁。

(3) 诗前原有小序："魏明帝青龙元年八月，诏宫官牵车西取汉孝武捧露盘仙人，欲立置前殿。宫官既拆盘，仙人临载，乃潸然泪下。唐诸王孙李长吉遂作《金铜仙人辞汉歌》。"李贺，字长吉，因自己有皇室血亲的远房先人，故自称"诸王孙"（诸，多人中的一个）。汉孝武，汉武帝的别称。小序英译如下：

It was in the eighth month of the first year of the *Qinglong era,* during the reign of Emperor *Ming* of the *Wei* Dynasty. A palace officer was ordered to ride west and bring back the gilded bronze statue of an "immortal" that held a disc to catch dew, and that had been erected in the *Chang'an* Palace during the years of Emperor *Wu* of the *Han* Dynasty. The statue was to be moved to the new capital, and to be set up in the front courtyard. When the palace officer removed the disc and loaded the statue on to the cart, the bronze figure shed tears. So Li Changji, descended from a prince of the House of *Tang*, wrote this song *The Bronze Statue Taking His Leave.*

泊秦淮

杜牧（803—882？）

烟笼寒水月笼沙，夜泊秦淮近酒家。
商女不知亡国恨，隔江犹唱《后庭花》。

〖评注〗

(1) 秦淮，穿过古城金陵（今南京）、注入长江的秦淮河；河畔多歌舞场。商女，商家特别是酒楼女子。亡国，本指六朝建都金陵的南朝各国的灭亡；但寓意是对大唐王朝的警告。晚唐时期，皇室颓靡，宦官篡政、藩镇乱国，民变四起，败亡已迫在眉睫。

(2) About Backyard Flowers see p.204, Note 4.

《后庭花》，是隋前六朝最后误国之君陈后主所制靡靡之音。参见 204页 王安石《桂枝香·金陵怀古》评注3，310页 萨都剌《满江红·金陵怀古》评注3。

(3) 白居易是 846年逝世的，中唐其他主要诗人，先已作古，包括比白居易出生晚得多的李贺。其后，便是一般所说的“晚唐”时期了。杜牧是晚唐诗人中较早的一位。他所写以夜色为背景的哀怨小诗，还有著名的《秋夕》(*Autumn Night*)：“银烛秋光冷画屏，轻罗小扇扑流萤。天街夜色凉如水，卧看牵牛织女星。” 诗中只有清冷画屏为伴、

Mooring on the *Qinhuai* [1]

Enveloped in mist the water cold, in moonlight the shores. [6音步]
At night my boat, on the *Qinhuai*, beside a tavern moors.
The singsong girl not sensing yet the conquest's sting,
Still singing "*Backyard Flowers*," left by the fallen King[2].

闲捕萤火虫的主人公是谁呢？皇宫通道即白石铺砌的"天街"上，深夜无人了，她回去还不能入睡，躺在床上孤单注视秋空的牛郎和织女！

With autumn coming, the painted screen is chilling,
The light 'pon a silver candlestick now dimming.
In hand a silken fan so thin and small,
With that you try some fireflies to catch for sport.
Paved paths seem steeped in water cold as it's getting late.
In bed you watch the stars, the Cowherd and the Weaving Maid[4].

(4) About the Cowherd & the Weaving Maid, see p.38, Note 2.

金谷园

杜 牧

繁华事散逐香尘，流水无情草自春。
日暮东风怨啼鸟，落花犹似坠楼人。

〖评注〗

(1) 相当于 The flows running as heartlessly as of old。下行 flourishing，第一个和第三个音节都重读，后接轻读的 as。

(2) belov'd 表示词尾中读 [id] 的元音在此不发音，以合节律。

The owner of the Garden, Shi Chong of the *Jin* Dynasty(265-419), a most wealthy noble, was to be arrested and put to death. The singer of the house, Luzhu(Green Pearl), ended her own life by jumping off the tower from which her lord Shi and she herself had seen the soldiers forcing open the gate.

靠抢劫起家的富豪石崇，被抄家将死，还迫使歌女绿珠为他坠楼。在大男子主宰的漫长历史中，女性总是牺牲品。春秋西施（174页）、汉朝昭君（92页/202页）、班婕妤（160页）、西晋绿珠（本篇）、唐代杜秋娘（124页）、南宋徐君宝妻（280页）……甚至显赫一时的杨玉环，39岁就做了替罪羊。晚唐郑畋写《马嵬坡》(*Emperor Xuanzong Passing Mawei Mound*)："玄宗回马杨妃死，云雨难忘日月新；终是圣明天子事，景阳宫井又何人？"（宫井故事见311页）

The Emp'ror, returning on horseback, the revolt suppressed,
Now passes where his concubine hanged herself.
O what intense and tender attachments he recalls!
Yet gone are days of gaiety and glee of yore.
We deem His Maj'sty wiser in giving up,
Compared with King of *Chen*, imprisoned with his love!

Golden Dale Garden in Ruins

O pomp and vanity vanish swift, [4音步]
To follow the fragrant dust adrift.
As heartlessly running as of old the flows,[1]
There flourishing as ever the lawns.
The sun declines, a breeze arising;
Some mournful birds are bitterly crying.
Now falling blossoms suggest a belov'd —[2]
Green Pearl, the singer plunging from above!

过华清宫（其一）

杜 牧

长安回望绣成堆，山顶千门次第开；
一骑红尘妃子笑，无人知是荔枝来。

〖今译〗

从长安城回头望去，堆堆锦绣是别宫的花木亭台；
忽然在那高山顶上，千百道宫门都依次大敞开来。
一匹如飞的快马扬起红尘滚滚，让妃子笑逐颜开；
谁知是鲜美荔枝经多少骑手接力，来自迢迢域外！

Passing by *Huaqing* Palace on *Mount Li*

Behold, from *Chang'an*, Mount *Li* gorgeous and gay! [5音步]
O seems it not embroid'ry works on display?
Unnumbered gates on high are presently seen
Being thrown so widely open in quickest turn.

Thro' reddish rising dust there comes a horse;
Now Lady Yang's to give a smile so broad.
Yet none's aware: it's litchi arriving fresh,
Passed on and on by racing riders' relays[1].

〖评注〗

(1) relay 重音可在后：PASSED ON and ON by RAC-ing RID-er's re-LAYS。

《新唐书·杨贵妃传》："妃嗜荔枝，必欲生致之，乃置骑传送，走数千里，味未变，已至京师。"荔枝以广东、福建为主要产地，四川也有一些。东汉第四代皇帝和帝永元年间，一度从广东向京城洛阳进贡荔枝，也是在驿站间以人马接力、日夜兼程传送，当时就常有死伤。一下级官吏唐伯游，不顾自己地位低微，直接上书皇帝，陈明这样传送荔枝，实属扰民弊政。和帝下令免贡。唐玄宗天宝年间，奸相李林甫为笼络贵妃，又令人传送荔枝，但这是涪州（今四川涪陵）一带所产。该地距长安约一千五百华里，以快马接传，每昼夜跑五百里，三昼夜可到。宋苏轼的《荔枝叹》写道："十里一置飞尘灰，五里一堠兵火催。颠坑仆谷相枕藉，知是荔枝龙眼来。飞车跨山鹘横海，风枝露叶如新采。宫中美人一破颜，惊尘溅血流千载。"（一置、一堠，大小驿站；颠坑仆谷相枕藉，摔死的人马重叠险坑、深谷中；鹘(gǔ)，鹘鸠，古书所记的一种善飞候鸟；破颜，露出笑脸。）

陇西行

陈陶（812?—885?）

誓扫匈奴不顾身，五千貂锦丧胡尘。
可怜无定河边骨，犹是春闺梦里人。

〖评注〗

(1) Huns，匈奴人。前两行是以 All 为逻辑主语的过去分词与形容词独立结构，pledged 和 regardless of self 是逻辑谓语。这独立结构作状语，修饰下面句子主体 five thousand warriors were lost …。

五千貂锦，以西汉李陵事为典型，像征当代的征战悲剧。汉武帝晚年，派贰师将军李广利征讨不断犯边的匈奴。原令李陵押运辎重，而李陵自请分出一支奇兵为主力牵制强敌。汉武帝同意，并派大将路博德率部担当其后援。李陵转战千里，杀敌数倍于己，被八万敌军追逐，陷于深谷，箭支净尽。而汉军主力迟迟不发。路博德更因嫉人之功，按兵不动，致使李陵全军覆没。

李陵当晚对部下说："兵败，死矣！"部下劝慰他，举例说，赵破奴曾两次落入匈奴、两次立功返汉。李陵道："公止！吾不死，非壮士也！"（《汉书》）按其素日英勇，这决心应是真的。被俘或者说投降后，没有马上死去，或许真像司马迁所说，他"欲得其当而报汉"。文天祥在《指南录后序》中也讲到自己被执之初、未即时"引决"，是"将有以为也"。然而，大节岂容暧昧迟误，甚至因波折而动摇？

汉武帝认为司马迁为李陵辩解，是攻击自己所信赖的贰师将军，影射自己调遣不当，立即治司马迁以"宫刑"。后又听信谣言，说是李陵在为匈奴练兵。汉武帝偏听偏信，当即杀害了李陵老母和其全家。李陵终于作为降将，甘留匈奴至死。

By a River West of Mount *Long*

All pledged to beat the brutal invading Huns, [5音步]
Regardless of self, defending motherland,[1]
As one, five thousand warriors sable-clad
Were lost forever on remotest sullen sands.

O sadly, the bones already dried and white
That're now on the shore of the *Wuding* River scattered
Should still appear the youths of vigor and valor,
In springtime soothing dreams of the wishful wives.

梦泽

李商隐（813—858）

梦泽悲风动白茅，楚王葬尽满城娇。
未知歌舞能多少，虚减宫厨为细腰。

〖今译〗

凄凉梦泽，无边的茅草，秋风里茅草摇撼着白梢。
纤纤之美，楚王的偏爱，一时间京城葬尽了娇娆。
都弄不清，能为君王歌舞的，将有几位、待到几时？
只悄悄然，在宫中节食忍饿，竞相减损细细的腰肢。

〖评注〗

(1) 洞庭以南广大沼泽称梦泽。楚灵王爱细腰，使梦泽荒原埋葬着楚国渴望为王歌舞的一代少女。与此诗类同的晚唐张祜《何满子》(*The Dying Singer's Song* "*Heman*") 也写宫中歌女，那少女却是为临死缠她不放的昏君唱歌、过于激愤而毙命："故国三千里，深宫二十年。一声《何满子》，双泪落君前。"

O home deserted thousands of *li* away,
Confined in deepest of palaces for twenty years,
On singing the "*Heman*", the dying singer's lay,
Before the throne I can't help shedding tears.

Dreamy Marshland[1]

O'er Dreamy Marshland swaying are white-head reeds in wailing wind. [7音步]
The king of *Chu* has had the girls of his whole dominion ruined.
Not knowing how to get their chances to sing and dance in the court,
To reduce their waists e'er slender and slender they starved themselves for naught.

据南宋计有功《唐诗纪事》，此诗为悼念孟才人（“才人”是嫔妃称号）而作。诗中没提孟才人之死。但在另一七绝《孟才人叹》中张祜写明：“偶因歌态咏娇嚬，选入宫中二十春。却为一声《何满子》，下泉须吊旧才人。”事实是：武宗病危懊恼，把孟才人找来唱歌。他对那才人表示，自己死也舍不得她，如何是好。孟才人明白皇帝有意让她陪葬，便答称奴家甘愿自缢相陪。可以想见，她自幼进宫，远离家乡，与世隔绝，二十多年，忽然要为昏君而死。积压已久的满腔悲愤，猛地涌起。她提出先给皇上唱一曲《何满子》。她唱得悲悲切切、哽哽咽咽。一曲未了，她就跌倒在地、气绝而亡。《何满子》本是以唐玄宗年间沧州歌女之名为曲名的长歌，那歌女含冤被定死罪，临刑唱一曲哀歌，申述委屈，要求重新审判，竟未得准许。

无 题

李商隐

相见时难别亦难，东风无力百花残。
春蚕到死丝方尽，蜡炬成灰泪始干。
晓镜但愁云鬓改，夜吟应觉月光寒。
蓬莱此去无多路，青鸟殷勤为探看。

〖评注〗

(1) 正装词序是The silkworm does not cease to spin his silk ... until he is utterly exhausted ...

(2) 意即 It's regrettable — hair locks in the morning mirror looking changed. 此行和下行看来是男女对话，各述彼此的关怀。晓镜但愁，是女子自述；夜吟应觉，是女对男的猜想（“应……”不会说自己“应该”觉得寒冷）。而上面“蚕丝”（“思”可属男）、“烛泪”（泪多属女），似乎分别喻指男女的情意。

如果理解成，二句都指一人，或都是泛指，就显得同义重复。好像只有从男女双方设想，这两句诗，才是深了又深、透了又透。因而，我们的英译，使用了 he 和 she 明明白白拟人，而且指示春蚕和蜡烛象征两性。

(3) a far cry 意思是“很远的地方”，以 too 修饰 far 时冠词 a 移到 far 之后。不说 * a too far cry 。

蓬莱，传说中的仙境。青鸟，传情通气的使者。参看 182页 李璟《摊破浣溪沙》：“青鸟不传云外信，丁香空结雨中愁”。

A Poem Untitled

'Tis hard for us to get together, harder to part. [6音步]
By a languid easterly wind, all blossoms blown apart.
O not until he's utterly exhausted late in Spring
Does he, the silkworm, cease his silk from bosom to spin.[1]
While she is not yet burnt herself into cinders dead,
The candle cannot help but hot tears shed and shed.

"Regrettable — in morning mirror hair locks looking changed,"[2]
"Thro' night recitals moonlight must be felt so chilled."
Although, in fact, my fairyland's not too far a cry,[3]
There's only the bluebird entrusted between us two to ply.

无题（二首之二）

李商隐

重帏深下莫愁堂，卧后清宵细细长。
神女生涯原是梦，小姑居处本无郎。
风波不信菱枝弱，月露谁教桂叶香？
直道相思了无益，未妨惆怅是清狂。

〖今译〗

莫愁姑娘的闺房，掩着层层帏幔；
你久久躺在床上，漫漫凉夜无眠。
神女同君王相会，原来只是梦幻；
闺中自怜的少女，至今无人相伴。
狂风掀涌起波澜，不理解菱枝细弱得可怜；
月夜洒遍了冷露，谁顾及桂叶芳香被遮断？
说到头来呵，一往情深无助于如人所愿，
你却任自己、如醉如痴浸渍于惆怅无边。

〖评注〗

(1) “莫愁”，乐府诗歌中民间女子名。

原文第三句“神女”，指未嫁而卒、成为巫山女神的炎帝之女瑶姬；宋玉《高唐赋》讲，楚庄王游山，曾在梦中与神女相会。

据清初著名校勘家何焯等指出，此诗抒发的是怀才不遇、报国无门之苦楚。以男女之情，喻爱国之心，常见于古典诗歌。屈原《离骚》（24页）有“恐美人之迟暮”、“众女嫉余之娥眉兮”，王安石《明妃曲》（202页）有“咫尺长门闭阿娇，人生失意无南北”。

The Second of Two Untitled Poems

Sheets and sheets of curtains in Mochou's chamber hanging low,[1] [扬抑7]
Sleepless lies the maiden, as long night hours, so cold, drag slow.
Tale of the Fairy meeting the King was the touring monarch's dream.
Never is broken her loneliness in her house obscure and drear.[2]

Blasts and billows brutal will dash on water lilies wretched;
Dewdrops dense in the night should shroud osmanthus foliage scented?[3]
Well she knows her lovesick heart is bleeding to no avail.
Yet to free herself from sickening yearnings she always fails!

李商隐屡次科举考试不中。八年后，欣赏其诗文的大臣令狐楚父子加以提携，他始得进士及第。等待分科复试期间，他暂应泾原（今甘肃泾川）节度使王茂元之聘担任书记。王茂元爱其才，嫁女给他。他没想到因王家与令狐家分属党争两派，令狐派认为李商隐投靠异己，马上从分科榜中勾销了已经录取的李商隐之名，并开始处处予以挟制打击。从此，他一生备受党争之害。

(2) 相当于Her loneliness（第一、三音节重读）in her house, which is obscure and dreary, is never broken.

(3) 上行will dash，本行should shroud，都用了情态动词，表“定要拍击”、“竟该包围”……。

“月露谁教桂叶香？”被很多人误会。比较合理的解释应是：在明月之夜、露水很重的夜晚，谁让你桂树的花、叶要吐露芬芳呢？你是难以如愿的。董乃斌在《李商隐诗选读》该诗注释5中说得明确：“风波、月露喻左右其命运的外界力量……她虽承受着月露的侵蚀，却偏像桂叶那样散放香气。”（见《中华活页文选》成人版第二辑1998年第23期）

嫦娥

李商隐

云母屏风烛影深，长河渐落晓星沉。
嫦娥应悔偷灵药，碧海青天夜夜心。

Lady of the Moon[1]

With the mica-sheeted screen by a candle dimly lit, [抑扬6]
While the Milky Way is fading, the Morning Star has set,
You'd suppose the Goddess regrets e' er stealing elixir of life,
As she contemplates the oceans of th' azure night after night.[2]

〖评注〗

(1) Chang'e was wife of the mighty archer Houyi(后羿), who had shot down nine surplus suns for the people and was awarded the elixir of life from the Queen Mother(西王母). While the archer was out, Chang'e swallowed all the miraculous potion meant for both husband and wife. She flew up in spite of herself until she reached the palace of the moon. From that day on she has been living alone there, as the Goddess of the Moon.

(2) contemplating，第一和第三个音节都要重读。从"云母屏风"等语看来，诗人在写一个女子，写其不眠之夜的幽思，因而译文有You would suppose 等语。

嫦娥，古神话"后羿"之妻，他俩原皆神仙；因远古时，空中有十个太阳，一起晒焦大地，后羿就用神弓射掉九个，又为民众除去长蛇等祸害，天帝命令他俩留在人间；昆仑山西王母给了后羿两份灵药，说二人吃了可在人世长生不老，一人吃了可升天再做神仙；嫦娥贪图天宫安乐，夜里独吃两份灵药，却不由自主地飞进了月亮上的广寒宫。

云母，片状半透明矿物，大片云母可以镶在屏风上。

清代文人纪晓岚（纪昀，字晓岚，曾主持编纂《四库全书》）说此诗"十分蕴藉"，认为可能是诗人的悼亡之作。刘逸生教授在《唐诗小扎》（广东人民出版社1978年版）中提出："诗人是在忆念他的亡妻或离他而去的恋人"，"从对面写来"。正如杜甫的《月夜》："今夜鄜州月，闺中只独看"。跳过了自己的情思，深入到对方的内心。"应悔"说的是不眠女子同情嫦娥呢？还是诗人设身处地、推想那境遇如嫦娥的女子之心呢？看来全诗都是诗人自语。"你虽抛下我走了，但我相信你一直孤独寂寞，像我一样在苦苦熬过一个个无寐的夜。"

夜雨寄北

李商隐

君问归期未有期，巴山夜雨涨秋池。
何当共剪西窗烛，却话巴山夜雨时？

〖评注〗

(1) 据信此诗是诗人写给妻子的。Is there yet ... not yet 对应原首句的部分反复“问归期”“未有期”，联结了你与我、北方与西南。第二行的 Rains thro nights amid these mounts（巴山夜雨），在第四行末尾重复，从我到你再回到我处、从西南到北方再回到西南边疆、从今夜到向往团圆再回忆起今夜。重读音节后即使是实词也自然轻读：is there YET, so you ASK, date for HOME? — no, not YET.

(2) 主语 Rains ...，谓语 get，后接复合宾语（get）autumn ponds brimming 。

巴山，大巴山脉，在四川中部，东南接巫山。这里泛指蜀中、今川中山区。

李商隐不仅写情动人心弦，其政治诗歌更是惊心动魄，如《龙池》：“龙池赐酒敞云屏，羯鼓声高众乐停。夜半宴归宫漏永，薛王沉醉寿王醒。”

A Rainy Night's Lines to Wife in the North

Is there yet, so you ask, date for home? — No, not yet.[1] [抑抑扬4]
Rains thro nights 'mid these mounts autumn ponds brimming get.[2]
Who knows when by our window we'll trim the candle bright,
And recall as we chat 'mid these mounts rains thro nights?

说的是，唐玄宗经奸相李林甫推荐、盯上了其子"寿王"之妻杨玉环（16岁嫁给玄宗第十三子寿王李瑁），硬讲她有道骨仙缘，令其进"太真宫"道观修行。后玄宗给寿王另娶一妻，自己60岁时把 27 岁的太真道姑封为贵妃。龙池大殿的家宴中，寿王等子女看着玄宗、贵妃欢饮作乐，为舞姬伴奏的鼓点声压倒丝竹音律。酒阑人散，宫漏迟迟，兄长"薛王"能够沉睡，失去娇妻的"寿王"怎能安然入睡呢？

宋代杨万里《武惠妃》(*The Orchid*) 诗云；"桂折秋风露折兰，千话无朵可天颜。寿王不忍金宫冷，独献明皇一玉环。"说皇后和武惠妃像桂花、兰花都在风露中凋谢了，几千佳丽无一让帝王称心；皇子怕为父冷清，慨然奉上绝色艳妻，温暖金宫。

The osmanthus withered in frost; the orchid, in a blast;
'Mid myriad flowers none after his noble heart.
For fear that your father be left for long forlorn,
You presented him this rose-like beauty of your own.

锦瑟

李商隐

锦瑟无端五十弦，一弦一柱思华年。
庄生晓梦迷蝴蝶，望帝春心托杜鹃。
沧海月明珠有泪，蓝田日暖玉生烟。
此情可待成追忆？只是当时已惘然。

〖今译〗

还有谁说得清，这锦纹古瑟，为什么偏偏如许密柱繁弦——
它在让五十颗柱、五十张弦，同咱风华岁月、事事牵连！
清晨梦断，我像庄生，不辨是身曾化蝶、还是蝶投人间；
春心恋旧，你如望帝，幽魂归为杜鹃，向故园啼血涟涟！
你似海上织绡的鲛女，满月夜圆润的珍珠，沾着你泪珠点点；
我曾种玉在蓝田山间，日暖时袅袅的香烟，赢得了你的欣羡。
哪堪直到你身后，再让此情此景，演为历历追念？
只恨就在你生前，总是聚少离多，早已心意惘然。

〖评注〗

(1) Master Zhuang Zhou was at a loss awaking from a dream, and so was the poet. King Wang died young and then his spirit returned home (embodied in the crying cuckoo), and in the poet's mind the spirit of his deceased wife did likewise. The poet was mourning his beloved, recalling their youth with both distresses (tears turning into pearls) and delights (sapphire's giving off scented vapor).

(2) 读作：KING Wang's(轻读) BLEE-ding HEART's re-STORED in the CUC-koo ap-PEAL-ing。上 ...or I （that）was dreaming 有省略。

Painted Zither

Who knows why the painted zither has fifty strings?[1] [扬抑6]
Each and every string or stop revives our springs.
Zhuang Zhou's puzzled: "Is it the butt'rfly or I was dreaming?"
King Wang's bleeding heart's restored in the cuckoo appealing.[2]

Moonlit pearls on oceans from tears out of mermaids' eyes.[3]
Sun-warmed sapphires in Jade Fields let their vapor rise.
Could such feelings stand recalling after the years?
— All too soon already bittered with cares and despairs.[4]

(3) out of 相连轻读。此句相当于 Moonlit pearls on oceans (come) from tears out of mermaids eyes。

(4) 本行有省略 All too soon (they were) already bittered ...。

本诗为诗人悼亡名篇，参见上海辞书出版社《唐诗鉴赏词典》周汝昌教授对该篇的翔实评介。庄子曾经梦见自己化作蝴蝶，醒来不知这是不是蝴蝶在梦中化作了人身。蜀国望帝英年早逝，魂灵变成杜鹃，春来回到故园，直啼得血溅山林。南海鲛女以所织鲛绡来人间易物，临行洒泪为珠以谢主人 —— 海上月满珠圆时，明珠仍含着泪光。蓝田学子曾得仙人指点种石生玉，风和日暖白璧生香引来佳偶 —— 学诗的成就导致自己同贤妻的良缘。几多典故全都喻指夫妻旧事。关于杜鹃，详见 290页《酹江月》 评注1 。

《锦瑟》是李商隐写给亡妻的诗篇，正好对应《锦瑟》的有他另诗《哀筝》写道："延颈全如鹤，柔肠素怯猿（古筝颈长似鹤，而声含至情；性如传说中的母猿那样，会为幼猿遭难而柔肠寸断）；湘波无限泪，蜀魄有余冤（舜妃沉江前泪染斑竹，蜀王早逝后魂化杜鹃）"；同这些形成对比的还有"逡巡又过潇湘雨，雨打湘灵五十弦"（《七月二十八日夜听雨后梦作》，湘灵即化为湘江女神的舜妃），这都可印证他寄托于弦索的永诀之痛。

第三章

唐、五代词

Chapter 3

Ci-Lyrics of theTang & the 5-Dynasties Times

望江南

敦煌曲子词

天上月，遥望是一团银。
夜久更阑风渐紧，
为奴吹散月边云，
照见负心人。

〖评注〗

(1) 后五行祈使句。下bring …to light 照亮。thankless, heartless 指 ungrateful, unfaithful…(fickle lover)。词牌《望江南》又名《忆江南》、《梦江南》。

从清朝光绪年间起，在气候干燥的甘肃敦煌东南断崖上密封暗窟中，陆续发现隋唐等古文物包括宗教文献。其中有大量民间词，形式比较自由，和后来文人词的词谱字数不尽相同。如这首“望江南”第二句6个字，异于文人各行字数惯例 35775: “江南忆， 最忆是杭州。山寺月中寻桂子，郡亭枕上看潮头。何日更重游？”（白居易《忆江南》之二） “兰烬落，屏上暗红蕉。闲梦江南梅熟日，夜船吹笛雨萧萧。人语驿边桥。”（晚唐皇甫松《梦江南》之一）

To the Tune *South of the Yangtze*

Like a plate of silver bright,[抑扬3]
The moon's so high in the sky.
O Wind, with the deepening of night,
Yet harder and harder you blow,[1]
Disperse the clouds afloat,
For the moon to bring to light
That thankless, heartless guy!

《菩萨蛮》如韦庄的："洛阳城里春光好，洛阳才子他乡老。柳暗魏王堤，此时心转迷。桃花春水绿，水上鸳鸯浴。凝恨对斜晖，忆君君不知。"字数是7755-5555。但民间词《菩萨蛮》，字数就不那么固定；以下是敦煌石窟发现的一首，据研究属唐代较早流传的情歌："枕前发尽千般愿：要休且待青山烂，水面上秤砣浮，直待黄河彻底枯。白日参辰现，北斗回南面。休即未能休，且待三更见日头。"字数是7767-5557；参辰二星宿，此出彼没，永不并见，常用以喻指不可相会的人或事物，如苏武《诗四首》中："昔为鸳与鸯，今为参与辰"。

忆秦娥

李 白（701—762）

箫声咽，秦娥梦断秦楼月。
秦楼月，年年柳色，灞陵伤别。

乐游原上清秋节，咸阳古道音尘绝。
音尘绝，西风残照，汉家陵阙。

〖今译〗

是谁家吹出的这样凄迷、哽咽的箫声？
惊破秦楼女儿依依柔梦，空见月色分明。
月色分明，春来年年似旧；
柳色青青，灞桥折柳一别，忍泪伤情。

乐游原上旧地，又已洒遍、清秋冷露，
望尽咸阳古道，踪迹茫茫、断了音书。
断了音书，
唯有残阳暝暝，西风簌簌，
汉家帝王的古墓，黯淡凄楚。

To the Tune *Memories of the Qin Maid*

How sadly the flute keeps sobbing away! [4音步]
Awakened from dream is a *Qin* Town maid,
Who finds her loft in moonlight faint.
In moonlight faint the *Qin* Town's drear;
Its willows as verdant year after year,
As by *Baling* Road when departed her dear.[1]

On Pleasure Plain it's autumn late.[2]
She aches for word that shouldn't be delayed[3]
Through posts on roads from olden days.
O ne'er a word through the ancient posts —
In westerly wind, the sunset glows,
O'er royal tombs like barren knolls.

〖评注〗

(1) Its willows (are) as verdant year after year, as (they were) by *Baling* Road when off was her dear. 其中 *Baling* "灞陵"，汉文帝陵墓，在长安东（*Qin* Town 指该城），近有跨越灞水（渭水支流）的灞桥，旧时送人东去在此折柳赠别。关于"秦娥"、"秦楼"的故事和寓义，见 206页《秋波媚》评注。

(2) Pleasure Plain，长安东南的乐游原，这里可登高望远，又可俯临曲江池。

(3) word 表"音信"本不可数，aches for word 痛切盼望信息。下 never a word 强调 "只字皆无"。

菩萨蛮

李 白

平林漠漠烟如织，寒山一带伤心碧。
暝色入高楼，有人楼上愁。

玉阶空伫立，宿鸟归飞急。
何处是归程？长亭又短亭。

〖评注〗

(1) 相当于 … the woods sprawl beneath a hazy veil。诗歌中介词可以后置。

(2) a-flying：a-常加在名词或动名词前，构成表语形容词或副词。

(3) 唐代最早的文人词，除李白《忆秦娥》《菩萨蛮》外，有张志和（730?-810?）的《渔歌子》(*To the Tune Fisherman's Song*)："西塞山前白鹭飞，桃花流水鳜鱼肥。青箬笠，绿蓑衣，斜风细雨不须归。"

In front of the West Hill snow-white herons hover,
With peaches abloom by the river's running waters.
Our mandarin fish are fleshy, with a subtle flavor.
A broad, broad brimmed bamboo hat green I'm in,[4]
With a palm-bark cape o'er my back against the rain,
What need for a shelter, be there a drizzle steady,
A drizzle and a breeze a-driving brisk and slanted?

(4) 读作a BROAD broad bam-BOO hat GREEN I'm（I'm 轻读）IN。下be there 相当于 If there be，古旧虚拟形式，现代英语说 If there should be ...

To the Tune *Exotic Dancers*

As wearily sprawl the woods a hazy veil beneath,[1] [6音步]
A range of greenish hills looks dolefully dim and bleak.
The highest storey too is invaded by twilight's shades;
Therein is someone lonely, lost in grief and dismay.

On marble steps you linger and linger to no avail,
While watching flocks of birds to roost a-flying in haste.[2]
O where's the long, long way that leads to your home and hearth,
While visible are endless wayside pavilions small and large?

转应曲（胡马）

韦应物（731—790）

胡马，胡马，远放胭脂山下。
跑沙跑雪独嘶，东望西望路迷。
迷路，迷路，边草无穷日暮！

〖评注〗

(1) 原文“胡马”并非胡人的马，而是塞外所产马匹，汉族士兵也骑它、养它，因而英译作 frontier horse。词中“胡马”迷途像征：原曾为君王出力的士子如今流离失所。下Mount Rouge 是“胭脂山”意译，山在今甘肃中部，草木繁盛，所产红蓝花可制胭脂。这里西北胡人有民谣道：“怎又夺我胭脂山，使我妇女无颜色！”

(2)“跑沙、跑雪”的“跑”读阳平，意指用马蹄“刨”。即 be pawing sands/snows。此行形容雪原上失群胡马的烦恼无奈。若理解成“跑过” be running through …，就失去了深意。韦应物另一《转应曲》(*The Milky Way*) 道：“河汉，河汉，晓挂秋城漫漫。愁人起望相思，江南塞北别离。离别，离别，河汉虽同路绝。”

The Milky Way, the Milky Way!
At dawn it extendeth so pale, so pale;
O'er th' autumn fortress' tis seen to fade.
The wretched one is up and staring[3]
At the hazy horizon in earnest yearning.

A Frontier Horse

(To the Tune *Transpositions*)

A frontier horse alone, a frontier horse alone.[1] [6音步]
At the foot of Mount Rouge grazing aloof.[4音步]
The sands now pawing, the snows now pawing,[2]
It neighs and neighs, but ne'er to be heard.
On th' east now looking, on th' west now looking,
It's gone astray, too far from the herd.
The herd's away too far, the herd's away too far.[6音步]
Night falls 'pon endless frontier grass![4音步]

To the north of the Great Wall far thou art;
She, south of the *Yangtze*, stayeth apart.
Apart ye two, apart and remote,
Tho' the selfsame Milky Way ye behold,
Altogether blocked is the returning road.

(3) wretched后缀-ed中的元音发音[-id]，就像learned表示"有学问的"。

转应曲（边草）

戴叔伦（732—789）

边草，边草，边草尽来兵老。
山南山北雪晴，千里万里月明。
明月，明月，胡笳一声愁绝。

〖评注〗

(1) 上行drear等于dreary，诗歌用语。本行up it clears即it clears up，天晴了。

(2) strain，曲调，音乐片段；Tartar，鞑靼人的，可指"胡人的"；air，乐曲。

(3) biting, bitterness, bears, 辅音头韵；带定语不可数名词bitterness前加a, 强调"一种特定的……"。

胡笳，古时塞外的木管乐器。东汉末年，撰写《后汉书》的蔡邕被董卓胁迫任职。司徒王允买通吕布刺杀董卓的政变后，蔡邕遭人连累死于狱中。他的独生女儿蔡琰（字文姬）随即在战乱中被虏到匈奴，不得不归于匈奴左贤王。久后曹操平定北方，用黄金白璧把她赎回，她写了《胡笳十八拍》——胡笳伴唱的诗篇18节，叙述多年流落边荒、归来不得不留下12年间所生两个孩儿：

Border Grass

(To the Tune *Transpositions***)**

Our border grass, our border grass! [4音步]
Where border grass has come to its end,
Our men are getting old in their camps.
To the north and the south of the mountains drear,
The snow has stopped and up it clears[1].
For tens of thousands of *li* o'er hill-lands,
A lonely moon is rising brilliant.
A brilliant moon, a brilliant moon!
There's a strain of the bugle, a Tartar air,[2]
O what a biting bitt'rness it bears![3]

"我生之初尚无为，我生之后汉祚（zuò皇统）衰。天不仁兮降乱离，地不仁兮使我逢此时！……为天有眼兮何不见我独飘流？为神有灵兮何事处我天南海北头？我不负天兮天何配我殊匹（非同类的配偶）？我不负神兮神何殛我越荒州？……不谓残生兮却得选归，抚抱胡儿兮泣下沾衣；焉得羽翼兮将汝归？一步一远兮足难移！今别子兮归故乡，旧怨平兮新怨长。泣血仰天兮诉苍苍，胡为生兮独罹此殃？胡与汉兮异域殊风，天与地兮子西母东。苦我怨气兮浩于长空，六合虽广兮受之应不容！"

转应曲（团扇）

王建（766?—830?）

团扇，团扇，美人病来遮面。
玉容憔悴三年，谁复商量管弦？
弦管，弦管，春草昭阳路断！

〖评注〗

(1) 这“团扇”词基于班婕妤故事（婕妤是宫人称号）。班婕妤是才女，《汉书》作者班固的祖姑。汉成帝专宠赵飞燕后，她自请去服侍太后。她写《秋扇怨》(*A Fan's Grievance*）道：“新裂齐纨素，皎洁如霜雪；裁作合欢扇，团圆如满月。出入君怀袖，动摇微风发。常恐秋节至，凉飚夺炎热。弃捐箧笥中，恩情中道绝！”

The new silk, snow-white, is cut to make a fan moon-like;
O you moon-fan of the Lord, a congenial companion, his prize!
When gently you're waved, a refreshing breeze will quietly arise.
But autumn'll come, cool wind's to chase the heat away.
Then away you'll be cast — to deplore your fate in the plaited case.

(2) 盛唐王长龄的绝句《长信宫词》也记述其事：“奉帚平明金殿

The Round Silk Fan
(To the Tune *Transpositions*)

The round silk fan hand-made, the round silk fan hand-made,[1] [6音步]
With which the Fair may hide her face! [4音步]
Her complexion's been fading with passing springs.
No longer is her Lord to listen to her sing;
— No more those tunes on pipes or strings!
O strings or pipes ne'er again proposed,
O strings or pipes ne'er again proposed.
There vernal grass that footpath has choked![2]

开，暂将团扇共徘徊。玉容不及寒鸦色，犹带昭阳日影来。"诗词原文"昭阳"，指新立皇后赵飞燕所居昭阳宫。"昭阳路断"即因无人行走，通往那里的小径为春草遮没。

赵飞燕自己不生育，并把汉宫怀孕的嫔妃一一害死。成帝崩后，她被废为庶人，自杀。辛弃疾《摸鱼儿》词："长门事，准拟佳期又误。蛾眉曾有人妒。千金纵买相如赋，脉脉此情谁诉？君莫舞，君不见玉环、飞燕皆尘土！"先借用皇后阿娇冷落长门宫旧事，随之并提杨贵妃和赵飞燕之迷惑君王，显然在抒发忧国伤时的满腔忠愤，和屈原《离骚》的"众女嫉余之蛾眉兮"是同等沉痛。本词作者王建出身寒门，虽曾中举，却因无缘于朝廷权贵，一生落魄。他的词中也含类似寓意。

潇湘神

刘禹锡（772—842）

湘水流，湘水流，九嶷云物至今愁。
君问二妃何处所？零陵香草露中秋。
斑竹枝，斑竹枝，泪痕点点寄相思。
楚客欲听瑶瑟怨，潇湘深夜月明时。

〖今译〗

湘江水呵，流呵流，
九嶷山云烟景色，至今还流露着哀愁。
要问娥皇、女英两位妃子于今何处，
沾着中秋清露如珠，踏过零陵芳草清幽。

斑竹枝呵，泪斑斑，
点点泪痕寄托着无尽的思念。
湖湘过客要听那瑶瑟哀弦，
弦音生于月明深夜，在这潇水湘江之畔。

To the tune *Goddess of the Xiang River*

On and on the River *Xiang* pours forth. [扬抑5]
All Nine Similar Mountains fore'er in remorse.[1]
Where're the two, the princesses, seeking their lord?
Over dew-wet meads by mid-autumn shores!

Mottled, O mottled bamboos being dotted with tears!
Teardrop stains are signs of devotion of theirs.
Travelers wishing to hear their plaintive strains,
Come 'neath a bright moon, the river rippling faint.

〖评注〗

(1) King Shun died of fatigue inspecting the South. He fell down under the *Jiuyi*, which name means Nine Similar (Mountains). His two wives wandering up and down failing to find his remains, cried bloody tears and the bamboos became mottled. The two, after drowning themselves in the river and becoming goddesses of the *Xiang* and the *Xiao*(a tributary of the *Xiang*), used to play the zither in the night to give expression to their grief. 舜帝让位给治水的大禹后，亲自南巡，殉职于九嶷山下。娥皇、女英赶来追寻丈夫遗骨而不见，血泪染遍高下竹林。二人携手投身湘水，成为江神。深夜江上瑶瑟的凄凄哀诉，便是她俩在寄托深重悲思。

忆江南

刘禹锡

春去也，多谢洛城人！
弱柳从风疑举袂，丛兰裛露似沾巾。
独坐亦含颦。

〖今译〗

归去了，春光！
春之过客感谢你，洛阳姑娘！
见那柔嫩柳条随风飘拂，还疑心是你在挥袖起舞；
见那丛丛兰草含着清露，好似你滴落纱巾的泪珠。
就是让你独坐片时，眉宇间也暗藏着离别的愁苦。

To the Tune *South of the Yangtze*

Off is Spring! As well, my leave I took. [扬抑5]
"Thanks, O thanks a lot, my hostess in *Luo*[1]!
Willow twigs afloat in gentle breeze —
Dancing are you with graceful swinging sleeves?
Orchid clusters wetted with dewdrops sparkling —
Dripping are you unbidden tears on departing?
Brows of yours are often knitted, [4音步]
Even at times when alone you're seated."

〖评注〗

(1) *Luo*, or *LuoYang*, situated not far to the east of *Chang'an*, and said to be the "Eastern Capital", was the biggest city except the capital *Chang'an.* 洛城（洛阳）是唐代的"东都"，除长安外最繁华的城市。

《忆江南》又名《望江南》，可比较李煜《望江南》："多少恨，昨夜梦魂中？还似旧时游上苑，车如流水马如龙，花月正春风！"

What regret and remorse it revives,
Such a dream as I dreamed last night!
All the same as in days of old.
Blooming royal orchards we roamed —
Flows of carriages surging on and on;
Dragon-like horses riding along, along.
Vernal breeze on faces refreshed, radiant;
Moonlight floods o'er flowers fair and fragrant!

竹枝词（九首之二）

刘禹锡

山桃红花满上头，蜀江春水拍山流。
花红易衰似郎意，水流无限似侬愁。

〖评注〗

(1) 词似民歌。比较刘禹锡《浪淘沙》(*Waves Scouring Sands*)："汴水东流虎眼文，清淮晓色鸭头春。君看渡口淘沙处，渡却人间多少人？"

东泻的汴水中，涡流闪耀着虎眼样明亮的纹章，
澄清的淮河上，晨曦泛起鸭头绿般春水的光芒。
你看那滔滔渡口、冲刷沙粒的滚滚波浪，
浪花送多少世人、渡过河去了彼岸他方？

The River *Bian* with whirls like oxeyes eastward streams.
The limpid *Huai* on fresh spring mornings is duck-head green.
Behold the crossing where waves are forever washing the shoals —
What myriads of folks've been sent across by the ferryboats!

汴水，古运河，原西北接于黄河、东南通入淮河，在今河南、江苏两省之间；古城汴州在该河上，即今河南开封。清淮：唐代时淮河本是很清的，宋代黄河决口，夺取淮河旧道东流入海，泥沙淤塞河

To the Tune *Bamboo Twigs*

O'er hillsides, luxuriant peach trees are blooming pink and red, [抑扬6]
While springtime surging waves 'gainst hillocks dash and splash.
How quick do colorful blossoms fade, as my lover's ardor!
Yet endlessly the river waters flow, like longings I harbor.[1]

道；六百多年后清代中期，黄河又北迁，仍从山东入海；今江苏北部淮河入海故道已不通，淮河水南流，经洪泽湖注入长江。

波浪送多少人渡过……，暗含何等意味？淡淡一问，不那样直白，有时比直说更为深远。苏轼《念奴娇》（216页）道："浪淘尽，千古风流人物"；杨慎《临江仙》（312页）问："滚滚长江东逝水，浪花淘尽英雄；……青山依旧在，几度夕阳红？"；许浑《咸阳城东楼晚眺》（218页 评注）则说："行人莫问当年事，故国东来渭水流。"

竹枝词（四首之一）

白居易（772—846）

瞿塘峡口冷烟低，白帝城头月向西。
唱到《竹枝》声咽处，寒猿暗鸟一时啼。

〖今译〗

瞿塘峡险峻山口间，冷冷烟雾低低压向江中；
白帝城高高城楼上，朦朦胧胧是西下的月影。
一曲《竹枝》唱到最高亢处，突然凄紧失声，
苦寒的猿猴、暗藏的宿鸟，一时都放声哀鸣。

To the Tune *Bamboo Twigs*

A stagnant haze is hanging o'er *Qu Tang* Gorge. [5音步]
The setting moon comes closer to White-King Fort.[1]
As *Song of Bamboos* is choked at its highest thrills,
Out cry all birds and monkeys by night dew chilled.

〖评注〗

(1) 单音节介词常轻读；重读音节后虽实词也轻读：a STAG-nant HAZE is HANG-ing o'er *QU-Tang* GORGE. / the SET-ting MOON comes CLOS-er to WHITE king FORT.

(2) 白居易民歌风格小词还有《杨柳枝》*(Willow Twigs)*八首，选译"八首之七"："叶含浓露如啼眼，枝袅轻风似舞腰。小树不禁攀折苦，乞君留取两三条。"

Her leaves with dewdrops — shining eyes in tears.
Her twigs in light breeze — flexible arms of dancers'.
"I'm hardly a tree, so mis'rable, meager and drear.
Pray you, please spare my last surviving branches."

(3) 《竹枝》、《杨柳枝》原为长江流域民歌曲名，歌词每句七字，压平声韵，可与绝句形式相同（白居易这两首词就形同绝句）；但风格全属民间，通俗而亲切，文人写《竹枝》、《杨柳枝》时，各拍平仄也可不尽相对、相粘。例如刘禹锡《竹枝》（166页）"山桃红花满上头，蜀江春水拍山流。花红易衰似郎意……"里边，"山桃红花"两拍末尾的"桃""花"，在绝句中应该平仄相对；"花红易衰"的第三句和"蜀江春水"的第二句，在绝句中应该平仄相同（相粘）。民歌和民歌体的"词"中，可以不管那些。

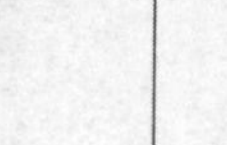

更漏子

温庭筠（812?—880?）

玉炉香，红蜡泪，偏照画堂秋思。
眉翠薄，鬓云残，夜长衾枕寒。

梧桐树，三更雨，不道离情正苦。
一叶叶，一声声，空阶滴到明。

〖今译〗

玉炉香烟袅袅，红烛泪珠涟涟；
烛光偏偏照见，画堂凉秋，愁思惨淡。
眉黛早已轻浅，鬓发任它缭乱；
渐觉夜长漫漫，孤枕薄被，清冷难眠。

梧桐树靠门庭，连夜雨过三更；
它哪里理会你，苦于离忧深重？
残叶一片片，冷雨一声声，
空荡荡的阶前，一直滴嗒到天明。

To the Tune *Hourglass*

The emerald censer fragrance spreads; [4音步]
The crimson candle teardrops sheds,
Her autumn chamber lonesome getting.
In pencilled eyebrows the color's fading.
The pillow her fancy tresses dishev'ling.[1]
The night so long, the quilt so chilling.

'Gainst withering Chinese plane trees beats
The midnight rain, incessant and drear.[2]
O heedless of parting sorrow of hers,
These drops and drops in dullest drone,
On each and every leaf forlorn,
Keep pattering beyond the steps till dawn!

〖评注〗

(1) fancy tresses 花样发式。disheveling 弄乱（多指使头发蓬乱）。

(2) 梧桐似原欧洲plane法国梧桐，译作Chinese plane tree。温庭筠另词《望江南》："梳洗罢，独倚望江楼。过尽千帆皆不是，斜晖脉脉水悠悠。肠断白蘋洲。"

In dainty dress, with afternoon makeup on,
I lean 'gainst rails above the river alone.
A thousand sails come hither, ne'er the awaited boat.
The dusk gets fainter, fainter; quiet, quiet run the flows .
' Pon Duckweed Islet in flower, my heart is sunk in woe.

浣溪沙

韦庄（836?—910）

夜夜相思更漏残，伤心明月凭栏杆。
想君思我枕衾寒。
咫尺画堂深似海，忆来唯把旧书看。
几时携手入长安？

〖今译〗

每夜每夜思念，守得更漏滴断；
明月下暗伤心，为你独倚栏杆。
料你也在挂牵，想着我绣被难耐天寒。

近在咫尺堂前，竟像在海底深不可探；
相忆时我只能、把旧时书信一再翻看。
要等什么时候，我们手携手同返长安？

〖评注〗

(1) 据说此词作者晚唐诗人韦庄，入蜀在节度使王建部下任职之初，王建以请进府中教授家眷文墨为名，夺走韦庄所爱，韦庄因之作此词。王建后趁势占据全蜀，被唐室封为蜀王；唐大将朱温灭唐建后梁之年(907)，王建在蜀称帝，史称前蜀（五代十国时期的十国之一）。中唐另有诗人王建，诗《望夫石》（84页评注）、词《转应曲》（160页）的作者。

(2) small hours 是后夜一两点钟。

(3) “想君思我枕衾寒，”从我方想到女方对自己的想念，可以比较李商隐《无题》“夜吟应觉月光寒”（138页），同样是诗人所思念女子对自己的挂念。

To the Tune *Gauze-Rinsing Brook*

I miss you each and every long, long night[1], [5音步]
Awake through small hours of secret, heavy sighs.[2]
In moonlight ofttimes dreary and weary I lean on rails. [6音步]
I know you share in my feeling forlorn in my icy quilt.

That chamber of yours is beyond the seas to me, [5音步]
Although that majestic mansion is nearby, indeed.
I can but read your letters of old, while longing for you. [6音步]
When can we wend our way home hand in hand, we two?

浣溪沙·西施去处

薛昭蕴（生卒年代不详）

倾国倾城恨有余，几多红泪泣姑苏？
倚风斜睇雪肌肤。

吴主山河空落日，越王宫殿半平芜；
藕花菱蔓满重湖。

〖今译〗

纵灭他吴国，纵毁他京城，你自怀抱着幽恨重重，
长辞了故乡，长别了亲人，多少胭脂泪暗洒吴宫？
谁解你流波顾盼，雪白的肌肤，迎着秋风？

空留下落日斜晖，还抹过大王夫差的江山，
几尽是丘荒草乱，难辨认霸主勾践的宫殿；
姑苏太湖一湾湾——仍旧是荷花滟滟，菱蔓连连。

〖评注〗

(1) 上行You had in view ...，你料想到的是。此行读作 BIT-terly EV-er your GRIEV-ance kept GNAW-ing at your SOUL. 最后重读音节前轻读处是三个较短音节。

(2) 此行读作 WHAT were you GLANC-ing at, FAIR arms on RAILS in the GUST? 两实词紧连时，后一实词自然也属轻读（FAIR arms on ...）。

(3) 上面隔行 re-conjure“使……再现脑际，使人想起”。末后二行，相当于 All that are left on the lake(you often strolled on its shore) are flowers of lotus and tendrils of waternuts afloat.

Meeting Your Fate
(To the Tune *Gauze-Rinsing Brook*)

Ruin of his capital, and ruin of his realm you'd in view; [扬抑抑5]
Bitterly ever your grievance kept gnawing at your soul[1].
Tears unobserved down your rouge after parties would gush.
What were you glancing at, fair arms on rails in the gust[2]?

Sunsets in vain over King-of-*Wu's* country now glow;
Debris can hardly re-conjure the *Yue* Court of old.
All that are left on the lake round whose shore you oft strolled:
Flowers of lotus and tendrils of waternuts afloat[3].

In the poem, "you" refers to Xi Shi, a beauty who avenged her country.

During the later years of the"Spring and Autumn Era"(770-475 BC), the state of *Yue* was vanquished by the neighboring state of *Wu*. King Goujian of *Yue*, taken prisoner, had to serve Fuchai, King of *Wu*, as a humiliated slave. Three years later he was permitted to return to his homeland. He looked for a most beautiful maiden to be presented to King Fuchai, and Xi Shi was discovered. She was conscious of the idea of her King and ready to sacrifice herself. Scarcely had Xi Shi arrived at *Gusu*, the capital of *Wu*, when King Fuchai was enamoured of her. From then on Fuchai abandoned himself to a life of worldly pleasures and neglected the administration of his country. The state of *Wu* was declining in strength. Ten years later, *Yue* completely wiped out and annexed *Wu*. King Fuchai committed suicide.

Xi Shi is said to have been killed just before the war was ended.

曹雪芹《红楼梦》借黛玉之笔所写《西施》有和此诗同样的感叹："一代倾城逐浪花，吴宫空自忆儿家。效颦莫笑东村女，头白溪边尚浣纱。"

南乡子

李珣（855?—930?）

相见处，晚晴天；
刺桐花下越台前。
暗里回眸深属意；
遗双翠，骑象背人先过水。

〖今译〗

会面在晚来雨晴的清凉时光，
古老越王台前，开满刺桐花的路旁。
暗中回头一望，目光传送情意悠悠。
你特意把一双翠玉手镯，丢在身后。
转脸不再看他，先自骑象涉过清流。

To the Tune *Southern Song*

What time and where did they meet?[抑扬3]
At dusk when the drizzle ceased.
'Fore the Terrace, flowering trees of Indian planes.[1] [5音步]
On the quiet she turned to give a wistful glance.
A pair of emerald bracelets aground she dropped;
On wading elephant's back, the brook she crossed.

〖评注〗

(1) Terrace开头大写表示这是著名地点。Indian plane (trees)刺桐树。

五代十国时，前蜀出现的回族词人李珣，是波斯人后裔，他写南疆风情的18首《南乡子》颇有特色，如"愁听猩猩啼瘴雨"、"玉纤遥指花深处，争回顾，孔雀双双迎日舞"、"暗里回眸深属意，遗双翠，骑象背人先过水"。

唐末天灾人祸迫使多处贫民起义。公元890年底，黄巢义军在居民夹道欢迎中进入长安，但一年多后被围撤离，兵败泰山，黄巢自尽。降唐的黄巢部将朱温，在与各地军阀混战中占了上风，于907年，代唐称帝，国号梁，史称后梁。朱温当了五年皇上就被其子所杀，接着是黄河流域王朝的迅速更替：923年换作后唐，936年换作后晋，946年换作后汉，951年又换作后周——即所谓"五代"。同时，其他地区还有过十个割据政权，所谓"十国"。

五代十国期间，各自地区平时渐较晚唐稳定，文人"曲子词"有所发展。不过前段作品多不离闺情，追求华丽，而失真意。众多词人中，前蜀秀才李珣颇有特色，是他在民间影响下，重新着眼于真挚民情与乡土风味。

巫山一段云

李 珣

古庙依青嶂，行宫枕碧流。
水声山色锁妆楼，往事思悠悠。

云雨朝还暮，烟花春复秋。
啼猿何必近孤舟？行客自多愁。

〖今译〗

神女的古寺，背靠青翠的山头；
楚王的行宫，前临碧绿的清流。
水声山色中，藏有瑶姬的妆楼，
想起往事桩桩，令人思绪悠悠。

云霞拂晓，雨水薄暮，总在巫山山头；
野花年年，如烟似雾，一春又是一秋。
那悲切的啼猿，何必挨近孤零零的小舟？
这舟中的旅人呵，本来已满怀哀愁。

To the Tune *Cloud on Mount Wu*

An ancient temple under the wooded peak;[1] [5音步]
A royal abode on shore of the verdant creek.
O where's the Fairy-of-Mount-*Wu's* boudoir of old?
Beyond the winding waters, blossoming slopes.
What stories remote, remote are revived for all!

For ever gone are the days of King Huai's call.
What point in gorgeous flowers spring through fall?
In vain cloud-drifts, rain-drips both eves and morns.[2]
Why must the crying apes come close to my boat?
Enough, while I roam, regret and remorse of my own!

〖评注〗

(1) "temple" — the temple to the Fairy-of-Mount-*Wu*（神女庙）。传说巫山神女是与黄帝同时的炎帝之女，名叫瑶姬，未嫁而死，葬于"巫山之阳、高丘之岨" (岨[jū]，有土的石山)。巫山朝朝暮暮的云霞雨露，便是她精魂的萦回。她曾经劈开大山，消除洪水；至今挺立为巫山最高峰，引导水路行人迂回艰险航道之间。

据说是屈原弟子的宋玉作有《高唐赋》，其《高唐赋序》讲述，楚襄王同宋玉出游，遥见高山上有绮丽云霞，楚王惊问宋玉，宋玉解释说，先君怀王曾登临高丘，梦中与神女相会，她自称旦为朝云，暮为行雨，朝朝暮暮，萦绕巫山。译诗第二节开头King Huai's call就指传说中怀王对巫山的访问。

（2）eves and morns，诗歌用语，(in the) evenings and mornings。

归国谣

冯延巳（903—960）

江水碧，江上何人吹玉笛？
扁舟远送潇湘客，芦花千里霜月白。
伤行色，明朝便是关山隔！

〖评注〗

(1) 原义 on 的前缀 a- 常加于名词或动名词，构成表语形容词（可作后位定语），见 154页《菩萨蛮》，评注2。

冯延巳是五代十国时期建都金陵的南唐大臣，比南唐中主李璟大13岁。他们君臣常常议论词作。他有一首《谒金门》“风乍起，吹皱一池春水。闲引鸳鸯芳径里，手挼红杏蕊……”，被李璟当作玩笑，问他：“吹皱一池春水，干卿何事？”

建都洛阳的后唐皇帝庄宗李存勖制《忆仙姿》词，中有“如梦，如梦”等句，该词牌后改为《如梦令》。后唐朝中，有词人牛希济，其《生查子》(*To the Tune Hawthorn Fruit*) 传诵颇广：“春山烟欲收，天淡星稀小。残月脸边明，别泪临清晓。语已多，情未了。回首犹重道：‘记得绿罗裙，处处怜芳草！’”

To the Tune *Back to Homeland*

So green are the river waters a-flow.[1] [4音步]
From whom come the thrilling strains of flute?
A tiny boat with its passenger leaves
For the South, to cover thousands of *li*,
With catkins all along from reeds,
'Mid hoary frost in moonlight bleak.
What parting pain at the thought — the morrow means [5音步]
Apart, with all the mountains and passes in between!

Spring hills, now stripped of mists, appearing faint.
Night sky is paling, stars seem farther between.
The waning moonlight lingers on your face 'fore parting —
The dewy dawn sees tears unceasingly pouring.
Though much exchanged, still more is left to be said.
On turning round again you expressively stressed:
"Remember my silken skirt of this green, green hue;
And care for gracious grasses wherever they grow!"

摊破浣溪沙

李璟（南唐中主，916—961）

手卷珠帘上玉钩，依前春恨锁重楼。
风里落花谁是主？思悠悠！

青鸟不传云外信，丁香空结雨中愁。
回首绿波三峡暮，接天流！

〖评注〗

(1) 词调“摊破浣溪沙”是把原“浣溪沙”上下片末句“摊开”，实加三字，韵移其后（原来上下片各三个七字句）。

(2) dreary, dreary depression，以一串辅音头韵传达原文叠词“（思）悠悠”。这里的悠悠，不是“悠然自得”，而趋近“沉沉难解”。李璟28岁继位为建都金陵的南唐皇帝。但不久，北方的北周渐渐强大，使他不得不遣使奉表，愿以国为附庸，削去帝号，改称南唐国主。他一直生活在强权的威胁中。他去世前，赵匡胤已篡夺北周政权，建立宋朝。他的六子李煜（后主）嗣位，终于败亡归宋。李璟的感伤小令，不能不说是风雨飘摇、家国不保的写照。后来，李清照评论他的词说：“语虽甚奇，所谓‘亡国之音哀以思’也。”（《词论》）

下片“丁香空结雨中愁”句是现代诗人戴望舒名作《雨巷》所本（“撑着油纸伞，独自徘徊在悠长，悠长又寂寞的雨巷，我希望遇着一个丁香一样地结着愁怨的姑娘。”）

(3) the Gorges 专指三峡。暮色中下泻的峡江，可是大势所趋、无力回天的象征？

To the Tune *Rinsing Brook* (Extended)[1]

The bead-string screen up rolled; on the hook it's fixed. [5音步]
As always, the mansions're in springtime's miserable mists.
Who should have falling flowers from scattering spared?
What dreary, dreary depression for me to bear?[2]

The messenger bird from afar ne'er coming again,
O lilac buds won't unfold in the dismal rain.
Look back at the waters, in the Gorges dark'ning at dusk
From the very horizon, endlessly pouring down![3]

相见欢

李煜（南唐后主，937—978）

林花谢了春红，太匆匆；
最怕朝来寒雨晚来风。

胭脂泪，相留醉，几时重？
自是人生常恨水常东。

〖今译〗

林间花树失落了春日的嫣红，
岂不是过于匆匆？
最怕偏偏：
清晨每连连冷雨，夜晚又阵阵疾风。

像滴雨花枝，任泪水冲开胭脂，
你曾劝我尽醉，殷切相留。
但想旧梦重温，几时能够？
人世间苦恨从不休，长江水永远向东流！

To the Tune *Joy at Meeting*

Florescence in woods is shedding its colors of spring,[5音步]
Already! What haste it's in! What haste and hastening!
From chilling morning rains there's no escaping;
Nor keeping away from evening flurries's sweeping![1]

Your rouge-stained tears down cheeks have me detained.
I drink, in doubt about chances of meeting again.
As rivers are bound to be flowing endlessly east,
So is life endowed with endless regret and grief.[2]

〖评注〗

(1) 此行是一个省略句：Nor (is there) keeping away from evening flurries's sweeping.

(2) "常恨""常东"，传达以这两行中endless 的反复。另有endowed, endless, regret, grief 的元辅音头韵。

李煜继先人所统治的南唐被新兴宋朝吞并，他从金陵来汴梁作俘虏。在农历七月初七之夜过生日时，让同来的歌女演唱，声传于外。"故国不堪回首"（见190页）等怨言传到宋太宗那里。太宗让李煜旧臣徐炫去探望。李煜一见徐炫大哭，叹道："我真后悔当时下令捕杀潘佑！"潘佑曾劝谏后主戒声色、图自强。徐炫回朝见宋太宗，太宗询问时，徐炫不敢隐瞒，将李煜的话如实奏明。于是在第二年李煜42岁的生日，也是七夕之夜，宋太宗派中使给李煜送去酒宴，酒中有毒，李煜饮后，头脚相就数十次而死。这种毒药叫做"牵机药"。

乌夜啼

李 煜

无言独上西楼，月如钩；
寂寞梧桐深院锁清秋。

剪不断，理还乱，是离愁；
别有一般滋味在心头。

〖评注〗

(1) 梧桐，英语称Chinese plane, 因类似欧洲plane tree 悬铃木，法国梧桐。

(2) by SUL-len AU-tumn its SHA-dows and SHADES locked UP.（locked轻读）

(3) 比较 It is biting vexation to be parted；It引导词，to be parted是实际主语。后二行读作 O（轻读） WHAT ve-XA-tion it IS to be PART-ed — un-SPEAK-able TASTE to the TEN-der-HEART-ed 。

《乌夜啼》词牌亦即《相见欢》。如所写为夜晚伤情，自然应题作《乌夜啼》；如咏聚会而且不是夜间，宜于以《相见欢》为题。

李煜写寂寞之夜的另有《捣练子》(To the Tune *Pounding Cotton Stuffs*)：“深院静，小庭空，断续寒砧断续风。无奈夜长人不寐，数声和月到帘栊。”

To the Tune *Crows Croaking at Night*

In silence, alone, the Western Tower I climb. [5音步]
There hangs, like a hook, a crescent moon in the sky.
Secluded courtyard, dimmed with plane trees dull,[1]
By sullen autumn its shadows and shades locked up.[2]

Though snipped and snipped, it intact remains;[4音步]
Untied and untied, it tangles again.
O what vexation it is to be parted —[3]
Unspeakable taste to the tender-hearted!

Quiet it is, in the compound's depth;
Void it is, the small yard aback.
On and off the puff of snappy nocturnal gusts;
On and off the pounding of winter cotton stuffs.[4]
Helpless sleepless all night long by the noise perturbed,
Hearing it again and again thro' curtains in moonlight immersed.

(4) Coarse cotton stuffs are beaten with clubs to be made flexible before making winter clothes.

浪淘沙

李 煜

帘外雨潺潺，春意阑珊。
罗衾不耐五更寒。
梦里不知身是客，一晌贪欢。

独自莫凭栏，无限江山。
别时容易见时难。
流水落花春去也，天上人间！

〖今译〗

帘外雨声潺潺，春色渐觉凋残；
薄薄的被子啊，怎抵五更风寒？
睡梦里不知道，自己寄人篱下；
一时间还如旧，只是作乐寻欢。

不要独自倚栏望远——
故国啊，你空有江山无限！
离开你那般容易，再见你怕已万难。
随着流水落花，春天啊，一去不返。
从天上的乐园，丢下我到凄苦人间！

To the Tune *Waves Scouring Sands*

It drizzling, drizzling, beyond the curtain dim,[5音步]
Though lingering, lingering, spring's retiring again.
The chill of small hours pierces my quilt so thin.
Now broken is the dream in which I was carried away;
A merry-maker turns back an exile dismayed.[1]
O no more staring vacant on rails alone!
Immense as you stretch, homeland dear of my own,[2]
You're easy to part with, hard to come before!
See, off are vernal flowers on rushing flows.
From Heaven's bliss, I'm down in a pit forlorn!

〖评注〗

(1) 上行 broken is the dream，强调倒装，突出短暂梦境之猛然破灭。本行 turns back，联系动词短语，exile 为表语，取其名词之义"背井离乡的人"。

(2) 上行是对自己的命令句，读作 o(轻读) NO more STAR-ing VA-cant on RAILS a-LONE! 形容词代替副词vacant(ly) 。No构成命令，如 No smoking/more nonsense!

对"无限江山"自家亲切土地的呼唤，译成第二人称呼语引导之句。as 相当于though：Though you stretch immensely, you are easy to part with, hard to come before!

虞美人

李 煜

春花秋月何时了？往事知多少！
小楼昨夜又东风，故国不堪回首月明中。

雕栏玉砌应犹在，只是朱颜改。
问君能有几多愁？恰似一江春水向东流！

〖评注〗

(1) 读作when'd BE（或WHEN'd be）an END to SPRING flo-RES-cence and AU-tumn MOON? with THEM, what MAS-ses of ME-mories UP in my MIND would LOOM。loom up（表"浮现"）是常用搭配。

(2) 这二行有略。(There was) ... an easterly wind ... , It was unbearable missing ...

(3) If asked 即If I were asked之略。I'd(would) say, 虚拟语气。最前When'd be 也属虚拟。

(4) well动词，"涌起""涌流"，相搭配的 away表示"持续不断地"，在此不表"离开"。

风花雪月，尤其是花、月动人情思，包括牵引乡愁。李煜是亡国之君，永作阶下囚，固然难忘家国之恨。李白从唐宫被"赐金放归"，潦倒流浪、以至放逐夜郎，思乡之心，想也异样浓重。李白诗《夜思》(*Still-Night Musing*) 单写望月怀乡："床前明月光，疑是地上霜。举头望明月，低头思故乡。"

The pool of moonlight that's my bed before,
I took for hoary frost upon the floor.
Head raised, I gaze at the moon on high;
Head bowed, my yearnings homeward fly.

To the Tune *Yu the Famous Beauty*

When'd be an end to Spring florescence and Autumn moon?[6音步]
With them, what masses of memories up in my mind would loom![1]
On the hostel balcony an easterly wind again at night,
'Twas unbearable missing my homeland remote in moonlight bright.[2]

The carven rails and marble steps should remain as glorious;
Alas, one's flowery cheeks alone are no more florid!
If asked like what it is, this anguish of mine, I'd say,[3]
It swells as a swollen river in springtime, welling away![4]

第四章
宋代诗词

Chapter 4

Poems & Ci-Lyrics of the Song Dynasty

雨霖铃

柳 永（987？－1053？）

寒蝉凄切，对长亭晚，骤雨初歇。
都门帐饮无绪，方留恋处，兰舟催发。
执手相看泪眼，竟无语凝噎。
念去去千里烟波，暮霭沉沉楚天阔。

多情自古伤离别，更哪堪冷落清秋节？
今宵酒醒何处？
杨柳岸，晓风残月。
此去经年，应是良辰好景虚设：
便纵有千种风情，更与何人说？

〖评注〗

(1) bear on，压在……上面。

(2) 相当于It is worse to be parted in frosty, forlorn autumnal days.

(3) 省略句用于回答：(I will be) by a willowed bank ...

To the Tune *Bells in the Rain*

A violent shower has barely come to a lull. [5音步]
And parting pavilions look so dull at dusk.
Cicadas' chirping sounds a chilling complaint.
Just having had some joyless drinks in the tent,
Beside the City Gate in vain we're delaying,
When there the boatman urges: "Time for sailing!"

Both tearful, face to face and hand in hand,
Our words all choked in sobbing, silent we stand.
Ahead for me are boundless waves to plough,
While mists at sunset bear on horizon remote![1]

Departure's all the times been cruel for the tender-hearted. [6音步]
'Tis worse in frosty, forlorn autumnal days to be parted.[2]
O where'll I be when waking up from inebriate dreams?
By a willowy bank, the moon declining in daybreak breeze.[3]
Long years will vainly elapse, though glorious seasons be there —
And what a shame for my myriad sentiments with none to share!

渔家傲

范仲淹（989–1052）

塞下秋来风景异，衡阳雁去无留意。
四面边声连角起。
千嶂里，长烟落日孤城闭。

浊酒一杯家万里，燕然未勒归无计。
羌管悠悠霜满地。
人不寐，将军白发征夫泪。

〖评注〗

（1）此行为一省略句：(I drink) A cup of turbid wine, a myriad miles (away) from home.

（2）意思是 (I am) yet to inscribe our victory on *Yanran*（我还得把克敌制胜的经过刻写在燕然山巅）。The *Yanran* Mountains lie along the boundary. On top of the highest peak, the general after having conquered the predatory tribesmen would be due to inscribe his victory on a big piece of rock.

范仲淹，北宋最早的政治革新家，为保守派围攻，革新失败。在边防吃紧的关头，范仲淹带兵御敌，连西夏敌手也为他的威望折服。他最著名的作品是《岳阳楼记》，是应另一位被贬同僚之请而写的。文章结尾道："北通巫峡，南极潇湘，迁客骚人，多会于此，览物之情，得无异乎？不以物喜，不以己悲；居庙堂之高则忧其民，处江湖之远则忧其君。是进亦忧、退亦忧，然则何时而乐耶？其必曰：'先天下之忧而忧，后天下之乐而乐'乎！"

Frontier Citadel
(To the Tune *Contented Fisherman*)

With autumn's coming the frontier scenery's bleak. [5音步]
Departing wild geese are ne'er to loiter at ease.
From all around come drones with bugles resounding.
'Mid thousands of peaks, with haze the air pervading,
At sunset the lonely castle's gates are latching.

A cup of turbid wine, from home a myriad miles.[1] [6音步]
Return I can't — on *Yanran* our victory yet to inscribe.[2]
A Tartar flute's bewailing, frost all o'er the place.
The night's already deep; yet none has gone to sleep —
Your homesick soldiers with tears, your hair is turning grey!

苏幕遮

范仲淹

碧云天，黄叶地；
秋色连波，波上寒烟翠。
山映斜阳天接水；
芳草无情，更在斜阳外。

黯乡魂，追旅思；
夜夜除非，好梦留人睡。
明月楼高休独倚；
酒入愁肠，化作相思泪。

〖今译〗

天上碧云缥渺，地上黄叶飘扬；
凄凄秋色萧条，接着冷冷秋波荡漾。
波光上的寒烟，凝作薄薄翠幛。
山间辉映斜阳，水天一片茫茫。
芳草不解你的忧伤，绵延到斜晖后难忘的远方。

家园远、黯黯心神牵，旅途难、萦萦愁做伴，
每夜呵每夜，不得安眠，
除非有好梦，引入深深眷恋。
明月下高高的楼头，莫去独倚楼栏：
一杯酒才要把愁肠浇灌，已化作相思的泪水涟涟！

To the Tune *Painted Hat* [1]

With lucid cloudlets strewn in azure skies, [5音步]
The motley land is decked with yellow leaves.
On waters autumn tinge extending serene;
Thereupon a greenish haze is hanging faint.
Hills tinted in sunset, horizon just o'er waves,
E'er farther are grasses sprawling unfeeling away.

O gloomy's my helpless soul in pining for home,
And haunting me are cares as I trudge my road!
There'd ne'er be a peaceful rest from night to night,
Unless some comforting dream prevails a while.
Watch not from the height the vast in moonlight bright —
Wine taken would turn to lovesick tears at the sight!

〖评注〗

(1)《苏幕遮》是西域乐曲名称的音译，原指舞女所戴涂有油漆的帽子。

浣溪沙

晏殊（991—1055）

一曲新词酒一杯，去年天气旧亭台。
夕阳西下几时回？

无可奈何花落去，似曾相识燕归来。
小园香径独徘徊。

〖评注〗

⑴ 即 (I have been) renewing the lines to the music, while drinking a cup of wine.

⑵ 北宋初期的主要词人，除柳永、晏殊、范仲淹外，还有较晚的欧阳修。唐宋古文八大家当中，唐朝人只有韩愈、柳宗元两位，宋朝的第一人就是欧阳修，欧阳修为主考官期间，首先荐举了王安石，随后陆续提拔了苏洵、苏轼、苏辙父子兄弟和自己的门生曾巩。欧阳修（1007-1072）创立了复兴古文的历史功绩，他的格律诗也很古朴；但他的小词，却是温柔婉转，如《生查子》(*To the Tune Hawthorn Fruit*)：“去年元夜时，花市灯如昼。月上柳梢头，人约黄昏后。今年元夜时，月与灯依旧。不见去年人，泪湿春衫袖。”

To the Tune *Gauze-Rinsing Brook*

To the music renewing the lines, o'er cup of wine.[1] [5音步]
Last year's pavilion and terrace, the day as fine.
Like the sun in the west that's bound to set at dusk,
Just when will your warmth come round to me, my belov'd?

Declining flowers from scatt'ring may not be spared.
Returned swallows seem to be oldtime pairs.
Yet along the fragrant path of the garden small,
Alas, alone I'm left for my dreary stroll!

On last year's Lantern Festival night,
The firework shows were dazzling bright.
The moon on top of willows glowed,
For lovers to meet at their rendezvous.
Round comes the Festival night this year.[3]
Both moon and firework as glorious as e'er.
But where's the one so dear to me?
With tears are soaked my vernal sleeves.

(3) rendezvous 约会地，首尾重读。 comes round，又到来了。

明妃曲（之一）

王安石（1021—1086）

明妃初出汉宫时，泪湿春风鬓脚垂。
低回顾影无颜色，犹得君王不自持。
归来却怪丹青手，入眼平生未曾有。
意态由来画不成，当时枉杀毛延寿。
一去心知更不归，可怜着尽汉宫衣。
寄声欲问塞南事，只有年年鸿雁飞。
家人万里传消息，好在毡城莫相忆。
君不见咫尺长门闭阿娇，人生失意无南北。

〖评注〗

(1) 相当于 It was folly (that) the artist Mao was sent to be executed 常见形式。其中executed 第一、三音节都重读。

Wang Zhaojun, or Lady Ming, as she was called later, was a beautiful palace maid during the reign of Emperor Yuan(48-33 BC) of the Western *Han* Dynasty. The official painter Mao Yanshou was ordered to paint the maids' portraits, on the basis of which the sovereign was to make his choice of consorts. So the maids all bribed the painter for having a nicer portrait to be presented. But Wang Zhaojun would not stoop to such sordid measures, and had, it was said, a somewhat distorted portrait produced.

Then a Tartar king came on a visit to the capital *Chang'an*, and asked the Emperor for a wife. The Emperor had this proclaimed in his harem, and called for a volunteer. Wang Zhaojun, preferring spending her whole life with nomadic tribesfolks to remaining neglected and humiliated hopelessly in the deep palace, availed herself of the chance.

It was not until her departure with the Tartar king that Emperor Yuan saw her and was struck by her seraphic beauty and tranquil grace. But it was

Lady Ming Leaving Her Homeland

Now Lady Ming was about to leave her country for e'er, [6音步]
In tears her face, at her temples coming loose her hair.
At a loss, her head hung low, she was utterly pallid, depressed,
Yet the Emperor failed to conceal, at her peerless beauty, his surprise.

On coming back the unfaithful portrait-maker he cursed.
He saw a goddess, for the first time in life, in her.
That graceful air is nothing depictable in any event.
'Twas folly the artist Mao to be executed was sent[1].

You knew you'd not for life be back to kindred folks.
What misery soon were all worn out your clothes from home!
You wondered how the inland people were getting along,
While perceiving from thither yearly coming wild geese alone.[2]
Your parents' message from a myriad miles away advised:
"No use being homesick, and make the best of your yurt-town life.
You've heard of Queen Jiao deserted within a mere stone's cast.
There's many a wretch in the South as well as on wastelands vast!"

---

too late. Furious, he had the painter Mao Yanshou beheaded after the tearful bride-to-be embarked on a long trek north outside the Great Wall.

据说,"元帝后宫既多，不得常见，乃使画工图形，案图召幸之。诸宫人皆赂画工。独王嫱不与，遂不得见。匈奴入朝，求美人为阏氏。于是帝案图以昭君行。及去，召见。貌为后宫第一，善应对，举止娴雅。帝悔之。而名籍已定，帝重信于外国，故不复更人。乃穷案其事，画工皆弃市。"（东晋葛洪所编《西京杂记》）此诗中，王安石借明妃旧恨，寄托失志之憾。

(2) While perceiving ... wild geese alone coming 是状语，修饰前面句子主体 You wondered how ... 。

桂枝香·金陵怀古

王安石

登临送目，正故国晚秋，天气初肃。
千里澄江似练，翠峰如簇。
归帆去棹残阳里，背西风，酒旗斜矗。
彩舟云淡，星河鹭起，画图难足。

念往昔，繁华竞逐。
叹门外楼头，悲恨相续。
千古凭高对此，漫嗟荣辱。
六朝旧事如流水，但寒烟衰草凝绿。
至今商女，时时犹唱，《后庭》遗曲。

〖评注〗

(1) a ribbon of a river, 意思是 a river like a ribbon 。又如 a giant of a man（巨人般男子）,a mountain of a wave（如山巨浪）。

(2) (The) Isle (of) Egrets(白鹭洲) soaring and gliding thro' the Milky Way，现在分词独立结构，修饰前面 the boats look florid ... 。thro'是 through 的缩略。

有些译者把此处的喻指误会为实指。彩舟云淡：并非实指彩船，而是淡红云霞对船只的渲染。星河鹭起：不是真见鹭飞；而是指南京（古名金陵）西南长江中的白鹭洲，词人把白鹭洲看作腾飞的白鹭，翱翔于薄暮时银河般的江水之上。

(3) curses 代表屈辱，而crowns 代表荣耀（如谚语说 He that had no cross deserves no crown, 不经苦难，不配王冠）。原诗“门外楼头”：南北朝南朝最后一个君主是陈后主陈叔宝，他在位时北方新建的隋王朝

Recalling *Jinling's* Stories
(To the Tune *Fragrant Cassia Twigs*)

The height I scale, the vast I contemplate, [5音步]
In face of the Capital ancient, in autumn late;
Already becoming cool and serene the days.
For thousands of *li*, a ribbon of a river clear.[1]
In dozens of clumps, the bush-like mountains sheer.
With sunset glowing, sails are going and coming.
'Fore west wind wine shop flags aslant keep flutt'ring.
The boats look florid among some cloudlets pale,
Isle "Egret" soaring and gliding thro' Milky Way.[2]
The picture's hard for artists in colors to paint.

In bygone days, after luxury one with another racing. [6音步]
By the gate came the foe, upstairs they kept on merry making.
In what a rapid succession ensued regrets and remorse!
So people on railing high have ever since been in thoughts —
Not any use complaining of curses replacing crowns.[3]
As each of the transient Dynasties is gone with the streams,
O only haze o'er grass remains in gloomy green!
To the very day there ofttimes singing our singsong girls[4]
The song by the late king "Back Yard Flowers Dew-Impearled".

迅速强大，而他仍然沉缅声色，不理政事。公元589年，隋将韩擒虎从"朱雀门"破建康入城，陈后主还在宠妃张丽华的"结绮楼"上寻欢作乐。唐杜牧《台城曲》写道："整整复斜斜，隋旗簇晚沙。门外韩擒虎，楼头张丽华。谁怜容足地？却羡井中蛙！"陈叔宝等躲藏在景阳宫井内，被搜出做了俘虏，囚禁至死。末句《后庭》遗曲指陈所作艳歌。参见310页《满江红·金陵怀古》评注 3 。

(4) ofttimes属文学用语，相当于often 。

秋波媚

王雱（王安石之子，生卒年代不详）

杨柳丝丝弄轻柔，烟缕织成愁。
海棠未雨，梨花先雪，一半春休。

而今往事难记省，归梦绕秦楼。
相思只在，丁香枝上，豆蔻梢头。

〖今译〗

丝丝碧条轻软，摆弄满眼婆娑，
柳色如缕如烟，织成一片寂寞。
海棠未像冷雨般洒落，梨花先如飞雪般飘泊。
可怜珍贵春光，已把一半消磨。

如今再难清楚记起，旧日相依的欢乐，
惟有一缕梦魂归去，萦绕秦娥的楼阁。
深深的思念呵，只能凝注枝头花间：
向丁香一簇簇，向那豆蔻呵一朵朵。

〖评注〗

(1) 省略了联系动词，意思是 Dear attachments of yore (are) now hardly remembered.

原诗"秦楼"本指春秋时秦穆公的女儿弄玉的住所；传说萧史善吹箫，可作鸾凤之鸣，弄玉也爱吹箫，穆公将其嫁给萧史，后二人分乘龙凤，升空而去；这里，王雱用秦楼指妻子的住处，因他体弱多病，婚后更甚，其父王安石令他们夫妇分居；又过些年，他还是过早病故了，时年32岁。

To the Tune *Charming Eyes*

With twigs and twigs so tender, tender twined, [5音步]
How weeping willows are weaving a sorry screen!
Our apples abloom their petals not yet raining,
The pears are scattering blossoms about like snowing.
O half of the spring is o'er, as youth is fleeting.

Now hardly remembered — dear attachments of yore,[1]
My dream in vain our chamber haunts and haunts.
Alas, what's there for my yearnings to rest upon?
Upon those shrubs of purple lilacs thither,
Or just these sprigs of yellow cardamoms hither?

临江仙

晏几道（1030？—1106？）

梦后楼台高锁，酒醒帘幕低垂。
去年春恨却来时，
落花人独立，微雨燕双飞。

记得小蘋初见，两重心字罗衣。
琵琶弦上说相思。
当时明月在，曾照彩云归。

〖今译〗

睡梦觉来，高高楼台空锁凄寂，
宿醉方醒，窗口遮起帘幕低低。
忆起去年别离，春怨涌上心扉。
落花阵阵处，有人影孑然独立，
微雨蒙蒙里，看燕侣比翼双飞。

记得那一天，最初和小蘋相聚，
那绣着叠字“心心”相印的绸衣。
琵琶弦上，流露出缠绵的情意。
当时有明月相随，正清光如洗：
送她像彩云一朵，她飘然归去。

〖评注〗

(1) afloat ... fair，辅音头韵；前面还有slender silken。

To the Tune *Fairy Upon the River*

Awake from dream, disappointed, I find [4音步]
Pavilion and tower locked up high.
When drunk'ness does abate I see
But curtains down in shade so bleak.
That springtime grief of the previous year
Returns to me with the season and the scene.
While lonely I stand 'mid flowers drifting,
In pairs the swallows hover, it drizzling.

I remember my first encounter with her,
Xiaoping by name, so few her words.
She wore a slender silken dress
With double hearts embroidered abreast.
Her touches on strings were never failing
To tell in music of tender feelings.
The moon at the full then sees her away
— A rosy cloud afloat, so fair.[1]

鹧鸪天

晏几道

彩袖殷勤捧玉钟，当年拚却醉颜红；
舞低杨柳楼心月，歌尽桃花扇底风。

从别后，忆相逢，几回魂梦与君同。
今宵剩把银釭照，犹恐相逢在梦中。

〖今译〗

挽起绚丽的衣袖，素手频频，再捧上酒盏；
当年伴同我饮宴，你不怕染上嫣红的醉颜。
悠悠的舞步让杨柳楼前，明月也低徊窥看，
萦绕的歌声使桃花扇底，和风也忘情沉缅。

自从分别以后，回忆旧日盛情，
多少次在梦中，我同你一再相逢。
今晚该把银灯，照亮你的面容，
还恐怕这相逢，仍是在迷梦之中。

〖评注〗

(1) oft 是 often 的古旧形式，常用于诗歌之中。

To the Tune *Quails in the Sky*

Your embroidered sleeves you tucked and tucked, [4音步]
To fill and refill my emerald cup.
You readily risked the influence of wine;
Your cheeks were tinted rosy as were mine.
You danced and danced while the moon came low
'Pon the chamber in shades of willows enclosed.
You sang and sang till the wafts lulled quiet —
From the peach-in-blossom fan I held.

Since parted were we so long, long ago,
I've been living with memories dear and old.
How oft with joy I've been able to share[1]
The same dreams as dreams you were having there.
Tonight uphold the lamp I do,
The brilliant silver lamp to you,
For fear that even now and here
Are we in a dream, though sweet yet queer .

⑵ 上片说“歌尽桃花扇底风”的是男方，讲女子连连歌唱，使自己忘却再挥彩扇（不会指歌者摇扇与否）。 因而所接下片“与君同”中“君”是男对女的尊称（如李商隐《夜雨寄北》“君问归期”），尽管更多情况是女对男称“君”。否则，上是男子言，下是女郎语？

江城子·记梦

苏轼（1037—1101）

十年生死两茫茫，
不思量，自难忘。
千里孤坟，无处话凄凉。
纵使相逢应不识，
尘满面，鬓如霜。
夜来幽梦忽还乡，
小轩窗，正梳妆。
相顾无言，惟有泪千行。
料得年年肠断处，
明月夜，短松冈。

〖评注〗

(1) 这两行相当于For ten years I've felt myself in a (bedimming) haze not perceiving your world — (that is) some realm in a haze as bedimming, I believe. 十年了，我处在茫茫境地，也感觉不到你的世界，我想那是同样茫茫的所在。

Last Night's Dream (To the Tune *Town on the River*)

Ten years I've felt myself in a haze not perceiving [5音步]
Your world — some realm, I believe, in a haze as bedimming.[1]
I needn't at all on purpose recollect;
'Tis hardly ever possible for me to forget.
Your lonely grave is a thousand *li* away.
O how and with whom can I give vent to my grief?
You wouldn't recognize me, were we to meet —
My wrinkled face with dusty specks is smeared,
My hair o'er the temples white as frost severe.

Last night my dream returns as of old. [4音步]
Before the window in th' room of your own,
To make your toilet you're seated alone.
We each keep looking at th' other, in a hush;
From eyes of both but teardrops gush.
Though year after year my heart so aches,
I cherish the image of your burial place —
In silent and brilliant moonlit nights,
That knoll enclosed with stubby pines.

水调歌头·中秋

苏 轼

明月几时有？把酒问青天。
不知天上宫阙，今夕是何年。
我欲乘风归去，惟恐琼楼玉宇，
高处不胜寒。
起舞弄清影，何似在人间！
转朱阁，低绮户，照无眠。
不应有恨，何事长向别时圆？
人有悲欢离合，月有阴晴圆缺，
此事古难全。
但愿人长久，千里共婵娟。

〖评注〗

(1) 两行相当于I doubt, however: isn't the chill above 'mid the air ... too severe to bear? 该doubt趋于"否定"后述，估计并非不太冷，还是很冷。

(2) 上行dainty tinged，正常顺序是 tinged dainty,"（被月色）濡染得如此清雅秀丽的"。

(3) peereth 所带是旧词尾-eth，现用-(e)s， 如 peers； 比较最前一行 hast thou (have you)，下行的cherisheth 。

(4) foul and fine, on the wax then wane, 辅音头韵，下有 thro(ugh) weal and woe 。

(5) each of our folks be ... enjoying 属虚拟语气，后(be) in lunar beauty rejoicing，有省略。重读音节后自然轻读，这两行读作 just

Mid-Autumn Festival
(To the Tune *Prelude to the Waters*)

O glorious Moon, since when hast thou been there? [5音步]
With wine cup raised, I inquire of th' azure sky,
While wondering: of what a calendar year of theirs,
This night of nights, in palaces up so high?
To be gone with the wind — I'd like to have a try.

I doubt, however, isn't the chill above 'mid the air [6音步]
In marble towers and jade halls too severe to bear?[1]
I rise and dance to sport with my shadow, dainty tinged[2]
Am I in a humans' world or fairies' land quite strange?

Now high around the chambers 'neath crimson eaves, [5音步]
Now lower down the windows' embroidered drapes,
She peereth inside at those deprived of sleep.[3]
There shouldn't be any ill against us she cherisheth at heart. [6音步]
Yet why at the full is she beaming on dear ones severed afar?

There's weather foul and fine, her phase on the wax then wane,[4]
As sure as we part and unite again, thro' weal and woe.
'Tis simply impossible for things to be perfect since of old.
Just pray that each of our folks be long, long good health enjoying;
Tho' thousands of miles apart, now in lunar beauty rejoicing![5]

PRAY that EACH of our FOLKS be LONG, long GOOD health en-JOY-ing; tho' THOU-sands of MILES a-PART, now in LUN-ar BEAU-ty re-JOIC-ing. 其中 tho' 是though之缩略。

念奴娇·赤壁怀古

苏 轼

大江东去，浪淘尽，千古风流人物。
故垒西边，人道是，三国周郎赤壁。
乱石穿云，惊涛拍岸，卷起千堆雪。
江山如画，一时多少豪杰！

遥想公瑾当年，小乔初嫁了，雄姿英发。
羽扇纶巾，谈笑间，强虏灰飞烟灭。
故国神游，多情应笑我，早生华发。
人生如梦，一樽还酹江月！

〖今译〗

大江东流滚滚，让千古风流人物在波涛中荡涤净尽。
古老营垒西边，人们说就是赤壁，三国周瑜在这里大破曹军。
乱石直插浮云，惊涛击裂岩岸，飞起无数浪花，像瑞雪纷纷。
江山美如图画，一时间多少豪杰粉墨登临。

设想当年的周郎公瑾，刚刚从国丈府里迎亲，雄姿英俊，
手挥羽扇，头戴纶巾，谈笑间令强敌在烟火中化为灰烬。
心驰神往，故国亲临，有人会嘲笑我吧，如此情深，早早白了双鬓。
人生犹如梦寐，还是高举起美酒一杯，祭洒这江月如轮！

〖评注〗

(1) “The youthful Lord” refers to(指上文) Zhou. 其后recollect 第一三音节重读。

Crimson Cliff
(To the Tune *The Pretty Singer*)

The mighty river eastward flows; [4音步]
Its surging waves have washed away
The worthies of all the times of old.
To the west of the ancient fort, they say,
Is a battlefield of the Kingdoms Three,
The Crimson Cliff, renowned for Zhou.

While jagged cliffs o'ershadowing clouds afloat, [5音步]
Appalling billows are madly dashing at the shore —
Behold, a thousand drifts of snows up roll.
An enchanting picture of landscape and waters is the scene.
There what a host of bygone heroes have been!

The youthful Lord, I recollect those days,[1] [5音步]
Was brightly beaming then with gallant grace.
Soon after the wedding with Younger Qiao so charming,
A plume-fan wafting, a silken kerchief wearing.
'Mid chatter easy and laughter gay he reduced
Formidable fleet of the foe to ashes and dust.[2]

While ancient kingdoms I travel in fancy, [4音步]
I must be laughed at because of my folly —
My hair becoming grey so early!
O life like a dream is passing soon.
Let's pour a libation to river and moon!

---

(2) 这四行是一句，after the wedding ... , ... wafting, ... wearing 是三个短语，修饰句子主体 he reduced formidable fleet ... to ashes and dust。

题西林壁

苏 轼

横看成岭侧成峰，远近高低各不同。
不识庐山真面目，只缘身在此山中。

〖评注〗

(1) (They are) Whole ranges, as seen from beside; few peaks, (as you see them) if you've rounded the corner. 从旁看是条条山岭，转角看是几座山峰。

(2) 'Tis 是 It is 的缩略形式。To be made out，被认清。

(3) nothing but,(不是别的）正是…（your staying amid …你之处身大山之中挡住你的视线）。

“不识庐山真面目”已经化为成语。正如陆游的“柳暗花明又一村”（见246页《游山西村》）；又如许浑的“山雨欲来风满楼”。

中唐许浑（生卒年代不详）登上咸阳城楼，他遥见古城之外，只有寂寞渭水沿着东行的古道流逝远方，身感高楼之上更加晚风凄紧，便以“莫问当年”概括过去遗憾，“山雨欲来”提示面前危机，写七律《咸阳城东楼晚眺》(*At Dusk on the East Gate-Tower of XianYang*)，向世人发出警报：“一上高城万里愁，蒹葭杨柳似汀洲。溪云初起日沉阁，山雨欲来风满楼。鸟下绿芜秦苑夕，蝉鸣黄叶汉宫秋。行人莫问当年事，故国东来渭水流。”其英译可为：

Written on the Wall of West Forest Temple

Whole ranges, as seen from beside; few peaks, if you've rounded
the corner.[1] [6音步]
From afar, nearby, below or above, e'er diff'rent to the roamer!
'Tis never to be made out what Lu Mountains are really like,[2]
For nothing but your staying 'mid the Massifs stops your sight.[3]

O' erwhelmed by woe is the one on this tower high,
With reeds and willows down across the isles.
' Pon the waters clouds emerge as daylight fades,
A mountain storm being foretold by the sweeping gale.
Qin palaces hushed, and birds now unseen in gloomy trees,
Han pavilions bleak, and cicadas wail 'mong yellow leaves.
O no, please don' t refer to the bygone glorious feats,
While only the Old *Wei*, the dreary river flows on east.

蝶恋花

苏 轼

花褪残红青杏小，燕子飞时，绿水人家绕。
枝上柳绵吹又少，天涯何处无芳草？

墙里秋千墙外道，墙外行人，墙里佳人笑。
笑渐不闻声渐悄，多情却被无情恼。

〖今译〗

花丛间残留的嫣红已渐渐消减，
杏树梢青青的小杏才斑斑点点；
燕子飞去飞来，碧水环绕家园；
枝头毛茸茸柳绵已不厚密，渐飘零失散；
看远方处处，哪里没有、芳草绿遍天边？

墙外一条路，墙里荡着秋千，
行人要走过，正好佳人笑语呢喃；
驻足细听，这一声声多娇多甜，
笑声软语，却又远去再听不见；
你这个自作多情的人儿呵，
枉然被无情惹下满心幽怨。

To the Tune *Butterflies Love Blossoms*

What's left of the pink and red is rapidly fading [5音步]
On branches, apricots tiny and green appearing.
With swallows here and there beginning hovering
About the villas streams are swelling and wavering.
Remaining willow down gets thinner in blasts;
Where'er o'er th' earth is not there flourishing grass?

Inside the wall a swing hangs high; [4音步]
Outside, an alley goes on quiet.
A passenger's passing and list'ning intent,
The maidens giggling to their heart's content.
Afar from the listener retreating the bevy —
By th' uncaring the caring is left dejected.[1]

〖评注〗

(1)"多情却被无情恼"：据清代张宗棣《词林纪事》，苏轼此词作于被远贬岭南惠州期间，隐寓为国为民横遭排挤之恨。"天涯何处无芳草"应似《离骚》："何所独无芳草兮，尔何怀乎故宅？"苏轼先讲芳草天涯，后说多情墙下，表明他像屈原被迫浪迹边陲，却仍心系故国，"虽九死其犹未悔！" 比《蝶恋花》明显是他的《卜算子》："缺月挂疏桐，漏断人初静……拣尽寒枝不肯栖，寂寞沙洲冷。"

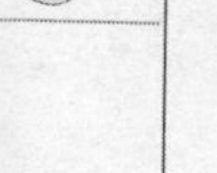

卜算子

李之仪（1038?—1117?）

君住长江头，妾住长江尾；
日日思君不见君，共饮长江水。
此水几时休？此恨何时已？
只愿君心似妾心，定不负相思意。

〖今译〗

你家紧邻长江江口，我家依傍涓涓上游。
天天忘不掉你呀，却无缘重聚，
这同饮的江水白白连成一气。

这江水悠悠何日能够流干？
这幽怨绵绵何时才会消散？
盼你能和我有同样的心愿，
我定要真诚报答你的爱怜！

To the Tune *Fortune Telling*

I live up the long, long river's tail. [4音步]
And you, by its mouth, so far away.
Though daily I'm longing, no chance again with you to meet! [6音步]
You drinking as well as I from the selfsame river great.

O when will the waters cease to flow? [4音步]
And when will my languishing heart be consoled?
If only your feelings were as warm as mine,
Repayment from me you'd be sure to divine![1]

〖评注〗

(1) 相当于 You would be sure to divine（预料）repayment from me（我的报答）。

"定不负，相思意"是说"如果……，我一定不会辜负你的厚爱。"有人误解为"（但盼你能和我有同样的心愿，）你一定不负我的心意"，那就又是无谓重复，又是重大缺欠。

末句开头的"定"字，很重要，如无此字，就失去了"我就……"的转折。而且这是一个多加出来的字。此词上片，末句是5个字。夏完淳的《卜算子》（322页）上下片字数都是 5575。

踏莎行·郴州旅舍

秦观（1049—1100）

雾失楼台，月迷津渡，桃源望断无觅处。
可堪孤馆闭春寒，杜鹃声里斜阳暮！

驿寄梅花，鱼传尺素，砌成此恨无重数。
郴江幸自绕郴山，为谁流下潇湘去？

〖今译〗

暮霭茫茫淹没层楼，月色昏黄迷失渡口。
极目望不到，那当日的桃花溪头。
哪堪这孤寂旅舍里、沉滞的早春寒气，
杜鹃哀啼，斜阳落去，暮色这样凄凄！

路寻驿使、寄以梅枝，遥追踪迹、书简频传，
积蓄起这层层叠叠、无穷的哀怨。
郴江之水呵，你原该好好地环绕郴山，
又为谁要奔向那迢迢潇湘，愈流愈远？

At an Inn in *Chenzhou*
(To the Tune *Treading through Weeds*)

With spreading mist, pavilion and terrace dimming,[5音步]
In moonshine befogged up the river the ferry is lost.
I seek for a trace of the Peach Dale, never finding,
With dusk descending and care-laden cuckoos crying.
The lonesome inn in spring night's cold is locked.

I sent some twigs of winter-sweet by post to my beloved,[1] [6音步]
And tender letters writ for fish to bring to her brook,[2]
Yet only to have my yearnings turned to mountains of grief![3]
Alas! Let River *Chenjiang* girding Mount *Chen* stay,
Why ever, down to *Xiao-Xiang*, must it break away?[4]

〖评注〗

(1) winter-sweet 是梅花俗称。有人用 plum flower指梅花，它更常指李树花。

(2) And tender letters (were) writ(ten)，其中writ是written的古旧形式，常用于诗歌里。For fish to bring to her brook: It was believed that fish are able to carry messages for people — letters from afar may be called fish-carried messages"鱼书". That's why the original poem says "鱼传尺素"。

(3) only to have my yearnings turned to ...，结果状语，表示极端的失望。

(4) 作者被长期贬逐，死于归来途中。他的师长和好友苏轼听到这噩耗时，把"郴江幸自绕郴山，为谁流下潇湘去？"写在扇面上，悼念同病相怜的受难者。

卖花声·题岳阳楼壁

张舜民（生卒年代不详）

木叶下君山，空水漫漫。
十分斟酒敛芳颜。
不是渭城西去客，休唱《阳关》。

醉袖抚危栏，天淡云闲。
何人此路得生还？
回首夕阳红尽处，应是长安！

〖今译〗

秋叶纷纷飘落，铺遍湖心的君山。
水茫茫，天渺渺，水天无边。
酒家姑娘斟得你的酒杯满满，
但她也因你去国离乡，脸色凄然。
如果不是为了远客、辞渭城向长途漫漫，
那悲凉的阳关离歌，不要唱向樽前！

迷醉之人啊，衣袖拂过高高楼头的栏杆；
你兀自远眺，长空淡淡，浮云翩翩：
能有几位经此去后，活着返回家园？
等到日落时分，回望晚霞渐渐阴暗——
那天边应该是，你一心怀念的长安！

Written on the Wall of Yueyang Tower
(To the Tune *Hawking Flowers*)

O' er *Jun* the Islet leaves a-withering flake. [5音步]
Immense extend the skies and waters of the lake.
The waitress fills up my cup with wine to the brim;
Her angelic face in a shadow grave and grim.
Sing not that Song of *Yangguan*, the plaintive tune,
Except for travelers to remotest countries unknown.

Inebriated, I lean against the dizzy rails.
Afloat are leisurely cloudlets, dim and pale;
The vault of heaven stretches dull and high.
O tramping beyond, whoe'er shall return alive?
Behold the last of bloody glows on horizon —
' Tis our homeland e'er so dear, tho' away we're driven![1]

〖评注〗

(1) 相当于 It(轻读) is our HOME-land EV-er so DEAR (to US), though a-WAY we are DRIV-en. 作者是建都汴梁的宋朝时人，词中"长安"、"渭城"（靠长安西）、"阳关"（从长安去西域的疆界上）都是喻指，描述自己和正直士人包括师友苏轼、秦观等，在被弄权奸人排挤迫害，远赴蛮荒边陲，无望返回中土。

采桑子

吕本中（1084—1145）

恨君不似江楼月，
南北东西，南北东西，
只有相随无别离。

恨君却似江楼月，
暂满还亏，暂满还亏，
待到团圆是几时？

〖评注〗

(1) 即：If only you would behave as the moon over the waterside tower (behaves)!

江楼，这二字很关键。只有这里，眺望江面与江滨，才可看到月光一泻千里。这种境界，因为没有遮拦，人走到哪里，都有月亮跟随到那里。所以，译文也不能缺少 o'er the waterside tower（江楼上空）的明月。

(2) 原文"南北东西"指人走月跟。(Going) South, north — east, west, / One never fails to enjoy her attendance 。一个人到处走动，总享有月亮伴随。李白古诗《下终南山过斛斯山人宿置酒》"暮从碧山下，山月随人归。"

(3) 相当于 It is a shame that you are just as varying as the moon does change.

(4) be round 相当于 come round "再度来到某人处"。union 传达"团圆"之意。round, full, union 结成联想。行内韵有 fail, way，shame, wane 等；辅音头韵有 waterside, west, way, wax, wane 等。

Watching the Moon
(To the Tune *Picking Mulberries*)

If only as the moon o'er the waterside tower you'd behave![1] [5音步]
South, north — east, west, [2音步]
South, north — east, west,
One never fails to enjoy her attendance on one's way.[2] [5音步]

A shame you're just as varying as the moon does change:[3]
On the wax — on the wane, [2音步]
On the wax — on the wane!
What time you'd be round for a union as it's full again?[4] [5音步]

长相思·雨

万俟永（北宋末，生卒年代不详）

一声声，一更更，
窗外芭蕉窗里灯，
此时无限情。

梦难成，恨难平，
不道愁人不喜听，
空阶滴到明。

〖评注〗

(1) rooted regrets … to be rid of，含r- 头韵。最前有 splashes … strike and strike 。

(2) towards light, 接近天明的时候。这两行，Defying, dolorous, dislike … dripping，含 d- 头韵，以传达原文之反复。下面末行的 stark secluded（全然与世隔绝的） steps（门前台阶）也用了重复的辅音或辅音连缀。

南宋林逋《长相思》(*Missing You Ever Since*)"吴山青，越山青；两岸青山相送迎。谁知别离情？君泪盈，妾泪盈；罗带同心结未成。江头潮已平！"

Lush are hills on the Northern bank.
Lush are those of the Southern land.
All are lined up to see me off.
None, however, knows our woe.
Swollen with tears are eyes of thine.
Swollen with tears are those of mine.
Why should it slip, our love knot tight?
What regret to be gone with the tide!

Rain
(To the Tune *Missing You Ever Since*)

It drips, and drips, and splashes. [3音步]
Then strike, and strike, night watches.
Outside, banana leaves a-pattering, [4音步]
Inside the window the lamp a-fading .
O what emotion is meantime surging!

'Tis hard for dreams to come at quiet.
As hard to be rid of are rooted regrets.[1]
Defying the dolorous wretch's dislike,
It goes on dripping, while night wears on,[2]
My stark secluded steps upon.

如梦令

李清照（1084—1151?）

昨夜雨疏风骤，浓睡不消残酒。
试问卷帘人，却道“海棠依旧”。
“知否？知否？应是绿肥红瘦。”

〖评注〗

(1) The scarlet (would be) wearily wearing away, 后三词中用辅音头韵。

李清照，号易安居士，济南人。她自幼多才，18岁时嫁给太学生赵明诚。每逢旧历初一、十五，太学休假，夫妻就把衣物当几百钱，踱到相国寺市场，买些碑文，回家共同赏玩。有人拿一幅名画《牡丹图》来卖，要二十万钱，他们留了几天，但凑不够钱，归还后相对惋惜了很久。赵明诚在青州（今山东益都）做官时，李清照同来。夫妇陆续买了不少书画、铜器、石刻。闲时就沏好香茶，打赌某事在某书某卷某页某行，胜者饮茶，往往举杯大笑，把茶全洒在怀中。

赵明诚出外作官，过九九重阳节，李清照写了《醉花荫》（236页）词寄给丈夫。赵明诚很想作词胜过妻子，就闭门谢客，废寝忘食，三天写五十几首，和妻子的混在一起给朋友看。那人反复吟味，最后说：“只有三句绝佳。”问他是哪三句。友人答道：“莫道不销魂，帘卷西风，人比黄花瘦。”正是李清照《醉花荫》的结尾。

李清照44岁时，金灭北宋。丈夫随其他官员，已先南渡，李清照把15车书画等珍品运到江南；青州还锁有收藏，被金兵付之一炬。二年后赵明诚在战乱中病死。金兵又渡江攻占临安（今杭州）。李清照想把剩下的收藏献给南宋皇帝，皇帝也一再逃跑。她没有子嗣，独自辗转飘泊，珍藏丢尽，潦倒落魄，死于临安。

To the Tune *Like a Dream*

Last night tho' slight was the rain, the wind was blowing wild [6音步]
A slumber profound has not dispelled effects of the wine.
In earnest I question the maid who my curtains has rolled. [5音步]
She replies: "The crab-apple blossoms remain as before."
"O don't you see," I can't but retort. [4音步]
"O don't you see for sure at all?
The green'd be swelling merry and gay,
The scarlet wearily wearing away!"[1]

一剪梅

李清照

红藕香残玉簟秋。
轻解罗裳，独上兰舟。
云中谁寄锦书来？
雁字回时，月满西楼。

花自飘零水自流。
一种相思，两处闲愁。
此情无计可消除：
才下眉头，又上心头！

〖今译〗

红莲凋谢，再无芳香；素净蒲席凉初透。
轻轻脱掉长丝裙，独自登上木兰舟。
早就瞩望高天，会有锦书一封，寄于远来的云头？
见到人字排开、传书鸿雁重来，月光已洒满西楼。

无奈何花朵飘落，河水呵自是奔流。
同样的相思心意，两地的恼人烦愁。
这牢牢情结，竟无法解除：
刚脱开眉头，又缠上心头。

〖评注〗

(1) Wild geese were supposed to be entrusted to carry letters for people as carrier pigeons are assigned the task. 据说大雁像信鸽那样能为人传递书信。

To the Tune *One Winter-Sweet Sprig*

Our lotuses pink decay, their fragrance fails. [5音步]
The cattail mat a little chilly feels.
My lengthy silken skirt unloosening quiet,
Alone I set my rowing boat adrift.
'Tis a cordial letter coming in clouds for me?
In neat array arriving the messenger-geese,[1]
The Western Tower is steeped in lunar beams.

With fallen flowers following the flows, [4音步]
Unceasing streams ne'er heed us folk.
One common longing, of both our souls,
Has each one languishing, severed remote.
The nuisance you're never able to elude —
From brows it's been hardly driven apart,
It'd come at once to gnaw at your heart.

醉花荫

李清照

薄雾浓云愁永昼，瑞脑销金兽。
佳节又重阳，玉枕纱厨，半夜凉初透。

东篱把酒黄昏后，有暗香盈袖。
莫道不销魂，帘卷西风，人比黄花瘦。

〖评注〗

(1) linger，迟疑不去，时间拖长。

(2) “gold-lion” censer 金狮子形状的香炉。coiled incense 盘旋起来的“瑞香”，即“瑞脑”；瑞香是一种芳香灌木，开花外紫内白，可作香料。

(3) 常说的It serves you right! 意思是“你活该！” 但 serve somebody right 也可不含贬义，表示“为某人做得很好”。

(4) affecting 使人动心的，可怜的。这两行直译：在东篱边花丛之上举着酒杯，到黄昏已使我的衣袖充满令人感念的芳香（因伤感而断肠）。

(5) you … blues 行内韵。the blues 忧伤（情绪）。译文社《英汉大词典》melt条有“（心）软，伤心”等注释。

(6) the Zephyr（诗歌用语）西风（拟人化）。英语常用拟人说法，something sees …： This coat of mine has seen hard wear.（牛津高级英语词典第四版）我这件上衣经受了多少磨损。

To the Tune *Drunk Beneath Blossoms*

With mists thin or clouds thick, lingers the dreary day;[1] [5音步]
In the "gold-lion" censer, burns coiled incense away.[2]
Shouldn't be cheered the returning Double Ninth?
Jade pillow and gauze net no longer serving me right,[3]
Allowing the first chill to steal in, deep in the night.

O'er blossoms by eastern hedge a wine cup lifting,
By dusk, has filled my sleeves with aroma affecting.[4]
Don't say, will you? My heart isn't melting in the blues![5]
Up-rolling the curtain, the Zephyr sees a figure —[6]
Compared with the yellow flowers, she's the thinner!

声声慢

李清照

寻寻觅觅，冷冷清清，凄凄惨惨戚戚。
乍暖还寒时候，最难将息。
三杯两盏淡酒，怎敌他、晚来风急？
雁过也，正伤心，却是旧时相识。

满地黄花堆积，憔悴损，如今有谁堪摘？
守着窗儿，独自怎生得黑？
梧桐更兼细雨，到黄昏、点点滴滴。
这次第，怎一个“愁”字了得？

〖评注〗

(1) 第一行读作 O(轻读) WHAT'S it I'm(轻读) SEEK-ing, SEEK-ing，是分裂句（特殊强调句）的疑问形式，句中省略了 that，比较 It is companionship (that) I am seeking 。第二行修饰上文，相当于 as I'm peeping and peeping all around，在我四处窥探之际。第四行主语 one 置动词 remains 后，保持诗句各音节轻重相间，sick'ning 省略一个音节也为合律。

原文全词97字竟有57个是舌齿音，76个是趋于闭口、音质低迷的“阴性字”，特别是开头这类语音构成七对叠词，揭示了词人愁肠百结、欲说还休的深沉抑郁。英译所用叠词、头韵中也多舌齿辅音与合口、半合口元音：peeping, seeking, sickening, depressing, despairing 。

(2) 此句 Warm 前省略了It is 。e'er 是 ever之略。

(3) 本行 faded away, decayed, dismay 构成元音行内韵和辅音头韵。

To the Tune *Slow, Slow Strains*

O what's it I'm seeking, seeking,[3音步]
All around as I'm peeping, peeping?
With ev'rything depressing, depressing,
Remains one sick'ning, sick'ning, despairing, despairing![1] [5音步]

Warm just a while, and chilly e'er and anon.[2]
'Tis hard to keep from feeling afflicted and forlorn.
What little warmth my sorry wine's begetting,
Ne'er guards me 'gainst the gale at dusk a-raging!
Wild geese are crying past, and ruffling my thoughts;
They're acquaintances of old, I then find out.

About the ground are yellow petals bestrewn,
All faded away, decayed in dismay so soon.[3]
Just where is a spray remaining unspoilt so far,
To be plucked and brought to me, displayed in my vase?

Beside the window, sitting in anguish stark,
How could I bear this solitude till dark?[4]
On drying leaves of plane trees should there be
A drizzle pattering, pattering towards the eve!
How could the saddest of sad words not be failing
To depict this train of saddening scenes I'm facing?

末后一行有 saddening scences ... facing，辅音头韵。

下行的 Where is a spray ... to be plucked? "有谁堪摘":有哪一枝可以摘来？"谁"可指哪个或什么。

(4) 读作 how COULD I(轻读) BEAR this SO-li-TUDE till DARK?

武陵春

李清照

风住尘香花已尽，日晚倦梳头。
物是人非事事休，欲语泪先流。

闻道双溪春尚好，也拟泛轻舟。
又恐双溪舴艋舟，载不动，许多愁。

〖评注〗

(1) 不同于suspect 对所猜疑趋于肯定，译文所用的 doubt 对存疑事项趋于否定。这里要对"船儿不小"(the boat isn't too tiny to keep afloat) 加以否定。如果使用 suspect，要说 I suspect that the boat is too tiny to keep afloat, with me … ，但那又不是原意那样翻来覆去、犹疑再三。

双溪，是作者旅居江南时，听说的一个野游去处。"又恐双溪舴艋舟，载不动，许多愁"，比较王实甫《西厢记·长亭送别》（296页）末尾："夕阳古道无人语，禾黍秋风听马嘶。四围山色中，一鞭残照里。遍人间烦恼填胸臆，量这般大小车儿如何载得起？"

To the Tune *Spring in Peach Dale*

The wind with scented dust has settled down,[5音步]
And all the fragrant flowers from branches are gone.
I'm not in the mood for my toilet, the dusk so drear.
Although what meets the eye the same appears,
The heart is bereft of all it cherished dear.
'Fore a word is uttered, out will gush my tears.

'Tis said the Joint Brook a scenic resort, [4音步]
Where spring excursions are enjoyable for all.
Not bad if I go adrift with flows.
I doubt, however, if isn't the boat,[1]
With me, too tiny to keep afloat —
My heart's so heavily laden with woe!

临江仙·夜登小阁，忆洛中旧游

陈与义（1090—1139）

忆昔午桥桥上饮，座中都是豪英。
长沟流月去无声。
杏花疏影里，吹笛到天明。

二十余年成一梦，此身虽在堪惊。
闲登小阁眺新晴。
古今多少事，渔唱起三更。

〖评注〗

(1) 相当于 (Those were) high feasts at *Wu Qiao* Bridge for jolly folks.

(2) 相当于 The brooklet (flowed) long, and the moonlit ripples (were) cool.

(3) 'Mid 是Amid 之略。重读音节后，自然轻读（即使是实词）。本行读作 a FLUTE tune vi-BRA-ting the WHOLE night, FLOAT-ing a-FAR 。这也是省略句，可相当于 a flute tune (kept) vibrating the whole night ...

Luoyang Pleasures Recalled at Night
(To the Tune *Fairy Upon the River*)

High feasts at *Wu Qiao* Bridge for jolly folks,[1] [5音步]
And all were talents and worthies of the Capital Old!
The brooklet long, and the moonlit ripples cool,[2]
'Mid apricot flowers, whose shadows so slender and smart,
A flute tune vibrating the whole night, floating afar.[3]

These twenty years have proved a nightmare grim.
Remaining alive, yet how I'm aghast and grieved![4]
Ascending the loft I watch it clearing again.
What lots of tales since ancient ages have made
But songs of fishers sung at the break of day![5]

---

(4) 分词短语表让步，(Though) Remaining alive, yet how I am aghast（惊骇的）and grieved!

(5) have made but(just) songs，只是(被)编成歌曲。but 是副词，相当于 only, merely 之类。三更在此不确指半夜，犹言起得很早。

小重山

岳飞（1103—1142）

昨夜寒蛩不住鸣，惊回千里梦，已三更。
起来独自绕阶行。
人悄悄，帘外月胧明。

白发为功名，旧山松竹老，阻归程。
欲将心事付瑶筝。
知音少，弦断有谁听？

〖评注〗

(1) Return I can't ... 是I can't return (home), while bamboos and pines … grow old. 的强调倒装。

The author is one of the greatest and most tragic national heroes of China. In the year of 1129, the *Jin* invaders(Golden Tartars) seized the *Song* Dynasty's capital *Bianliang*, and then drove south to conquer more and more lands. Yue Fei, a native of the middle plain, joined the resisting army and launched one after another victorious battles, forcing the enemy to withdraw to the north of the Yellow River. But the remnants of the imperial family had set up in the South another *Song* regime, the Southern *Song* court, which was for "peace" at any price. Yue Fei's army was officially under the control of the capitulationist court. They forcefully summoned Yue Fei back to the new capital *Hangzhou*, where awaiting him was a false accusation of treason. He was soon murdered with poison without any formal sentence being announced, at the age of 39. Some 20 years after that, under pressure of mounting public indignation, a later emperor admitted the injustice done to him. A temple to his memory was put up by the West Lake in *Hangzhou*.

To thc Tune *Hills Beyond Hills*

'Twas deep in the night the autumn crickets chirped and chirped. [6音步]
When all of a sudden out of my long march dream I was stirred.
I rose and took a stroll around the courtyard alone.
No other soul was about, but brightly the moonlight shone.

I'm growing gray-haired striving for honor, vainly though.
Return I can't, while bamboos and pines round my farm grow old.[1]
To the zither I wish to commit my yearning dear and sincere;
O broken might my strings be struck, but who'd lend an ear?

游山西村

陆 游 (1125–1210)

莫笑农家腊酒浑，丰年待客足鸡豚。
山重水复疑无路，柳暗花明又一村。
箫鼓追随春社近，衣裳简朴古风存。
从今若许闲乘月，拄杖无时夜扣门。

〖评注〗

(1) People used to offer sacrifices to the God of Earth twice a year, on some day after 立春(the Beginning of Spring) and another day after 立秋(the Beginning of Autumn). "社" 指土地神或祭神庙堂、或祭祀之日。春社 (Spring/Vernal Sacrifice)，在立春后第五个戊日。

"山重水复疑无路，柳暗花明又一村"，后来作为成语，常说"山穷水尽疑无路，柳暗花明又一村"，简单说："山穷水尽，柳暗花明"。

成语"求之不得"，出自诗经《关雎》："求之不得，寤寐思服；悠哉悠哉，辗转反侧。"

"九死一生"出自屈原《离骚》："亦余心之所善兮，虽九死其犹未悔。"

"四面楚歌"出自虞姬《和项王歌》："汉军已略地，四面楚歌声。"

"青梅竹马，两小无猜"，出自李白《长干行》："妾发初覆额，折花门前剧；郎骑竹马来，绕床弄青梅。同居长干里，两小无嫌猜。"

Visiting the Village Across Western Hills

Sneer not at lees in year-end wine at the farmer's house. [6音步]
A bumper harvest provides the guests with pork and fowl.
Where's the way ahead, with hills and waters doubling back?
O another village! Willows shadowy, blossoms bright!

The Vernal Sacrifice is greeted by gleeful drums and pipes.[1]
In caps and clothes plain, by ancient custom you abide.
When free some moonlit evening of any later day,
I'll come around, supported by a stick, to knock at your gate.

钗头凤

陆游

红酥手，黄縢酒，满城春色宫墙柳。
东风恶，欢情薄，
一怀愁绪，几年离索。
错！错！错！

春如旧，人空瘦，泪痕红浥鲛绡透。
桃花落，闲池阁，
山盟虽在，锦书难托。
莫！莫！莫！

〖今译〗

当年你润红的双手啊，为我斟上藤黄美酒。
正当满城春色，宫墙边垂着婆娑碧柳。
狂暴的东风乍起猛扑，欢乐的日子那么短促。
剩一腔愁惨的思绪，多少年离别的悲苦。
这情景全然错误啊，全然错误！

春天还如旧时一样娇艳，人却白白消瘦，不似当年；
让涔涔的泪水，湿透你嫣红的丝绢。
桃花又被吹打飘零，池阁中间空空荡荡。
海誓山盟虽铭记不忘，深情书信却难以寄上。
这命运怎么来讲啊，怎么来讲？

To the Tune *Phoenix Hairpin*

Your pinky creamy hands so fine, [4音步]
Our orange-golden cupfuls of wine.
The city entire with vernal radiance shined; [5音步]
The Palace walls by willows lovely lined.
Of a sudden a raging gale then swooped and swept;[1]
And there our heart-felt joy was snatched and snapped.
Suffusing my heart, my bitter longings thronged;
We parted asunder, thro lonely years prolonged.
'Tis wrong, 'tis wrong, 'tis wrong! [3音步]

While Spring awakens alive again, [4音步]
Your figure's losing its bloom in vain.
With rouge down washed, your teardrops roll and roll, [5音步]
At once that kerchief silken stained and soaked.[2]
As peach trees all bereft of fleeting flowers,
So pond and pavilion both forsaken, forlorn.[3]
Though standing true those solemn vows of ours,
Impassioned words may not be exchanged as of yore,[4]
No more, no more, no more! [3音步]

〖评注〗

(1) "a raging gale swooped" hints at the mother's forcing a divorce upon the poet and his wife. 陆游以"东风恶"暗指母亲当时的专横，强迫自己和妻子离婚。

(2) 诗中handkerchief 可略作 kerchief 。本行 silken stained ... soaked，辅音头韵；上有 awaken alive again，元音头韵 。

(3) As peach trees (are) all bereft ... So pond and pavilion (are) both forsaken ...，两句都省略了are。

(4) of yore（与上forlorn押近似韵），相当于of old。前flowers与ours隔行押韵。

陆游（1125-1210），越州山阴（今浙江绍兴）人，20岁时，与颇知诗文的表妹唐琬结婚。婚后，陆游两次科考不利。母亲认为是唐琬使陆游荒疏学业，强迫陆游休妻。陆游给唐琬另找一个住处。但不多时，此事被发现，母亲大闹一场，唐琬只好回到娘家。

陆游、唐琬虽各在父母指令下另有婚配，却始终怀念旧情。十年后陆游31岁，早已中举为官，从外地回到家乡，游于沈氏花园。碰巧，唐琬和后夫赵士程也在园中。唐琬得知陆游来园，劝说后夫派人给陆游送过酒肴。陆游感慨痛饮，酒后在园中墙上醉题《钗头凤》词而归。"红酥手，黄縢酒，满城春色宫墙柳"是在回忆十年多前的美好婚恋：陆游的家乡今绍兴，曾是古代越国的京城会稽，留有越王故宫；婚后二人走过故宫墙外柳荫，已是难忘的记忆了。随后，唐琬见到陆游题词，也和了一首《钗头凤》(见本书下一首唐琬词），辗转带给陆游。不久，她就悒悒而死。

二人写《钗头凤》过后四十多年，陆游走遍天涯，回到故乡。75岁的老叟，再度来到沈园，触景伤情，感慨系之,写下《沈园》二绝句和《沈园小阕》七律。又过多年，在逝世前四年 81岁岁暮，因梦中重游旧地，醒来悲痛，又写了《十二月二日梦游沈氏园亭》*(Dreaming of the Old Garden)*三绝句，下面这首就是其中之一：

城南亭榭锁闲坊，孤鹤归来只自伤。
尘渍苔侵数行墨，尔来谁为拂颓墙？

On Southern Skirts now pavilions and terraces forsaken, forlorn;
O lost in solitude a grievous crane returning alone.
While lines in ink with dust and moss altogether smeared,[5]
Just who is to mind the tumbling wall after long, long years?

(5) 行末smear，弄脏，使模糊。While 引导状语从句（...are altogether smeared省略are），可含让步意味"尽管..."，修饰下面主句Just who is to mind ...?

钗头凤

唐 琬（生卒年代不详）

世情薄，人情恶，雨送黄昏花易落。
晓风干，泪痕残；
欲笺心事，独倚斜栏。
难，难，难！

人成个，今非昨，病魂常似秋千索。
角声寒，夜阑珊；
怕人寻问，咽泪装欢。
瞒，瞒，瞒！

〖今译〗

世道冷冷漠漠，人心艰险莫测。
凄凉的黄昏更加冷雨，花朵怎能不纷纷洒落？
直到天明迎着苦涩的晨风，才把满脸的泪痕吹干扫净。
本想把心底千言写上信笺，却只能独自默默倚偏栏杆。
这境况真难啊，真难！

俩人各自孤单，当年一去不返。
多病的心魂像破旧的秋千，损耗的绳索哪一天会拉断？
号角的声调啊，分外凄惨，残灯能熬过这无眠的夜晚？
只怕他人，关心询问，强咽眼泪，装出笑脸。
怎堪总相瞒啊，相瞒！

To the Tune *Phoenix Hairpin*

A worldly world detached! [3音步]
No feeling's shown for a wretch.
A drizzle seeing fading the dreary even,[1] [5音步]
What plight for flowers rashly dropped and dampened!
A morning wind is drying [3音步]
My face, tearstained from crying.
If only my dear could be told what lies in my heart! [5音步]
I can but murmur to myself while watching afar.
'Tis hard, 'tis hard, 'tis hard ! [3音步]

I've been torn away from you;
And nothing's the same as of old.
My ailing soul will break 'neath strain one day, [5音步]
As ropes on a swing, through wearing, give away.
The horn keeps blowing chilly, [2] [3音步]
Night's waning, skies turn pallid.
In case of kind acquaintances inquiring, [5音步]
I choke my hot tears back, a forced smile wearing,
E'er lying, e'er lying, e'er lying! [3音步]

〖评注〗

(1) 第一行 ...worldly world (世俗的世界、人群) 是无谓语感叹句，相当于What a worldly world detached (it is)!。本行 even 为 evening 的原词，现属诗歌用语。三四行中drizzle, dreary, dropped, dampened, 辅音头韵。第四行What plight (it is) ...有省略。

(2) 相当于The horn is blowing sadly，诗歌中形容词（如sad）可代副词（如sadly）。

沈园二首（之一）

陆 游

城上斜阳画角哀，沈园非复旧池台。
伤心桥下春波绿，曾是惊鸿照影来。

〖今译〗

城头低落了斜阳，听角声阵阵凄清；
沈园的池塘、台榭已不是旧时情景。
最伤心那桥下春水，犹自碧波澄澄，
就是那水面上，映照过亲人的秀影。

The Shens' Garden

A drooping sun 'pon the city wall, [4音步]
Pathetic notes of the bugle call.[1]
Our old pavilion and pond so dear
Have vanished from this day's garden drear.[2]
My heart does ache as I see on the bridge, down there, [5音步]
Spring water verdant that mirrored her figure, so fair!

〖评注〗

(1) 主语是 notes, 谓语是 call, 上行 (With) A drooping sun 'pon the city wall 是独立结构作状语。

(2) drear，文学用语，相当于 dreary。

沈园二首（之二）

陆 游

梦断香消四十年，沈园柳老不飞绵，
此身行作稽山土，犹吊遗踪一泫然。

〖今译〗

旧梦摧残、香魂飘走，已有四十个春秋，
沈园衰颓的老柳，再没有轻絮飞下梢头。
自己也就快入土，给会稽山麓添一荒丘，
还在凭吊你的遗迹，还在为你泪湿襟袖。

〖评注〗

(1) is faded 表持续静态，可用 for 40 years 修饰。如为非持续动态 has faded 不可用for...修饰。

两首绝句是春天写的，大约在同年秋天，陆游再去沈园后又写七律《沈园小阙》（下篇）。

The Shens' Garden

I've been for ages out of the dreamland sweet.[5音步]
The blossom I adored is faded for forty years.[1]
In *Shenyuan* Garden willows are now [4音步]
Too old to scatter catkins about.
I myself am turning dust at the foot of Mount *Kuai Ji* ,[6音步]
Yet still my tears will drip for awakened memories in me!

沈园小阕

陆 游

枫叶初丹槲叶黄，河阳愁鬓怯新霜。
林亭感旧空回首，泉路凭谁说断肠？
坏壁醉题尘漠漠，断云幽梦事茫茫。
年来妄念消除尽，回向蒲龛一炷香。

〖评注〗

(1)“河阳”，在今洛阳北；西晋文人潘岳曾任河阳县官，因难以施展，作赋自伤青鬓愁损，终卷入八王之乱被杀，后代就常以“潘鬓”、“河阳愁鬓”指衰老鬓发。“怯新霜”，害怕新添的白发。“林亭”句说自己的回忆，“泉路”句说亲人在阴间。

A Short Poem on the Shens' Garden Wall

While maple leaves are tinted red and scarlet,[5音步]
Tree tops of Mongolian oaks are turned sallow.
On finding hair on my temples turning white,
I can't but feel alarmed and draw a sigh.[1]

With woods, pavilions of old in view again,
O what a lot of memories clustering in vain!
And thou in the Nether World, bewildering and wild,
'Fore whom art thou to lay those grievances of thine?

Beneath the pale, pale dust is the shabby wall
Retaining the poem which, mazed by drink, I scrawled,
What prized, prized recollections are haunting me
Of days we were clinging together dear and sweet!

Thro' years and years of bitter despairing dismay,
My fantastic fancies have all been worn away.
I'd care for nothing now but be home and kneel
At the shrine to raise my prayers to Buddha for thee.

小池

杨万里（1127—1206）

泉眼无声惜细流，树阴照水爱晴柔。
小荷才露尖尖角，早有蜻蜓立上头。

〖评注〗

(1) 动词spare习惯和of搭配，爱惜什么，说 spare of something 。

和南宋杨万里这首七绝中“小荷才露尖尖角”一句情趣相仿的，有北宋苏轼的名句“春江水暖鸭先知”。苏轼《题惠崇〈春江晚景〉》(*The Painting "Early Evening on Spring River"*)写道：“竹外桃花三两枝，春江水暖鸭先知。蒌蒿满地芦芽短，正是河豚欲上时。”写景写情又在说理：

The first few peach sprigs bursting abloom beyond the bamboos;
Spring river getting warm is first known to ducks afloat.
While wormwood is teeming and asparagus are shooting forth,
There comes the season when globefish savory upstream swarm.

什么情理？显然是——不觉泥水发新绿，无限风光出幼苗。

近代国学大师王国维说：“一切景语，都是情语”；“语语都在目前，就是不隔”(《人间词话》)。以景传情，更为明快。他评论陶渊明、苏东坡的诗词“不隔”，欧阳修以至姜夔的某些作品“则隔矣”，有如“雾里看花”，模模糊糊。

王国维《人间词话》又说：“诗人对宇宙、人生，须入乎其内，又须出乎其外。入乎其内，故有生气；出乎其外，故有高致。美成（北宋周邦彦）能入而不能出。白石（南宋姜夔）以降（以下词人），于此二事皆未梦见。”

苏轼的“天涯何处无芳草？”（220页）和陆游的“柳暗花明又一村”（246页），进入了情景，而又高出于物外——难得那一隅感知，升华为普遍哲理。

A Small Pool

The wellspring spares in silence of her streamlets trickling,[1] [5音步]
In her pool, the foliage sunny and supple mirroring.
A lotus' slim, slim bud on the surface emerges,
When a dragonfly, in no time coming, there perches.

菩萨蛮·书江西造口壁

辛弃疾（1140—1207）

郁孤台下清江水，中间多少行人泪？
西北望长安，可怜无数山。

青山遮不住，毕竟东流去。
江晚正愁予，山深闻鹧鸪。

〖评注〗

(1) *Zaokou* is a riverside village south of *Nanchang*, the biggest city of *Jiangxi* Province to the south of the middle reaches of the *Yangtze* River. In 1129, the Northern *Song* Dynasty met its doom when the capital *Bianliang*, on the Central Plains, was captured by the invading *Jin* troops(Golden Tartars from beyond the northern borders). The Emperor Qin Zong was taken prisoner. Some remnants of the *Song* imperial family escaped and set up a new regime, the Southern *Song*, making *Hangzhou* its capital. The savage invaders crossed the *Yangtze* River in a bid to occupy all of China. The Southern *Song* Emperor and his courtiers fled southward along the coast, while the empress dowager and some imperial kindred took flight on boats up the *Yangtze* and then the *Gangjiang* River. Two hordes of the Tartars chased after the two runaway groups. Some *Jin* savages drove as far as *Zaokou*, where most of the refugees were scattered or massacred. Thanks to the victorious battles fought

Written on a Wall at *Zaokou*
(To the Tune *Exotic Dancers*)[1]

Shed by refugees running-for-life, O torrents of tears [扬抑6]
Blended under Lonely Terrace with th' River Clear!
Towards the Northwest, from sight the Capital's lost, [5音步]
Screened by wretched ranges, and peaks atop[2].

Yet keeps rushing northeast th' angry stream,
Breaking thro' mountain ranges greenish with gleams.
Doleful me, on the flows the night is falling!
There the cuckoos, heard from dales, are calling[3]!

---

by Yue Fei's forces between the *Yangtze* and the Yellow River, the enemy intruding far into the South were forced to retreat. See p.245 Yue Fei's poem *To the Tune Hills Beyond Hills.*

(2) "长安"喻指故都，张舜民《卖花声》"夕阳红尽处，应是长安"（226页）。ranges,and peaks atop "重重叠叠的山和山峰"。

原诗"遮不住"、"东流去"喻指南宋人民反对投降、光复故园的意愿。

(3) 上行 Doleful me 感叹用语，类似的有 Woe is me! Unlucky me! 等。本行鹧鸪的确切译名应是 Chinese francolin，有人称之为 partridge(本指山鹑)。其啼声似杜鹃，同样令人思乡，译文可借用中外读者更熟悉的 cuckoo 。

贺新郎·别茂嘉十二弟

辛弃疾

绿树听鹈鴂，更哪堪，鹧鸪声住，杜鹃声切！
啼到春归无觅处，苦恨芳菲都歇：算未抵人间离别。
马上琵琶关塞黑，更长门翠辇辞金阙。
看燕燕，送归妾。

将军百战身名裂，向河梁，回头万里，故人长绝。
易水萧萧西风冷，满座衣冠似雪，正壮士悲歌未彻。
啼鸟还知如许恨，料不啼清泪长啼血。
谁共我，醉明月？

〖今译〗

听了碧荫中悲啼的鹈鴂，还怎能忍受，
鹧鸪啼唤凄楚，接着杜鹃声声凄切！
咕咕不歇，直啼到春光净尽的时节，
苦苦恼恨，那百花的芳菲都已完结。
但想来这层幽恨，哪里比得人间的离别：
马上琵琶低沉，关塞上云雾昏昏，
又从冷落深宫登车，辞别金灿灿的宫门。
看双燕萦绕殷殷，远送去国佳人。

将军啊曾经百战，到头来身败名裂，
向桥头路口回顾万里征途，故友分手便成永诀。
萧萧易水掠过西风凄寒，饯行席间全是雪白衣衫，
壮士唱起凄厉离歌，弦响怆然。
人世如许别恨，啼鸟若能理解，
料想它哀鸣时不是滴着清泪，而是洒着热血！
更有谁与我共此良夜，同我来痛饮送月？

Bidding Farewell to Brother Maojia
(To the Tune *Hailing Newly-Weds*)

Having listened to anis crying in foliage thick'ning,[1] [扬抑6]
How is one to tolerate hearing partridges whining,
Followed by cuckoos' harsh howls just like woeful wailing?
Not until altogether perished are flowers fair,
Would they stop complaining of spring elapsing in haste.
Birds' woe, however, is nothing compared with our parting grief!

Far ahead,the frontier passes in gloomy haze,
Music played on the *pipa* sending the princess away.
Once and again, alighting their carriage from palaces deep,
Beauties leaving their homeland for strangers' terrain bleak.[2]
Swallows hovering along, to see the travelers off.
Married to aliens, the brides were ne'er to be back to their folks.

Through with hundreds of battles, a general losing one[3]
Should have himself so hopelessly shamed and cursed and damned!
What regrets he suffered, while waving goodbye to his friend
Who was returning, leaving himself forever behind,
There, on a bridge across a foreign river remote,
Staring into the distance, myriads of miles from home!

Wav'ring, wav'ring waves of the *Yi* in autumn gales,[4]
Everyone was dressed in snow-white, mourning the day.
Warrior Jing was to pay his own for the despot's life.
Farewell songs were sung by comrades at pitches high.
Were the birds to know of how we're bereaved of our dear,
Sure they'd be crying bloody, instead of watery, tears.
— Why not stay for this moonlit night, O brother mine?
Who else's there to share my lament along with my wine?

〖评注〗

(1) “anis”, a rare kind of bird, similar to cuckoos. “鹈鴂”是很像杜鹃的一种啼鸟。

(2) About “beauties leaving their homeland” see p.202. note 1. Lady Ming's(or Zhao Jun's) story was the most well known among so many similar cases.

(3) be through with ... 表示“完成了某事”。(Being/Having been) Through with hundreds of battles（身经百战）作状语，修饰下面句子主体 a general losing one (battle) should have himself so hopelessly ... damned!（将军打一次败仗，竟会使自己身败名裂！）

“A general losing ... ” refers to General Li Ling(?-74 B.C.) of the *Han* Dynasty, who had achieved numerous feats for the state, but on losing one battle and captured by the Tartars, was ruthlessly condemned by the Emperor. His old mother and his wife at home, together with their children, were executed as a penalty for his “treachery”, and he was unable to set foot on his homeland again for life though he yearned to. His friend Su Wu, as an envoy having been detained there for 19 years, at last succeeded in returning.

(4) The *Yi* (River) shore was the place where comrades saw the warrior Jing Ke (?-227 B.C.) off. 下句讲，荆轲要付出自己的生命去换取那暴君秦王的生命。

本词其他典故——马上琵琶：汉时多次嫁女给匈奴等外族，当时弹奏琵琶送其远嫁，包括出塞的昭君。

长门宫，汉武帝时失宠陈皇后的住所，这里，指被冷落的王昭君的住处，从“长门”到“翠辇辞金阙”即从冷宫远赴异国。

《诗经》名篇《燕燕》写送妹远嫁:“燕燕于飞，差池其羽。之子于归，远送于野。”该诗后文“仲氏”即妹妹。于归即出嫁。《汉广》(5页)有“之子于归”。“送归妾”借送妹远嫁故事，暗示汴京失陷时，宋室的皇后、嫔妃、宫女全被掳去。

后片辛弃疾写李陵、荆轲，一方面影射抗金将士李纲、岳飞等的遭遇；另一方面借以透露自己的满腔愤慨，一心复国，反遭诬陷，壮志难酬，前途险恶。

青玉案·元夕

辛弃疾

东风夜放花千树，更吹落，星如雨。
宝马雕车香满路。
凤箫声动，玉壶光转，一夜鱼龙舞。

蛾儿雪柳黄金缕，笑语盈盈暗香去。
众里寻他千百度。
蓦然回首，那人却在，灯光阑珊处。

〖今译〗

一夜春风吹度，照眼银花开遍千株万树；
东风凌空过处，更计繁星万千落地如注。
多少骏马轿车驱送芬芳，弥漫大路。
听凤鸣般箫韵飞扬，看玉壶般灯辉流转，整夜鱼龙翻舞。

披着雪柳丝、金树条，戴着颤巍巍的扑灯蛾，
姑娘们更显眼，笑语轻盈，飘着幽香走过。
但在人群中，百回千回只寻找那一个，
猛然回头，她竟独自站在灯火稀疏、清静的角落。

The Lantern Festival Night
(To the Tune *Green Jade Table*)

Th' east wind at night has flowered a thousand trees, [扬抑5]
Bringing showers of glowing stars down streets,
Fleeting our scented chariots and stately steeds.
Phoenix-cooing flutes resounding, [4音步]
Jade-pot-flashing lanterns revolving,[1]
Dolphins and dragons are dancing away —
All night long it's bright as day.

See the grain moths silvern, the tassels golden? [5音步]
See the snow-clad willow twigs of the maidens
Passing with laughter gurgling, fragrance floating?[2]
Far and near, among the crowds e'er surging
Tens of thousands of rounds for one I've been searching;
Only on a glance cast backward do I behold:
There she is, where lights are burning so low![3]

〖评注〗

（1）Phoenix-cooing flutes, exquisite flutes that sound like the phoenix cooing.（似凤鸣之箫）Jade-pot-flashing lanterns, lanterns that shine like jade pots flashing. 这里玉壶指洁白闪亮(舞动)的灯笼。宋末周密撰《武林旧事》（武林为南宋首府临安的别名，该城西面有武林山）"元夜"条："灯之品极多……后福州所进，则纯用白玉，如清冰玉壶，爽澈心目。" resounding 和 revolving，辅音元音头韵兼尾韵；属头韵或行内韵的前有 stars, streets, stately steeds, phoenix, flutes, flashing，后有 night, bright, fragrance floating 。

(2) "黄金缕"，鲜嫩树条，冯延巳《鹊踏枝》"杨柳风轻，展尽黄金缕"；在此是装饰丝绦。下"寻他"：古"他"兼指现用的她。

(3) "那人却在灯火阑珊处"，近代思想家梁启超为之感叹："自怜幽独，伤心人别有怀抱"。辛弃疾矢志复国、横遭诬陷，其《摸鱼儿》道："娥眉曾有人妒。千金纵买相如赋，脉脉此情谁诉？"这一寓意继承了屈原以来"香草""美人"之喻。

(4) 辛弃疾《清平乐》(*To the Tune Serene Music*)以浓烈闺情象征复国热望："春宵睡重，梦里还相送。枕边起寻双玉凤，半晌才知是梦。一从卖翠人还，又无音信经年。便把泪来做水，流也流到伊边！"

O how profound is my sleep in the spring night sweet!
On seeing you off in a dream of some keepsake I'm thinking.
Up sitting by my pillow the emerald phoenixes I seek,
A long, long while remaining unaware I've been dreaming.
The maid was sent to town my jewels to sell last year,
There came a word from you, but no more ever since![5]
I can but weep my gushing tears, O gush, my tears!
The roaring torrents will reach you, remind you of me again!

(5) 词中"卖翠人还"同杜甫《佳人行》"侍婢卖珠还，牵萝补茅屋"寓意相仿。远从屈原美人香草的比喻开始，诗词中常以被遗弃的妇女喻指遭弃置的士子或庶人。卖掉珠翠，形容其困顿无依。辛弃疾这首词，尤其明显，抒发着这位南来北方志士代表北方遗民、申诉其光复沦陷国土的痴情梦想。

粉蝶儿·和晋臣赋落花

辛弃疾

昨日春如十三女儿学绣，
一枝枝、不教花瘦。
甚无情，便下得、雨僽风僽，
向园林、铺作地衣红绉。
而今春似轻薄荡子难久。
记前时、送春归后。
把春波都酿作、一江醇酎，
约清愁、杨柳岸边相候。

〖今译〗

先前春天像十三岁的女孩学着绣花，
每枝花都不情愿、绣得它不够饱满。
怎么就这么无情，连日来风雨连绵，
打尽繁花，任红绉铺满了林间地面。

如今这春天像轻薄的荡子难以久留，
记起去年也不得不含恨将春天送走，
再把一江粼粼春水，全都酿作春酒，
约来凄清愁怨，杨柳岸边尽醉方休。

To the Tune *White Butterflies*

Like a lass at her first embroidery works was Spring herself exerting, [抑扬7]
Presenting every flower on every sprig as chubby as charming.
Yet why's she bringing along her winds and rains so cruel, so mad,
As to deck the gardens' ground with crumpled carpets of petals red?

'Tis a lad unsteady bent on quitting, Spring today. [6音步]
Remember the previous year you saw him take his way?
Then mellow waves were brewed into a riverful of doping wine,
To which were invited your Moods on wat'rside willow-lined.[1]

〖评注〗

(1) 大写开头 Moods，拟人化的(personified)“愁苦”被请到 willow-lined waterside 来与诗人共饮。

(2) 这首词写春光消逝，象征复国大业之消沉，暗喻志士对朝廷大失所望。比较辛弃疾的《摸鱼儿》：

“更能消几番风雨，匆匆春又归去。惜春常怕花开早，何况落红无数。春且住，见说道、天涯芳草无归路。怨春不语。算只有、殷勤画檐蛛网，尽日惹飞絮。

长门事，准拟佳期又误。娥眉曾有人妒，千金纵买相如赋，脉脉此情谁诉？君莫舞，君不见、玉环飞燕皆尘土！闲愁最苦。休去倚危栏，斜阳正在，烟柳断肠处。”

采桑子

辛弃疾

少年不识愁滋味，爱上层楼。
爱上层楼，为赋新词强说愁。

而今识得愁滋味，欲说还休。
欲说还休，却道天凉好个秋！

〖评注〗

(1) take delight in something 是固定搭配(以……为乐)。部分倒装形成抑扬格五音步诗句。

(2) shouldn't 和 people 所带辅音连缀（dn, pl）构成音节，它们是双音节词。

《采桑子》上下片，都要求第二、第三两句，四字重复，如"欲说还休"。而吕本中的《采桑子》（228页），不仅二三句片内反复，而且上下片间，首句也是只换一字的强势重叠：

"恨君不似江楼月，南北东西，南北东西，只有相随无别离。
恨君却似江楼月，暂满还亏，暂满还亏，待到团圆是几时？"

尤其难得的是多种形式的反复，反复当中穿插着对应（《减字木兰

To the Tune *Picking Mulberries*

As a youth, not knowing the taste of mental plight, [5音步]
In climbing lofty towers I took delight[1].
I took delight in climbing towers high;
To fashion a few peculiar lyric lines,
I got myself to speak of a fancied plight.

Yet now I know the taste of mental plight.
About to speak of that but stop in time.
About to speak but stop — instead I cry:
O what refreshing coolness the days provide !
Why shouldn't people call this autumn nice[2] !

花》）：

"淮山隐隐，千里云峰千里恨。淮水悠悠，万顷烟波万顷愁。

山长水远，遮住行人东望眼。恨旧愁新，有泪无言对晚春！"

山对水、千对万；里对顷；隐隐对悠悠；云峰对烟波。淮山下是淮水。

前边山、水，引出后边山、水；上片恨、愁，接续下片恨、愁；长、远相比，旧、新相向，有、无相应，泪、言相对。

全词每两句一韵，共有平仄调换的四个韵脚。英译怎么办好？见278、279页 该词。

卜算子·海棠为风雨所损

刘克庄 (1187—1269)

片片蝶衣轻，点点腥红小。
道是天公不惜花？百种千般巧！

朝见树头繁，暮见枝头少。
道是天公果惜花？雨洗风吹了！

〖评注〗

(1) care for 爱护，下倒数第二行 feel for 怜惜，可隔开使用。

这首词也属忧国慨叹。辛弃疾另有《祝英台近·晚春》(*Late Spring*)：“宝钗分，桃叶渡，烟柳暗南浦。怕上层楼，十日九风雨。断肠片片飞红，都无人管，倩谁唤流莺声住？鬓边觑，试把花卜心期，才簪又重数。罗帐灯昏，呜咽梦中语！是他春带愁来，春归何处？却不解将愁归去！”

At Ferry of Peach Leaf my pin was split in two
To make souvenirs of th' attachment warm and true.
The Southern Shore enveloped in willows like clouds —
From upstairs the piteous place I hate to watch,
With lashing winds and rains more oft than not.

Apple Blossoms Spoiled by the Storm
(To the Tune *Fortune Telling*)

Petal and petal alike, as graceful as wings of a butterfly. [扬抑7]
Cluster and cluster above, as pretty as rubies bloody red.
Who would say that Heaven Great for flowers never cares?[1]
See, they're made in thousands of ways so fascinating, so fair!

Early at dawn was each of the branches thick with blossoms abloom.
Later by dusk get sparse the surviving ones, all drooping in gloom .
Who could say that Heaven Gracious for flowers always feels?
All are going, washed by rains and blown by blasts so fierce!

Innumerable petals drifting, my heart is aching.
There's none by my side to attend to this scene distressing.
And who's to stop the orioles' chitt'ring-chatt'ring?

I peer at and snatch the flowers to my temple pinned
For the petals' number to hint at the date you'll return.
I pin and snatch to count them again and again.
Beside my curtained bed the lamp burns faint;
In dreams my sobs oft choke my words of complaint!
'Tis Spring had brought along such troubles as these;
O why, since Spring's already taken her leave,
Would not she care to take these troubles from me?

虞美人

蒋 捷（1245?—1310?）

少年听雨歌楼上，红烛昏罗帐。
壮年听雨客舟中，江阔云低、断雁叫西风。

而今听雨僧庐下，鬓已星星也。
悲欢离合总无凭，一任阶前、点滴到天明。

〖今译〗

少年也曾听雨，歌楼宴罢人静，
有红烛融融，照向罗帐朦胧。
壮年又曾听雨，在那客船舱中，
江迷远岸，云暗低空，失群雁惊叫西风冷。

如今听雨已寄身僧庐，形影孤零，
空剩得这两鬓霜雪星星。
悲欢离合谁能测定？
任阶前檐水，滴滴嗒嗒，敲打到天明。

To the Tune *Yu the Famous Beauty*

In company of a singing girl, as a youngster, [抑扬4]
I used to listen to raindrops patter,
With candles flickering faintly red
Beside a cozy curtained bed.

I roamed afar while middle-aged;
On a boat so drear, I listened to the rain,
The river broad, the cloud banks low,
A lone goose crying in the west wind cold.

And now inside a Buddhist cottage,
I listen and listen to raindrops patter;
Increasing are hairs shimmering white,
Like silvern stars in a moonless sky.

Repeated distresses, rare delights —
For ever we're of quietness deprived.[1]
So, lying sleepless, heed not its drone:
The rain keeps dripping on steps till dawn.

〖评注〗

(1) distresses, delights, deprived，头韵和行内韵。下行有辅音 "l" 头韵 lying sleepless, let it alone ...

一剪梅

蒋 捷

一片春愁待酒浇，江上舟摇，楼上帘招。
秋娘渡与泰娘桥，风又飘飘，雨又萧萧。

何日归家洗客袍？银字笙调，心字香烧？
流光容易把人抛，红了樱桃，绿了芭蕉。

〖今译〗

春光撩人烦恼中烧，又要水酒来灌来浇？
随这江上扁舟轻摇，看那楼上酒旗频招。
漂过秋娘渡的渡口，穿过泰娘桥的江桥，
又飘拂起和风煦煦，更飘洒得细雨萧萧。

何日何时才能回转，换洗作客的长袍？
再把那银字笙调好，更把那心字香高烧？
流光这么悄悄溜掉，只抛下行人懊恼，
已急急地红了樱桃，又匆匆地绿了芭蕉。

To the Tune *One Winter-Sweet Sprig*

O springtime welling woe of mine, [4音步]
Is it to be drowned with abounding wine?
In the bosom of the rippling river the boat is rocking. [5音步]
From the restaurants' upper windows the streamers beck'ning.
The *Qiu* Maid Ferry is in no time left behind,
The *Tai* Maid Bridge ahead in sight you find.
As the wind for ever drifts and drifts, [4音步]
So the rain at the same time drips and drips![1]

When'll be a date for my traveller's robe[4音步]
To be taken off and washed at home,
My silver garnished reed-pipe be tuned again, [5音步]
And heart-curve curly incense lighted then?
Alas, while days and nights are slipping away,
We folks are easily lost and out of the way.
There turning green the banana bush, [4音步]
And dyeing crimson the cherry fruit.

〖评注〗

(1) drifts等，反复、头韵兼尾韵；前有welling/woe, flows/fronts，后有curve, curly。

减字木兰花

淮上女（南宋时人，姓名不详）

淮山隐隐，千里云峰千里恨。
淮水悠悠，万顷烟波万顷愁。

山长水远，遮住行人东望眼。
恨旧愁新，有泪无言对晚春！

〖评注〗

(1) The author of this poem was a Southern *Song* Dynasty girl who lived around the year 1220, when the *Jin* troops once more carried out a large-scale plundering operation. She was kidnapped from her homeland. This poem of hers was found on the wall of a roadside cottage. 金末词人元好问《续夷坚志》载，金国未被崛起的蒙族武力吞并前，金兵还屡次南来掠夺。“兴定（1220年前后）末，四都尉南征，掠淮上良家女北归，有题《木兰花》词逆旅间。”讲一女在被虏途中住地墙上题《减字木兰花》词。

(2) (lying) in betwixt，隔在(崇山峻岭与浩荡水面)中间。betwixst 相当于 between。 关于原文的对应与反复，见270页 评注；英译力求以相仿结构传达原作。

早在此作百年前，北宋末蒋兴祖任阳武县令；金兵南下夺取宋京

To the Tune *Lily Magnolia* (Shortened) [1]

The *Huaishan* Mounts go dimming, dimming far away; [6音步]
As peaks extend there endless, my grievance knows no bounds.
The *Huaihe* River on rolling, rolling from day to day;
As waves keep wavering boundless, my woe's as immense and profound.

Such mountain masses and waters' expanse in betwixt[2], [5音步]
One's not to see one's homeland staring east,
While meeting new distress 'pon old regrets,
With tears but not a word as spring gets late!

西北的阳武。蒋兴祖殉职，全家被杀，只剩一女，她和许多女子被俘北去。其《减字木兰花》To the Tune *Lily Magnolia* (Shortened)是题在雄州（今河北雄县）驿站墙上留下来的："朝云横度，辘辘车声如水去。白草黄沙，月照孤村三两家。鸿雁过也，百结愁肠无昼夜。渐近燕山，回首乡关归路难！"

The wheels keep grumbling, grumbling, gliding clouds across,
With nothing in view but sallow sands and bleaching grass.
Night falls on moonlit hamlets, on huts deplorable and sparse.
Some mess'nger-geese fly past us — helpless orphans' vans.
Thro torturing days and nights, we're farther, farther away.
Invisible our homeland, we turn our heads about in vain!

满庭芳

徐君宝妻（生卒年代不详）

汉上繁华，江南英俊，尚遗宣政风流。
绿窗朱户，十里烂银钩。
一旦刀兵齐举，旌旗拥、百万貔貅。
长驱入，歌楼舞榭，风卷落花愁。

清平三百载，典章人物，扫地都休。
幸此身未北，犹客南州。
破鉴徐郎何在？
空惆怅，相见无由。
从此后，断魂千里，夜夜岳阳楼。

〖今译〗

江汉何许繁华，南国几多俊杰；留有宣和政和太平年间的优雅风貌。
翠绿的窗棂，朱红的门楼，十里长街，家家帘角高挂着闪亮的银钩。
忽然间干戈临头，战旗急抖，拥来敌军百万如洪水猛兽。
长驱直入，人空舞榭，曲断歌楼，狂风里落花愁惨飘流。

三百载太平的年头，所有篇章文士，一扫而空，踪迹难留。
幸而自身未落北地，一时辗转南州。
半镜分携的徐郎，你在何处？我徒然惆怅，无法与你聚首。
从今我孤零零的魂魄呵——
将不远千里，夜夜飞向岳阳楼头。

To the Tune *Courtyard Full of Fragrance*

Along the shores of the *Han Jiang,* riches grouped, [5音步]
And over the land of the Southerners, worthies trooped,
Remaining the graceful ways of former reigns.
Streets lined by doors vermilion and windows green,
Long streets, where silver hooks on curtains gleamed.

The moment the tumult of war the town befalling,
There come a million brutes with colors flying.
Pavilions and halls for music and dance laid waste,
Forlorn fallen flowers whirl 'fore the gale.

Preserved thro' hundreds of peaceful years, we owned
Our talents of arts and masterpieces renowned.
Altogether now they are swept apart in chaos.
By luck I haven't been taken to Tartars' North,
A captive, driven from town to town in the South.

O where's my man, with half of the broken mirror in store?[1] [6音步]
Just how is this half of mine to unite with that of yours?
My spirit'll trudge all the way to the Tower of *Yueyang* Gate
Tonight and every coming night, for you I'll wait!

〖评注〗

(1) There is a story about a broken mirror helping to reunite a newly married couple driven apart by invading warlord troops. In North China, the Kingdom of *Sui* was growing more and more powerful. The *Chen* Kingdom in the South was on the point of being gobbled up by *Sui*. Xu Deyan, the husband of a *Chen* princess Le Chang, told his wife: "After the fall of the city *Nanking*, you're sure to be snatched by some *Sui* commander and be taken to their capital *Si'an*. Let's break this bronze mirror in two. You keep one half of it, leaving the other half to me. On the Lantern Festival night you may ask a servant to sell your half mirror at the market. And I'll find out where you are." In 589, the *Sui* warlord Yang Su occupied *Nanking*. The invaders captured lots of young women from the palace, and brought them to *Si'an*. Princess Le Chang was among those kept in Yang Su's mansion. Then it was the Lantern Festival night. The market was full of people displaying or watching the lanterns. An old servant was amid the crowd holding a broken half mirror for sale. Xu Deyan came up, bought that half, and gave to the servant his other half on which he wrote: "The half mirror has returned, but how could its owner come back?"

The old servant took it to Princess Le Chang. She cried and cried and from that time on refused to eat anything. The warlord Yang Su asked her the reason. On knowing the story of the broken mirror, Yang Su ordered the old servant to find Xu Deyan at the market place, to bring him home. The couple thanked Yang Su for allowing them to see each other. Yang Su, with a smile, let the wife return with her husband to their hometown.

So, in this lyric, by "my man, with half of the broken mirror in store", the woman author refers to her own husband from whom she had been seized.

南北朝时在以建康为都城的南朝，徐德言与陈后主陈叔宝之妹乐昌公主结亲后不久，陈在北方隋政权威协下，已朝不保夕。徐德言对

公主说：“亡国以后你必定流落在隋朝权贵人家。咱把铜镜打成两半；你可在正月十五元宵夜，求仆人到市上卖你那半片铜镜，那时我可能找到你。”陈都城陷落后，徐妻被隋将杨素带到隋都长安；徐德言也赶来于正月十五到市上。果然一老仆要卖半片铜镜，徐德言自己的半片，正好与之相合。徐买了妻子乐昌的半片，让老仆把自己那半片带给乐昌，上有题诗道：“镜与人俱去，镜归人未归。无复嫦娥影，空留明月辉。”（《归半镜》）

乐昌见到，悲泣绝食。杨素问明此事原委，把徐德言找到府中，与乐昌相见，并让她当场赋诗一首。她以《难言时》为题咏道：“今日何迁次？新官对旧官。啼笑俱不敢，方信作人难！”（今天是什么场合？新主人面前来了旧郎官。我既不敢哭、也不敢笑，才知道作人的难处了！）杨素解其真情，让他们重聚，欣然归去。

词中此处，从岳阳被掳的作者徐君宝妻借“破鉴徐郎”称（蒙古军灭南宋时）自己失散的丈夫徐君宝。经蒙古劫持者多次逼迫，她留下这首词，投河而死。

第五章

元明清诗词曲

Chapter 5

Poems, Ci-Lyrics & Qu-Verses From the Yuan Dynasty On

摸鱼儿

（金末元初）元好问（1190—1257）

问世间，情是何物？
直教生死相许！
天南地北双飞客，老翅几回寒暑？
欢乐趣、别离苦，就中更有痴儿女。
君应有语：
“渺万里层云，千山暮景，只影为谁去？”
横汾路，寂寞当年箫鼓，
荒烟依旧平楚。
招魂楚些何嗟及？山鬼暗啼风雨。
天也妒，未信与、莺儿燕子俱黄土。
千秋万古，
为留待骚人，狂歌痛饮，来访雁丘处！

〖评注〗

(1) The poet, traveling along the *Fen* River, saw a wild goose shot down dead by a hunter. Another wild goose, obviously the mate of the victim, was hovering around, crying bitterly. She refused to fly away, though the shooter tried and tried scaring and driving her aside. Then suddenly she dashed herself on the ground and ended her own life.

The poet bought these two wild geese from the hunter, buried them beside the *Fen* River, and piled up some stones as the mark of the grave. On the biggest stone, he engraved: "Wild Geese's Burial Mound".

元好问生活在隋、唐、北宋之后“南宋北金”的后期，为金国末

To the Tune *Groping for Fish*

Affection, oh, of what is affection comprised? [5音步]
Where from and how has it got the power like that
To impel you to live and die just side by side?
Tough travelers flying across those terrains wide,
What lots of summers and winters you've spent in flight,
While going thro' common pleasures, parting plight!
No wonder abiding couples are found thereby.
Alone, with the idea: "No point those troubles taking[1],
Laboring 'gainst clouds unending, o'er mountains dark'ning,
So lonely, a single shadow alongside casting."

On the site where Emperor Hanwu crossed the *Fen*,
No more are there his barges and music of his band[2].
Remaining dismal woods by a dim mist screened.
"Come back, you spirits!" we call again and again,
While lonely Maid Yao crying 'mid winds and rains[3].
With devotion envied by God, you're not the same
As orioles and swallows mortal, bound to decay.
In order that future poets raise their drinks to you,
The Mound I build here, a memorial to love so true!

年的文人，31岁中进士。他年轻时去并州（今山西省太原市）应试途中，见一猎人捕杀一雁，其伴侣盘旋哀鸣，不肯飞走，最后猛然撞地而死。他买了这两只死雁，埋葬在汾河之滨，堆石为记，称之为"雁丘"，并赋这首《摸鱼儿》词。

(There is) No point (in) taking those troubles, 费那些苦功毫无意义。

(2) About "Emperor Hanwu, his barges and music", see p.32 汉武帝《秋风辞》。下行原文"平楚"指"平林"。

(3) 些（sā），楚辞常用语助词；嗟，感叹。招魂楚些，楚辞招魂之歌。何嗟及，可叹哪里能及于（你的魂灵呢）？About "Maid Yao"（瑶姬），see p.22《山鬼》Note 1。'mid 是amid 之略。

鹧鸪天·题七真洞

耶律楚材（1190—1254）

花界倾颓事已迁，浩歌遥望意茫然。
山河王气空千劫，桃李春风又一年。
横翠嶂，架寒烟，野花平碧怨啼鹃。
不知何限人间梦，并触沉思到酒边。

〖今译〗

道观啊已经坍作瓦砾，繁华一去不返。
高歌远望天边，让我心绪茫然。
山河的主宰白白经受、千次万次劫难。
桃李匆匆开放，又把年华更换。

横亘着青翠山峦，笼罩着凄寒云烟。
野花碧草绵绵间，啼血的杜鹃声声愁惨。
谁知有没有尽头，屡屡破灭的人间梦幻？
幻灭濡染着思绪，随着这苦酒沾上唇边。

〖评注〗

(1) 原题中的“七真洞”，祭祀七位道教“真人”的洞府道观。这里以 temple 译“花界”，因该词本佛家用语，原指寺院。唐代罗邺诗有“花界登临转悟空”句。

(2) 原文“啼鹃”：传说啼血杜鹃是周代蜀国“望帝”杜宇的灵魂；杜宇本是猎人，因恶龙发水为患，他屠龙治水，被拥为帝；后为奸人陷害，冤魂化为杜鹃，每年春天归来，苦苦啼叫，叫得口流鲜

Written at the Seven Saints' Temple[1]
(To the Tune *Quails in the Sky*)

The temple in ruins, its glorious day is long, long past. [6音步]
Its elegy singing and gazing afar, in a mood I'm lost.
Those kings and kingdoms meeting one by one their doom;
These peach and apricot trees for another year are in bloom.

There greenish hills extend, by bleak haze veiled; [5音步]
Here cuckoos cry o'er the flower-dotted fields.[2]
O endless are fond dreams, rendering people bewildered,
That have me pond'ring, as I'm sipping my pungent liquor.

血。见下一篇《酹江月》评注 1 。About "cuckoos cry over the flower-dotted fields", see p.290, Note 1.

耶律楚材，字晋卿，号湛然居士，契丹人，辽国皇族后代，自幼接受汉文化教养，后任迅猛扩展的蒙古汗国中书令（相当于丞相）。开国大帝铁木真（尊称"成吉思汗"即强大汗王，后人给予谥号"元太祖"）对儿子窝阔台汗（后谥号"元太宗"）说，"耶律楚材是上天赐给我们的，军国大事只管靠他。"

蒙古大军攻破金国首府汴京，没有进行大屠杀，是听从了耶律楚材的劝阻。他使蒙古王室改变了"汉人无益于蒙古汗国"的观念，不再把汉人逐出家园、占其田地放牧牛羊，进而奖励农、工、商业。他倡导释放被俘士兵，起用汉族读书人，一次就通过考试选拔出四千多士子，其中千余原已由俘虏沦为奴隶。这些文明政策帮助奠定了改国号为"大元"之前建国的基础。

可惜窝阔台一死（1241），他便遭疏远，理想破灭，抑郁而终。平生劳瘁，并没有解决民族压迫、官僚肆虐的难题。

酹江月·和友《驿中言别》

文天祥（1236—1283）

乾坤能大，算蛟龙、原不是池中物。
风雨牢愁无著处，哪更寒蛩四壁！
横槊赋诗，登楼作赋，万事空中雪。
江流如此，方来还有英杰。

堪笑一叶飘零，重来淮水，正凉风新发。
镜里朱颜都变尽，只有丹心未灭。
去去龙沙，江山回首，一线青如发。
故人应念，杜鹃枝上残月！

〖评注〗

（1）第二节“横槊”等：也似曹操出战、手把长矛歌豪气，或如王粲登楼、斜倚栏杆赋情义……江流就是这样，后浪催送前浪，来日自有英豪，相随突兀崛起！末尾“去去……杜鹃”等：再一程就是荒漠凄凄；回望故国河山如青丝一缕。老友呵，你认得我的精魂吧，当残月低迷，枝头杜鹃还在哀泣！

The cuckoo, according to a Chinese legend, is the incarnation of a much-loved king of ancient times, King Wang. He, as a hunter, had killed a vicious dragon that had kept producing immense floods, and thus saved the people from calamity. So he was made their king. But before long, a wicked courtier murdered him out of jealousy. His spirit wouldn't bear being torn away from his homeland and his countrymen, and returned in the shape of the bird. The cuckoo cries and cries ceaselessly from the spring days on. His tongue bleeds. His blood splashes all about, staining the wilderness, and finally turning into bright red azalea flowers.

In Answer to Deng's Bidding Farewell
(To the Tune *Moon o'er River*)

O vast is the world, as all of us know, [4音步]
For dragons gliding high and low —
They're never confined to little pools.
Yet how can my grief in jail be allayed,
All windows blinded with winds and rains?
In corners, crickets wail their strains!

With a spear on my lap to chant my odes,
Or pieces in rhymes on towers to compose —
My longings are gone, as snowfiakes afloat.
For such is the way of things occurring
Just like the flows in rivers surging:
In my wake are future heroes emerging!

A drifting leaf, I'm back to the *Huai*,
On autumn breeze that's beginning to rise.
Ridiculous, piteous — this fate of mine.
Are there any more of the colors left
In mirror of the prime of my youthful life?
O no, not any, except that the heart
Remains as ardent, steady and fast.

Ahead is desert immense which shimmers.
Behind, my homeland dimmer and dimmer.
A green string afar it's soon becoming.
You know, as that bird I'll be reappearing,
My friend, when the crescent's setting and blushing,
And the cuckoo's crying, its tongue blade bleeding.[1]

《西厢记·春暮伤情》片段

（元初）王实甫（1230?—1310?）

恹恹瘦损，早是伤春，哪值残春？
罗衣宽褪，更能消几个黄昏？
……
无语凭栏杆，目断行云。
落红成阵，风飘万点正愁人。
池塘梦晓，兰槛辞春。
蝶粉轻沾飞絮雪，燕泥香惹落花尘。
系春心，情短柳丝长；
隔花阴，人远天涯近。

Late Spring Moods (opera songs, abridged)

E'er weak and weary, down I've been worn; [4音步]
I've long been grieved with spring forlorn.
Now even this spring declines 'fore me,
Its luster failing and fading away!
My silken dress is getting loose;
I'm feeling too weak for pulling through
These endless evenings ever in gloom.

On rails I lean alone and quiet,
With cloudlets floating out of my sight.
Behold, how faded flowers fly!
'Fore the wind are myriads of petals apart,
As if being torn to shreds is my heart.[1]

I'm woken up from my dream at dawn
By the pond in sunbeams fresh of the morn.
It's time for us adieu to bid
To Spring at our pavilion 'mid flowerbeds.

To wings of snow-white butterflies
Are fixed some flecks from fluff a-flight.[2]
In soil-crumbs making swallows' nests
Is mixed some scented blossoms' dust.

Such supple willow twigs there hanging.
They'd serve to fasten up one's feelings.
Yet feelings too sly to be firmly reined,
And fancies unbridled with any strings.

Tho' far he's not, who's dear to my heart,
— Beyond the bushes across the yard —
Than th' end of the world he seems much farther.[3]
For me to see him it's harder and harder![4]

〖今译〗

愁闷闷空瘦身，负春光早伤心，
更哪堪百花凋谢的残春？
绸衣渐松宽，腰肢渐疲软，
似这般能经受住、多少凄凉的黄昏？

倚向楼栏，默默无言，
只极目凝望、远飘天外的流云。
红英飞落，阵阵纷纷，
东风中漫天飘荡，怎不恼人！
池塘碧水边，春梦依稀觉清晨，
木兰窗棂外，送别归去的芳春。

蝴蝶翅膀的白粉间，轻轻沾上些柳絮的雪绒，
燕子筑巢的新泥中，细细搀和着落花的香尘。
柳丝绵长，待要系住春心，
偏偏不可捉摸，只这区区方寸；
天涯虽远，要比花荫遮处，
人儿不可相亲，天边相形还近！

〖评注〗

(1) 意即Myriads of petals are (torn) apart, as if my heart is being torn to shreds.

(2) 即 Some flecks from fluff on-flight are fixed to wings of snow-white butterflies.

(3) 此行接上，Though he is not far … (yet) he is even farther than the end of the world (因我难以同他相见)。the 在元音前可缩略为 th'。

(4) The *Western Chamber* is an opera written by Wang Shifu of the *Yuan* Dynasty.

Zhang Hong 张生, a young scholar who was traveling the South, met Cui Yingying 莺莺, a girl both pretty and bright, when he visited the Monastery of Salvation.

Yingying was the daughter of the late prime minister and, because of troubled times, was temporarily staying with her mother in the monastery. Young scholar Zhang was struck by Yingying's beauty, so he also remained in the monastery for the time being to seek the acquaintance of the girl. The west chamber was where he stayed. Suddenly the monastery was surrounded by some bandits whose chieftain, Flying Tiger, made it known that his sole intention was to make Yingying his wife and mistress of his camp. Panic stricken, Yingying's mother Madame Cui proclaimed to a gathering of the monks and the laity that whoever could induce the bandits to withdraw would get Yingying as his bride with a handsome dowry. (to be continued in comments below the next passage.)

一伙匪徒包围普救寺，要劫持前相国之女莺莺。寄居西厢的张生，设计降伏了匪帮。但老夫人自食其言，不再许亲。莺莺虽感念张生所表至诚，却也难违母命。张生愁闷难遣，抚琴直至深夜。莺莺也辗转不眠，来到院中，静听西厢琴音，引动了衷心共鸣。张生病倒了。侍女红娘责备莺莺，不该置卧病的恩人于不顾……

《西厢记·长亭送别》片段

王实甫

碧云天，黄花地，西风紧，北雁南飞。
晓来谁染霜林醉？总是离人泪！

恨相见得迟，怨归去得疾。
柳丝长玉骢难系。
恨不倩疏林挂住斜晖。
马儿迍迍地行，车儿快快地随……

下西风黄叶纷飞，
染寒烟衰草萋迷。
两意徘徊。
伯劳东去燕西飞，未登程先问归期。
虽然眼底人千里，且尽生前酒一杯。
未饮心先醉，眼中流血，心里成灰！……

荒村雨露宜眠早，野店风霜要起迟。
青山隔送行，疏林不做美，淡烟暮霭相遮蔽。
夕阳古道无人语，禾黍秋风听马嘶。
四围山色中，一鞭残照里。
遍人间烦恼填胸臆，量这般大小车儿如何载得起？

Farewell Feast (opera songs, abridged)

Lucid clouds in azure skies, [扬抑4]
Yellow flowers o'er the motley wilds.
Westerly wind 'pon moors and mounds;
Hurrying swans on high to the South.
What's it dyes the frosted trees
Red at sunrise as wine-flushed cheeks?
Tears from bleeding eyes of those
Leaving each the other in woe!

Pitiful, getting together so late;
Hateful, being disjoined in haste.
Long as the willow hangs its twigs,
Ne'er to be tied with them his steed.
Don't let the sun ascend apace,
Autumn woods, please have it stayed!
Slower, slower, that horse a-trotting;
Closer, closer, this carriage following.

Drying leaves disperse 'fore the breeze;
Withering grass looks grim in haze.
Ling'ring on parting as swallow and shrike,
Flying asunder far and wide.
Name in advance the date you'll be back,
'Fore your journey you actually take.
Soon you'll be far, once out of my sight.
Just from my hand a cup of wine
Drink to our future happy life!

There my head is mazed already.
Tears are gushed as if blood were jetted.
Heart is crushed into ashes chilly. ...
Early to bed at halfway hamlets.
Venture not into wretched weathers! ...
Yonder hills my carriage stop;
Shadowy woods my view now block.
Track and traveler are not to be seen;
Evening mist grows thick in between.

Ancient road at sunset hushed;
Not a single stir is heard,
Fading neighs of the horse except.[1]
Cornfield by gentle Zephyr swept.
Here and there are hillocks dull,
Carriage lonely returning at dusk.
All the woes of the world packed hard
Weighing down my helpless heart,
How could the tiny vehicle bear
Such a load too huge for her?

〖评注〗

(1) 即 Not a single stir is heard, except fading neighs of the horse. 介词可后置。

(continued) Scholar Zhang told Madame Cui to send her servant to ask Flying Tiger to wait just 3 days for Yingying "to go through some mourning rites for her father". In the meantime, Zhang wrote a letter to his friend General Du, Commander of an army guarding a nearby pass, requesting that he quickly come to the rescue of the besieged folks. The letter was delivered by a brave monk, who fought his way through. General Du arrived with his troops and Flying Tiger surrendered. But unexpectedly, at the dinner given by Madame Cui expressing her thanks to Zhang, she called Zhang"Yingying's elder brother", and informed him that during the lifetime of her husband, Yingying had been betrothed to a nephew of hers. Zhang's heart-breaking disappointment won the sympathy of Yingying and her maid Red Rose. Red Rose acted as a messenger in exchanging love poems between the girl and the young man. By and by Madame Cui came to see that things had gone too far for her to keep the two apart. At last, though reluctantly, she gave her consent to their union. However, she demanded that Zhang must become a successful candidate in the imperial examinations before they got married, and he must proceed to the capital the very next day, in spite of Yingying's parting sorrows.

在红娘撮合下，一对情人的结合，已势不可挡。老夫人便强令张生，立即进京赶考，取得功名，才能成为前相国家的女婿。别筵上，莺莺柔肠愁损，苦口叮咛。

天净沙·秋思[散曲]

马致远（1250?–1322?）

枯藤老树昏鸦。
小桥流水人家。
古道西风瘦马。
夕阴西下，断肠人在天涯。

〖评注〗

(1) traveling ...(及物动词分词短语)修饰上行One，这两行同上也是“主语句”，无谓语动词。

“枯藤老树昏鸦。小桥流水人家。古道西风瘦马。”三句并列9种事物；可以类比于晚唐温庭筠著名的五言诗《商山早行》：“晨起动征铎，客行悲故乡；鸡声茅店月，人迹板桥霜……”（动征铎，摇响了提醒旅客该要出发的大铃铛。有人理解征铎指车铃，似乎不对，因车上不装大铃。）鸡声、茅店、月亮、人迹、板桥、霜痕，两句6种名词。并列的形象却自然紧密结合为深广的图景。

我们从本篇开始，在四首元曲小令标题后，注明[散曲]（以别于下面更多词作与诗篇）。散曲是对应于元代及以后的戏剧曲词（成套曲作）而言。散曲和曲词，从元朝兴起，都属“元曲”。

“曲”有曲牌，和“词”有词牌相似，其“副题”也像词牌的副标题，标明所写主题。如本篇，“天净沙”是依照特定乐曲的曲牌，“秋思”是写的内容。

唐宋“词”的早期，词还叫做“曲子词”，按词牌所指曲谱，都可以唱。到后来，词渐渐脱离音乐。元曲，则是另一种新兴配乐文学，都可以唱。它和词不同的是，字数既可更多、也可更少；可在规定字数之外，添加衬字，不占主要节拍。平仄声字，可以相互押韵。相应散曲，可以组合成为套曲、以至中型或大型演唱或者戏剧。

To the Tune *Clear Skies O'er Sands*

Withered vines and ancient trees; [扬抑4]
Flocks of crows at twilight drear.
Tiny bridge across a stream;
Cottage small with nobody seen.
Highway ancient in chilly winds;
Rover on a shabby horse so lean.
Setting sun 'pon horizon gray.
One with broken heart on his way,
Traveling farthest lands in dismay.[1]

蟾宫曲·叹世[散曲]

马致远

咸阳百二山河：
两字“功名”，几阵干戈！
项废东吴，刘兴西蜀：
梦里南柯。

韩信功兀的般证果？
蒯通言哪尽是风魔？
成也萧何，败也萧何：
醉了由他！

〖今译〗

咸阳故都的屏障，百倍险阻的山河，
二字迷朦：功名；几番把戏：干戈。
项羽起兵于东吴，终遭败落，
刘邦封土于西蜀，得奏凯歌：
尽如云烟、同梦南柯！

韩信丰功伟绩，为何那般悲惨的后果？
蒯通怂恿反叛，哪里全属发疯、入魔？
飞黄腾达，也在于萧何，
身败名裂，也由于萧何。
我们举酒尽醉，悠悠然有何不可！

Regrets Over Earthly Events
(To the Tune *The Toad Palace*)

O mountains high and rivers wide, such sure defense; [抑扬6]
And that has served a single purpose — glories in vain.
And brought about but something bothering — battles at pains.
Just think of Liu the Emp'ror arising from the West[1],
His rival Xiang the Overlord biting the dust in the East:
Aren't both the stories as airy as those of which one dreams?

Why should what Han Xin'd achieved result in such a fate?
How might what Kuai Tong'd argued be deemed a madman's raves?
Success was due to Xiao, who understood you the best;
Downfall was due to the same, who helped to plot your death[2].
We would as well be tipplers — free from every stress!

〖评注〗

(1) About Liu and Xiang, see p.28 *The Last Song at Gaixia*, Comments.

(2) the same 指 the same person。 Han Xin was the leading general in the service of Liu Bang, who put an end to the *Qin* despotic regime and became the first emperor of a new imperial dynasty(206 BC). Han Xin helped Liu to defeat Liu's formidable rival Xiang Yu. But Han was groundlessly persecuted after the country was unified. Kuai Tong, a counselor of Han's, had advised him to break off from Liu Bang and create an empire of his own. Han did not listen to him. Xiao He was the prime minister. It was Xiao who at first recommended Han to be chief commander of Liu's troops. And finally it was Xiao himself who assisted Liu's wife to get Han trapped and killed. See p.30, Note 1.

塞鸿秋[散曲]

（元）张鸣善（生卒年代不详）

东边路、西边路、南边路，
五里铺、七里铺、十里铺。
走一步、盼一步、懒一步。

霎时间天也暮、日也暮、云也暮。
斜阳满地铺，回首生烟雾。
兀的不山无数、水无数、情无数！

〖评注〗

(1) expect another step and a third step (to be) no harder, 盼望下一步和再迈一步不要更加吃力。

(2) O all the rivers …! 无谓语的感叹句，叹这种事物之太多。(that) you have got to pass, 修饰 rivers and ranges 的定语从句。

“五里/七里/十里铺”的“铺”字，读第四声，是名词构成地名。“斜阳满地铺”的“铺”字读第一声，是动词表示铺展开来。这就有了仄声和平声间相通的尾韵。

从本篇语言，也可看出，“曲”比“词”更多使用民间口语，如“霎时间”、“兀的不”，上面《西厢记》“量这般大（的）小车儿如何载得起”（296页）、上篇《蟾宫曲·叹世》“兀的般证果”（302页），下《牡丹亭》“呖呖莺歌溜的圆”（314页）、《红楼梦》曲《枉凝眉》“想眼中能有多少泪珠儿”（329页），都是明显例证。

To the Tune *Wild Geese in Autumn*

O wandering east, or west, or southward on and on, [6音步]
One passes hamlets five or seven or ten *li* from town.
While making a step, you expect another and a third no harder;[1]
The sky turns dusky, the sun goes down, the clouds get darker.

The whole of the earth by twilight tinted gray, [5音步]
On turning your head you see but hovering haze.
O all the rivers and ranges you've got to pass![2]
And all the woes and worries wearying your heart!

山坡羊·潼关怀古[散曲]

（元）张养浩(1270—1329)

峰峦如聚，波涛如怒，山河表里潼关路。
望西都，意踌躇。
伤心秦汉经行处，宫阙万间都作了土。
兴，百姓苦！
亡，百姓苦！

〖评注〗

(1) as if arrayed 是 as if they were arrayed 之略。下 Below, billows 含辅音头韵和行内韵。

(2) 第三、四、五行Surrounded by ... shielded by ... guarded by ...都修饰第六行 The City is/comes in sight 。

(3) 这里 as 引导让步从句，相当于 Though the Ancient Capital used to be thought secure 。

(4) 前面用 down, 是强调倒装；正装词序是 Its palaces were burnt down ... 。

(5) 读作 how WOE-ful's the WAY-side WIL-d'rness THAT has SEEN … 其中wilderness用了缩略形式。

Thoughts upon Ancient Times
(To the Tune *Goats on Hillsides*)

O peaks above me look as if arrayed; [4音步]
Below them, billows seem to be enraged.[1]
Surrounded outside by rivers roaring,
And shielded within by mountains soaring,
And guarded by *Tongguan* the strongest Pass,
The City's in sight — I'm quite at a loss.[2]

Secure as the Ancient Capital used to be thought,[3] [5音步]
Yet down were its palaces burnt and brought to naught.[4]
How woeful's the wayside wild'rness that has seen[5]
The dynastics *Qin* and *Han*, the emp'rors and queens!
Alas, as they spring up, toiling like hell were the folks!
And then as they toppled, suff'ring to death were the folks!

满江红·金陵怀古

（元）萨都剌（1272—？）

六代繁华，春去也，更无消息。
空怅望，山川形胜，已非畴昔。
王谢堂前双燕子，乌衣巷口曾相识。
听夜深、寂寞打孤城，春潮急。

思往事，愁如织；怀故国，空陈迹。
但荒烟衰草，乱鸦斜日。
《玉树》歌残秋露冷，胭脂井坏寒螿泣。
到如今，唯有蒋山青，秦淮碧！

Meditations Over Jinling Ruins
(To the Tune *River All Red*)

Gone are all of the Southern Dynasties' dandy days! [扬抑6]
Gone as spring is, nowhere to be seen again or traced.
Grandiose sites, the land, the shores, now desolate,[1]
Not in the least resemble those of the bygone age.
Only pairs of swallows seem acquaintances of yore,
Flying out of the lane possessed by former lords.
Deep in the night, you hear the spring tide ceaseless striking,
Rash and rude, at the walls of the City lonely, declining.

Woe does weigh me down, with doleful events in thought.
Debris's drear, where royal riches are past recall.
Withering weeds enveloped in mists o'er mounds and knolls.
Swarms of hovering crows at sunset crying coarse.[2]
"Backyard Flowers" is sung no more 'mid autumn frost.[3]
Rouge-Wall Well in ruins, with cicadas whining in remorse.
See, just Wooded Hills are still so stately, serene;
Calm and cool, remains the *Qinhuai* River as green.

〖今译〗

短短六个王朝的珠光宝气、轻歌曼舞，
都像春风匆匆过路，一去全无踪影。
我枉自惆怅，眺望大好山河、天然盛境，
可怜眼前已远远不是，旧日的情景。
双双紫燕住过王家谢家的高耸门庭，
现在飞向寻常房檐，乌衣巷口又相逢。
如今夜深时分，只听长江春潮汹涌，
拍打着寂寞孤独、已不是为京都的古城。

回忆往事桩桩，惹人忧虑万端。
故国不堪回首，空留陈迹斑斑。
荒凉烟雾中，满目是衰颓野草连绵，
西斜落日里，只听得归巢鸦啼缭乱。
《后庭花》之歌，早在清冷秋露间消散，
“胭脂井”石壁，已在寒蝉哀泣中倒坍。
今朝但见，苍翠钟山依然，
秦淮流水，碧绿一如当年。

〖评注〗

(1) desolate，第一和第三个音节都重读。

(2) crows ... crying coarse(ly)，辅音头韵。上下各有 royal riches past recall, ... still so stately, serene 。关于上面两行所讲的燕子， 参见 115页《乌衣巷》（“旧时王谢堂前燕，飞入寻常百姓家”）评注。

(3) 玉树，指南朝末代君主陈叔宝《玉树后庭花》，“妖姬脸似花含露，玉树流光照后庭”。“Backyard Flowers” was a song composed by the last king of the short-lived *Chen* Dynasty. One day in 589, a few years after he had written the song and set it to music, the enemy troops invaded and were breaking into the palace. The king hurried, together with his concubine, to hide in a dried well in the palace

garden. They were captured in no time and brought to the North. The fallen king soon met his death in detention. The well where they hid themselves was called Rouge Wall Well. It was said that if one made a scratch on its wall, there would be a momentary rouge-like trace.

原文中的"胭脂井"，指陈后主与宠妃藏身其中的景阳宫"辱井"，他们在这里被找到后，成为俘虏，囚死异国；据说该井石壁用手一划，就出现胭脂痕迹。寒螀，秋蝉。蒋山，指金陵城东的钟山，也叫紫金山，蒋山，因东汉当地县尉蒋子文葬于山上。参见 204页《桂枝香・金陵怀古》评注 3 。

萨都剌的怀古之作，反映他对当代的思虑。

词中"王谢堂前双燕子"、"寂寞打孤城，春潮急"、"荒烟衰草，乱鸦斜日。《玉树》歌残秋露冷"等，分别取自刘禹锡《乌衣巷》《石头城》（116页）和王安石《桂枝香・金陵怀古》（204页），原是："旧时王谢堂前燕"，"潮打空城寂寞回"，"但寒烟、衰草凝绿。至今商女，时时犹唱、《后庭》遗曲"。

而所有前人语句，到这里全都融合无间，却也难得。

萨都剌另有《念奴娇》词，同是金陵怀古之作："石头城上，望天低吴楚，眼空无物…… 东风辇路，芳草年年发。落日无人松径里，鬼火高低明灭。歌舞尊前，繁华镜里，暗换青青发。伤心千古，秦淮一片明月！"

As seen from atop of the Stone Town, so low the vault of Heaven hangs;
Beneath, a blank expanse extending afar — the South-East lands.
Tracks left by monarchs' carriages yearly with green grass overgrown;
The sun goes down; 'mid pinewood shades not a single soul is found,
Where only will-o'-the-wisps are on and off, there up, here down.
No more are your singing and dancing, no more those mellow wines of yours,
With your shining mirrors wherein on the quiet your hair was turning hoary,
O leaving with later and later ages just mourning and the moon as glorious!

临江仙·说秦汉

（明）杨慎（1488–1559）

滚滚长江东逝水，浪花淘尽英雄。
是非成败转头空。
青山依旧在，几度夕阳红？

白发渔樵江渚上，惯看秋月春风。
一壶浊酒喜相逢。
古今多少事，都付笑谈中！

〖评注〗

(1) Sunsets have glowed, it seems, merely several times. 看来夕阳仅仅红过几次而已。

(2) to have chats/chitchats over jugs of wine 意思是“常常一面喝酒，一面闲谈”。

(3) to be bandied about，传过来、传过去，随便议论。

杨慎这首小令，被明末元初的小说家罗贯中借用，作为《三国演义》的开篇词，在那里，罗贯中并未注明词作的出处。因而有人误会，以为那就是罗贯中本人所作。翻阅所选比较全面的选集，不难找到杨慎的一系列咏史篇章，这一篇仅为其中之一、咏叹秦汉阶段的一首；由于《三国演义》的引用，使它广为人知。

“滚滚长江东逝水，浪花淘尽英雄”，使人想起苏轼的《念奴娇》

Chatting About *Qin* and *Han* Dynasties
(To the Tune *Fairy Upon the River*)

Rolling on and on e'er eastward the River Great, [扬抑6]
All those countless heroes by torrents are washed away,
Right or wrong, successes or losses, ending in smoke.
Mountains green alone remain from days of old.
Merely several times, it seems, havc sunsets glowed![1]

Hoar-haired fisher and woodcutter live by the riverside,
Vernal breeze and autumn moon refreshing their lives.
Cheerful chitchats they have o'er jugs of homemade wine.[2]
What a lot of momentous occurrences recent or remote
Now are bandied about with laughs, with amusing jokes![3]

（216页）“大江东去，浪淘尽，千古风流人物。”而“一壶浊酒喜相逢。古今多少事，都付笑谈中！”又好似陈与义的《临江仙》（242页）“闲登小阁看新晴。古今多少事，渔唱起三更。”

《牡丹亭·惊梦》片段

（明）汤显祖（1550–1616）

原来姹紫嫣红开遍，似这般都付与断井颓垣。
良辰美景奈何天，赏心乐事谁家院！
朝飞暮卷，云霞翠轩；
雨丝风片，烟波画船。
锦屏人忒看得这韶光贱！

遍青山啼红了杜鹃，荼蘼外烟丝醉软。
春香啊，牡丹虽好，他春归怎占得先？
“成对儿莺燕啊！”
闲凝眄，生生燕语明如翦，呖呖莺歌溜的圆。

〖今译〗

原来是千般姹紫、万种嫣红开满园，
只留给一眼枯井、几段残墙无人怜。
太稀少美好的辰光，不长存秀丽的景色，有谁奈何苍天。
既难得赏识的情意，更奇缺欢乐的因缘，曾在哪家庭院！
晨光中飞过彩云，暮色里卷起雨帘，云霞雨露飘洒在翠阁堂前，
丝丝的春霖，片片的风烟，迷茫烟波中泛来轻盈的画船；
可惜关在闺阁里的人啊，太不懂这韶光多值得欣羡！

洒遍青山，啼鹃之血化作杜鹃花，染红了大小山峦，
荼蘼花外，柳色如轻烟般连绵，柔丝似迷醉般娇软。
春香啊，虽然说牡丹无比地浓艳，春去百花残，岂不让她枉然争先？
“看那成双成对儿的莺莺燕燕！”恣意凝神细赏玩，
一声声燕语清清晰晰似言谈，一串串莺歌啁啁啾啾多宛转！

Garden Sight-Seeing
(songs from *The Peony Pavilion*[1])

See such abundance of flowers bursting out [抑扬5]
In all the shades of red bright and purple proud!
Alongside, however, of dilapidated wells[2]
And tumbling walls, amidst such woeful wastes.

O what a wondrous day with its wond'rful views
For us to enjoy our life by Nature bestowed!
In who else's sunny garden are sensible souls
To prize such hosts of pleasures as Heavens propose?

At dawn are colored cloudlets flying past;
By dusk like curtains lifts the overcast.
'Mid threads of rains and shreds of gentle wafts,
Adrift are painted barges on misty waves.
Yet kept behind, you maids, behind your screens,
Are letting slip this colorful season in vain.

With cuckoos crying and bleeding, tinted bloody
Are azaleas abloom across all hillsides so lushy![3]
Beyond the roseleaf raspberry, faint and fainter,
A mist of gossamer meanders and falters.

Though most alluring the peony will appear anon,
Too late she'll be to vie with flowers of spring!
I leisurely peer and pay attention around,
Hark! Swallows' chirps like cheerful chatter sound;[4]
And orioles' twitters trill so rich and round!

〖评注〗

(1) The Peony Pavilion is an opera written by Tang Xianzu of the *Ming* Dynasty. The drama tells of the "Love prevailing over Death" story of a maiden Du Liniang.

Liniang's parents were faithful observers of feudal ethical codes, denying her any pleasure of her flowering youth. Yet on an early-spring day after she had some stealthy garden sight-seeing, she felt tired, fell asleep and dreamed of meeting a young scholar to whom she felt dearly attached. Waking up from the dream she was quite at a loss.

She was taken badly ill with lovesickness, died and was buried beside the Peony Pavilion in the garden. Her parents moved to another town. A young scholar Liu Mengmei, none other than the one she had dreamed of, stayed at the former residence of Liniang's family. That place was now a monastery. He was staying there on his way to the capital to take part in the Imperial Examinations.

While he was studying deep into the night, Liniang's spirit came up to him, asking him to dig open her grave and help her come back to life. With the help of the monastery abbot, Liu did so, and Liniang really sat up in her coffin, revived and got out of her pit. Through the union of the two, Liniang's wildest dream came true.

(2) dilapidated、三节overcast、四节gossamers重读音节各二。

(3) The azaleas, in such bright red radiance blooming all over the wilderness, are said to be blood stains of the cuckoo. It is said that the cuckoo is the incarnation of an ancient time king, King Wang. To learn more about the king who died in the prime of his life and whose spirit returns in spring in the shape of the crying bird, see p.290, In Answer to Deng's Bidding Farewell, Note 1. 杜鹃本是古蜀国望帝的魂灵。望帝原是猎人，因屠龙治水、救民于灾难，被拥立为帝。但不久被害。其魂魄难舍故园，春来化鸟回乡，直啼得满口流血，血溅山林，化作鲜红杜鹃花。见290页 评注1 。

(4) 前"春香啊"、"成对儿莺燕啊"是侍女春香插话，其余是唱词。

《牡丹亭·寻梦》片段

汤显祖

最撩人春色是今年。
少什么低就高来粉画垣？
原来春心无处不飞悬。
哎，睡荼蘼抓住了裙衩线，恰便是花似人心好处牵。
这一湾流水呵！

为甚呵，玉真重溯武陵源？
也则为水点花飞在眼前。
是天公不费买花钱，则咱人心上有啼红怨。
咳，辜负了春三二月天。

那一答可是湖山石边？
这一答似牡丹亭畔。
嵌雕栏芍药芽儿浅。
一丝丝垂杨线，一丢丢榆荚钱。

那般形现，那般软绵。
忑一片撒花心的红影儿吊将来半天。
敢是咱梦魂儿厮缠？
咳，寻来寻去，都不见了。
牡丹亭、芍药栏，
怎生这样凄凉冷落，杳无人迹？
好不伤心也！

偶然间心似缱，梅树边。
这般花花草草由人恋，生生死死随人愿，
便酸酸楚楚无人怨！

Search for Dreamland
(opera songs, abridged)

Exceedingly tempting this very spring for me, [5音步]
The vernal scene suggesting a fabulous dream.
To what effect those white-washed garden walls,
Now higher, now lower, encircling bushes and lawns?
As is understood, there's no confining of such,
Such stirrings of love awak'ning with springtime buds.

O there the roseleaf raspberry seizes my skirt,
Like human souls preferring fantastic mirth.
Is Yuzhen returning to her fairyland stream, and why?[1]
'Tis just that fading petals're lavished wild;[2]
The peaceful surface of the lake is dotted thereby.

Though Heaven needn't pay for all the flowers
Being blown apart, let vanish as smoke and clouds,[3]
Yet those of tender hearts can't help themselves
Regretting in tears the decay of the pink and the red.
What piteous waste of the golden days of the year,
When youth should not be blessed with charm and cheer?

The rock'ry I dreamt of, appearing on the farther side?
And here's the spot, the Peony Pavilion by?[4]
Elm pods' coins — chains, and weeping willows — lines,
My dream showed peony in sprout by railing refined.
So striking, so melting: the feeling of floating away.[5]
Red petals' sudden dropping brought me awake.

Perchance by dream I've been under a delusion hurled?
O things I dreamt of are not to be recovered there,
And none to be seen, nor a whisper, a stir, to be heard.
Pavilion, flower beds, surrounding rails,
Altogether deserted, desolate is the place,
To my sad disillusionment and sour dismay.

Now somehow my straying heart is tightly drawn
To a nearby plum tree which I've known in my dream.[6]
Were blossoms and bushes abloom to be prized with our souls,
We living, dying and reviving by choice of our own,
Then ne'er would be given these grumbles, growls and groans!

〖评注〗

(1) Yuzhen, a fairy, met her lover by the fairyland stream when peach blossoms were abloom, and had him spend with her 6 happy months. Then in autumn the youth went back to his native village to see his parents. But later on returning to the fantastic fairyland, he failed to find the right stream amid so many mountains and valleys. Yuzhen also missed him and often came to stroll along the stream alone. Here by "Yuzhen", the maiden Du Liniang refers to herself, missing her beloved she met in her dream.

(2) wild 代替 wildly。'Tis that ... 可以回答 Why ...? 比较 Shakespeare 名句（It is) Not that I love Caesar less, but that I love Rome more.

上行"玉真重溯武陵源"指《神仙记》刘晨、阮肇遇仙的桃花水源；东汉时，刘、阮在天台山（今浙江东部）采药，遇二仙女，留居桃源洞府六个月，回乡看时，村庄零落，人间已过七世、三百多年。二人又向桃花溪水寻觅仙洞，再也找不到了。武陵源另指东晋陶潜《桃花源记》所写武陵（今湖南常德）渔人发现世外乐园处。

(3) Being blown apart, 是修饰上面 all the flowers 的现在分词短语；let vanish as smoke and clouds, 是 let 分词短语，修饰上 flowers 。

(4) 相当于 And here is the spot, by the Peony Pavilion?

(5) 上节说"梦"，上行主语是 My dream ， 因而这里 feeling 指梦境。

(6) My heart is tightly drawn to a plum tree nearby "心似缱，梅树边"，依恋梅树，暗示日后让她起死回生的是过路岭南书生柳梦梅，未来的丈夫。本篇与上篇都是女主人公杜丽娘的唱词。

小说《红楼梦》23回叙述：《牡丹亭》曲词"只为你如花美眷、似水流年……你在幽闺自怜"，在大观园梨香院女伶排练中、伴着悠扬笛音传到路边，触动黛玉衷情，使她"心痛神驰，眼中落泪"。

天仙子

陈子龙（1608—1647）

古道棠梨寒恻恻，子规满路东风湿。
留连好景为谁愁？
归潮急，暮云碧，
和雨和晴人不识。
北望音书迷故国，一江春雨无消息。
强将此恨问花枝，
嫣红积，莺如织，
侬泪未弹花泪滴。

〖今译〗

古道春寒犹厉，两行棠梨但觉凄寂；
一路子规哀啼，东风暗送阴湿气息。
大好春光，能几何时？留恋处为谁堆起愁绪？
潮水急急涨落，暮云层层染碧，
谁知天能开晴或只有雨水淋漓？
北望中原，故国音信沉迷；
鱼雁无踪，漫江飘洒春雨。
强打精神，试问花枝，这一腔幽恨你可知悉？
嫣红撒布遍地，黄莺惊飞来去；
我的泪水尚未涌出，残花间已是清泪滴滴！

To the Tune *Fairies' Song*

What sad, sad birches along the ancient road, [5音步]
With cuckoos crying, easterly wind so moist!
How come you're grieved? Regretting spring on the wane?[1]
The tide ebbs hastily, th' afterglow the horizon paints.
No telling whether it's going to clear or to rain.

With ne'er a message from North the dear old land,
Whole lot of the river veiled in vernal rains.
O whom am I to ask but the flowers on twigs?[2]
Yet petals fall apace while orioles quit.
From branches tears come dribbling 'fore mine would drip.

〖评注〗

(1) How (does it) come (that) you're grieved? 比…I'm grieved 更逼真。

(2) but 在此是介词表示"除了"（except, apart from）。

关于陈子龙和他的学生夏完淳的抗清事迹，见下322页夏完淳《卜算子》词评注 1 。下面末行 'fore 是 before 之略。

卜算子

夏完淳（1631—1647）

秋色到空闺，未扫梧桐叶。
谁料同心结不成，翻就相思结！

十二玉栏杆，风动灯明灭。
立尽黄昏泪几行？一片鸦啼月。

〖评注〗

(1) In the year 1644, the troops of the *Manchu* nationality marched south from their homeland in the Northeast. They established the *Qing* Dynasty, to replace the *Ming* Dynasty with *Han* nationality monarchs. Broad masses of the Han people put up bitter resistance against the plundering and slaughtering conquerors.

Chen Zilong(author of 《天仙子》 on p.320) and Xia Yunyi were two of the resistance leaders. Xia Yunyi was captured by the overwhelming enemy and killed. His son Xia Wanchun, only 14 years of age then, joined Chen Zilong in the struggle. Again their uprising failed and Chen died in the battle. The fighters were forced to scatter across the South provinces. Xia Wanchun, writer of this poem, was not long roving about. He was arrested, tortured, yet flatly refused to surrender, and kept silent about his comrades' whereabouts. The then 17-year-old young man met his death with great composure. And

To the Tune *Fortune Telling*

Your cheerless chamber'd be chilled by autumn shades;[1] [5音步]
The yard would be heaped with fallen plane leaves unswept.
What woe! A knot of attachment to tie we failed;
In the knot of pathos both are trapped by fate![2]

O'er rails now here now there you linger and linger;
In winds by the window a faint light flickers and flickers.
You'd stand in trickling tears till late in the night,
A crescent appearing, restless crows would cry![3]

---

this poem was to be left to his wife. The couple were married only less than a year before.

夏完淳之父夏允彝（1600?-1646），和陈子龙同是松江（今上海）人；夏允彝在二人第一次抗清起义失败时，已被俘殉国，留下遗嘱，让15岁的儿子夏完淳继承遗志。夏完淳12岁就“抵掌谈国事”，“千言立就”；14岁随父夏允彝、师陈子龙起兵，赋《即事》一诗（见70页《从军行》评注2）。在同老师陈子龙最后一次发动起义失败、老师牺牲后不久，他自己也被抓获。他被解送到南京，关押80天，怒斥企图软化他的降将洪承畴后从容就义，年仅17岁。《卜算子》是他写给妻子的，为自己牺牲之后闺中的凄寂先感痛心。

（2）knot 表姻缘或纠葛： a love knot, the knot of marriage, nerves in knots.

（3）restless crows would cry! 不安的乌鸦将会啼叫起来！

《桃花扇·寄扇》片段

（清）孔尚任（1648—1718）

寒风料峭绣帘薄，香炉懒去烧。血痕一缕在眉梢，胭脂红让娇。孤影怯，弱魂飘，春丝命一条。满楼霜月夜迢迢，天明恨不消。冷帐寒衾，……听那挂帘栊的钩儿兀自敲。记得一霎时，娇歌兴扫，……乱云、山风、高雁杳。

哪知道梅开有信，人去越遥。凭栏凝眺，把盈盈秋水，酸风冻了。欺负俺贱烟花薄命飘摇，倚仗他丞相府忒也骄傲。为保住这无瑕白玉身，免不得要撞碎如花貌。

……取出侯郎诗扇，展看一番。唉呀，都被血点污坏了，这怎么处？你看疏疏密密，浓浓淡淡，鲜血乱蘸。不是杜鹃抛；是脸上桃花洒红雨，点滴滴溅上冰绡。

叫奴家揉开云髻，折损宫腰。睡昏昏似妃葬坡平，血淋淋似妾坠楼高。怕旁人呼号，舍著俺软丢答的魂灵没人招。银镜里朱霞残照，鸳枕上红泪春潮。

Bloodstains Blossoms[1]

While silken curtains by chilling puffs are penetrated,[2] [6音步]
Too listless I am to have the incense burner lighted.
On tip of my brow remains that bloodstain, fresh and bright;
It looks so smart and showy as if rouge on purpose applied.

Alone with the shadow of my own, being ever torn and worn,
My soul is as frail as fluff a-flying 'fore springtime storm.[3]
The chamber steeped in frosty moonlight, long, long's the night —
And even with day now dawning, my anguish still resides.
My bed and curtain forlorn, my quilt e'er frigid feels;
Some hooks off window screens are knocking in winds so fierce.

What charming songs were cut short, coming the threatening news!
O'er mounts through winds and clouds like a wild goose gone were you!
While plums are in blossom timely, nothing from you has been heard.
I watched and watched on rails; by frost my eyes were hurt.

The so-called Premier sent his lackeys to snatch me from home —
I'm a mere down-trodden singsong girl, so humble and low.
For the sake of my perfect purity like a flawless jade,
I couldn't choose but spoil my fair, fair flowery face.
My companion's the fan with the poem sincere by you composed.
But, oh, that too was stained by drops of blood, behold!

Here thin, there thick, or light, or dark, all dotted round.
'Tis not from a cuckoo's bloody tears but my face's wound.
With high-rise coils disheveled, fragile body bent,
I dashed my head 'gainst the wall and, bleeding, lay in a faint.[4]

And Mom was to take my place on the sly to go with the rogues,
With anxiety — should I be left alone and cruelly ignored!
The mirror shows a cloudlet flushing in sunset's glow,
My embroidered pillow's flooded by bitter tears on the flow!

〖评注〗

(1) The *Peach Blossom Fan* is an opera written by Kong Shangren of the *Qing* Dynasty. The drama relates the true story of the union and parting of a singsong girl, Li Xiangjun, with a young scholar, Hou Fangyu. The *Ming* Dynasty was then about to be replaced by the *Qing* Dynasty set up by the *Manchu* nationality. Li Xiangjun showed her firmness and loyalty in love, struggling against the persecution of a handful of high-ranking *Ming* officials. Their lackeys came to grab her from her home with the intention of making her a concubine of one corrupt courtier. She dashed herself on the wall and, from the wound on her brow, blood was splashing all around. The fan her lover had given her as a souvenir of their betrothal was stained. But later on, one of their friends succeeded in completing a painting of peach blossoms on the fan making use of the bloody stains.

(2) penetrated 第一和第三音节重读，仍构成六音步诗行。

(3) fluff a-flying，英诗常在动名词前加-a（原义 on）。

(4) 原文“妃葬”“妾坠”借贵妃、绿珠之死（见130页）描绘香君撞昏，宜于意译。

蝶恋花

纳兰性德（1655—1685）

辛苦最怜天上月，一夕如盘，夕夕都成玦！
若似月轮终皎洁，不辞冰雪为卿热。

无那尘缘容易绝，燕子依然，软踏帘钩说。
唱罢秋坟愁未歇，春丛认取双飞蝶！

〖今译〗

天上月亮既是辛苦更为可怜：
只一夜如玉盘般圆满，剩下每夜每夜都残缺不全！
如果你能像满月般，永远皎洁在天，
我不怕霜空的凄寒，定把冰轮焐暖。

没奈何尘世姻缘被轻易割断，
空见旧宅燕子似当年，轻踩帘钩，软语呢喃。
凉秋坟前把挽歌唱完，愁思依然不断；
等向阳春花丛认得双蝶吧，你我化去翩翩！

To the Tune
Butterflies Love Blossoms

Toilful and doleful indeed is the Moon up there, [扬抑5]
Once a month a disk refined and fair,
Waning through all the other long, long nights.
Were the Moon fore'er at the full and bright,
Fearless of its icy chill as such was it made,
Warm it up I would for you, for your sake.

Helpless against the Fates destroying ties on earth, [扬抑6]
Cruelly the two are severed to belong to separate worlds.
Only a pair of swallows of yore seem still the same,
Each to th' other on curtain hooks keeps chirping away.[1]

Autumn elegy drawing to an end 'fore your grave, [扬抑5]
Yet there isn't an end to my anguish and grief.
Surely we'll turn into butterflies flitting along,
Side by side in spring 'mid bushes abloom![2]

〖评注〗

(1) 相当于 to each other 的 Each to the other 可保持"重-轻-重-轻"的节律。

(2) 如说 turn butterflies 其中 turn 是系词；这里turn into butterflies 中 turn 是不及物动词。

枉凝眉（《红楼梦》曲）

曹雪芹（1715?—1764）

一个是阆苑仙葩，一个是美玉无瑕。
若说没奇缘，今生偏又遇着他；
若说有奇缘，如何心事终虚化？
一个枉自嗟呀，一个空劳牵挂。
一个是水中月，一个是镜中花。
想眼中能有多少泪珠儿，
怎经得秋流到冬尽，春流到夏！

Bewailing in Vain

From a fairyland, thou formerly a flower divine, [抑抑扬4]
He, a disc of jade immaculate, refined.
Were it not for both of you predestined,
Ye'd meet again for this existence?[1]
Or yes, if predestined indeed, as is believed,
O why your yearning cometh to grief?[2]

Thou groanest, bemoanest, bewailest in vain;
He is worried and vexed to no avail.
For thee, he is a moon reflected in water;
For him, thou a blossom's image in mirror.
Could thou have such innumerable tears[3]
To well from thine eyes thro' autumn and winter severe, [抑扬5]
On streaming till spring and summer of another year?

〖评注〗

(1) In the novel *A Dream of the Red Mansions*, this poem is a song telling the story of Lin Daiyu, the leading girl character of the tragedy. Lin Daiyu is said to have been a fairyland flower in her previous existence; and her lover Jia Baoyu, to have been a divine jade, which took the shape of a youth. The youth has been watering that flower to save her from drought. So she owes him vast volumes of tears to be paid back in this present existence of hers. This novel is widely accepted as the most significant work throughout Chinese literary history. The author borrows some imaginary setting for sidelights only, and the essence or the highlight of the novel is the young rebels' — Daiyu and Baoyu's — desperate struggle against the formidable yet crumbling feudal system.

表"你们"古旧的 ye 属主格。Longfellow *Children*：Come to me, O ye children!

(2) your yearning cometh(comes),那your在旧日专表"你们的"（thy/thine,你的）。

(3) 末三行可印证，原著不同于高鹗续作，原 80 回后的残稿提示，黛玉是因为宝玉在抄家时被拘走，经秋冬春夏而不归，自己心疲泪尽而亡。

葬花吟

曹雪芹（《红楼梦》黛玉诗）

花谢花飞飞满天，红消香断有谁怜？
游丝软系飘春榭，落絮轻沾扑绣帘。
闺中女儿惜春暮，愁绪满怀无释处。
手把花锄出绣帘，忍踏落花来复去？
柳丝榆荚自芳菲，不管桃飘与李飞。
桃李明年能再发，明年闺中知有谁？
三月香巢初垒成，梁间燕子太无情！
明年花开虽可啄，却不道、人去梁空巢已倾。
一年三百六十日，风刀霜剑严相逼。
明媚鲜妍能几时？ 一朝飘泊难寻觅！
花开易见落难寻，阶前愁煞葬花人；
独把花锄暗洒泪，洒上空枝见血痕。
杜鹃无语正黄昏，荷锄归去掩重门。
青灯照壁人初睡，冷雨敲窗被未温。
怪侬底事倍伤神？半为怜春半恼春。
怜春忽至恼忽去，至又无言去不闻。
昨宵庭外悲歌发，知是花魂与鸟魂？
花魂鸟魂总难留，鸟自无言花自羞。
愿侬胁下生双翼，随花飞到天尽头。
天尽头，何处有香丘？
未若锦囊收艳骨，一抔净土掩风流。
质本洁来还洁去，不教污淖陷渠沟。

尔今死去侬收葬，未卜侬身何日丧。
侬今葬花人笑痴，他年葬侬知是谁？
试看春残花渐落，便是红颜老死时。
一朝春尽颜色老，花落人亡两不知！

〖略译〗

柳条和榆钱只管自己滋润蓬勃，
哪在意桃花李花纷纷凋谢飘泊？
桃花和李花，还能盼得明年花开，
闺房的主人呵，谁知她明年何在？
辛苦三月天，一座香巢刚刚建成，
梁上的燕子，为什么要离去匆匆？
明年即使、有新花开放可啄得香软，
闺阁空空，尘满屋梁，旧巢已无踪！

短短一年中间，这三百六十几天，
狂风呵，如尖刀！寒霜呵，似利剑！
将花枝劈砍、摧残！
能够何时，让你明媚鲜艳？
忽然间飘落凋零，寻不见你的容颜！
开时你在枝头，落去难以追寻，
香阶下愁坏了，为你相送的人。
花锄拿在手里，清泪滴在衣襟，
枝头也沾着泪痕，像血迹淋淋。

Burial of Fallen Flowers

As the flowers are falling and flying the azure across, [抑扬5]
Who's to pity the colors faded, the fragrance lost?[1]
O'er Spring's pavilions wafting gossamer light,
'Pon curtains embroidered fluff from willows quiet.

The retiring maid regretting for Spring to depart,
Unable to do away with woes from her heart.
Now hoe in hand, down portal and steps she goes —
She's loath to tread on petals to and fro!

Elm-pods and willow-floss, enjoying the day,
Care not if blossoms from peaches and plums would fade.
Next year the flowers will bloom again as fair;
Her chamber, alas, may fail to keep her there!

Thro' March your snug and scented nest is completed.
O Swallow heartless, why are you soon to leave?
Tho' next year the garden may offer petals as sweet,
Your hostess'd be gone, your nest be blown from the beam!

For all the hundreds of days around the year,
Let stabbed by storms, attacked by frostbite fierce,
How long can blossoms remain in bloom so bright?
Once blown away they're scattered far and wide!

Abloom, they're gay; all scattered, hard to trace.
With an aching heart, the maid's to dig them a grave.
Her hoe in hand, her secret teardrops gush,
And stain the bare sprays just like drops of blood.

Now silent is the cuckoo, as falls the shadowy night.
Her hoe back brought, all gates are shut at quiet.
A greenish light then sees her wearily in doze[2],
A chilly rain still pattering, bedclothes cold.

Why ever so overcome, overwhelmed am I by woe?
Because of missing and hating spring, of both —
So dearly I prize her, suddenly despaired by her flight.
On the sly she arrives; without a word she retires.

Last night, a sad song hovered the garden over.
Was it the soul of birds or the soul of flowers?
They're not to be stayed, all the souls of the bygone while,
For birds are shy, and flowers can never reply.

Could I this very day be winged to fly
With petals on winds to remotest corners of skies!
Yet even the horizon beyond, at the uttermost bound,[3]
Might there a fragrant mound for your burial be found?

I'd better get your remains in my silken pouch,
With clean earth piled above, your graces to shroud.
Since pure you came, as pure I'll see you go,
For you in mire or ditches not to be fouled.

Now dead you are and I come to bury you.
Who's there to tell what time I'm going too?
Let people laugh at my folly, my burying flowers.
Just who's to bury me on one of the morrows?[4]

Behold, there Spring is waning and flowers flying.
In wake of them the fair yet faded is dying!
Once flowers finished, the fair be faded out,
Whatever traces could ever remain thereabout?

〖评注〗

(1) the azure across，相当于 across the azure(the blue sky)。英诗中介词可后置，参见下边评注3。

(2) 英语文学语言常用无生命事物作 see 的主语，如说 My coat has seen five years of service.

(3) even the horizon beyond （介词后置）等于 even beyond the horizon 。参见8页《蒹葭》评注3 。

(4) morrow,诗歌用语，相当于 tomorrow 。on one of the morrows，最近哪一天。tomorrow也可用复数，如谚语：One today is worth two tomorrows.

比曹雪芹年龄略小、极可能是其友人的明义，读《红楼梦》手抄本前80回、并听说后40回梗概或见到下文片断之后，写了20首《题红楼梦》绝句，特别能够验证黛玉之死，是因宝玉被拘、远别经年，而不是像续书所说为自己得不到他。明义写这些绝句时，还没有高鹗的续书。下面是诗前小序及其中二首：

序："曹子雪芹出所撰《红楼梦》一部，……惜其书未传，世鲜知者，余见其抄本焉。" 题红楼梦之十八："伤心一首葬花词，似谶成真自不知；安得返魂香一缕，起卿沉痼续红丝？"（《葬花吟》暗含预示结局的谶语；但愿我能让黛玉从沉痼中复苏，让月老所牵红丝接续起来！）题红楼梦之二十："馔玉炊金未几春，王孙瘦损骨嶙峋；青蛾红粉归何处？惭愧当年石季伦。"贾府荣华未能经久，抄家导致门庭败落，宝玉潦倒憔悴；他像西晋的石崇石季伦，自愧获罪而累及所爱。（石崇故事见 130页《金谷园》评注）

"三月香巢初垒成，梁间燕子太无情"：原在阳春三月，宝、黛亲事已经说妥，秋天贾府就被抄家，宝玉被拘捕。根本原因是，一朝天子一朝臣，贾氏家族届时必然失宠。宝玉一去经年，困在"狱神庙"受苦。黛玉日夜悲啼，终于，以全部忠贞血泪，报答了自己平生唯一的知己。

唐多令·咏柳絮

曹雪芹（《红楼梦》黛玉词）

粉堕百花洲，香残燕子楼；
一团团、逐队成球。
飘泊还如人薄命，空缱绻，说风流！

草木也知愁，韶华竟白头；
叹今生、谁拾谁收？
嫁与东风春不管，凭尔去，忍淹留！

〖今译〗

百花洲前，零粉落英逐水流，
燕子楼外，残蕊余香到了头。
飞絮牵连成队，旋转如球。
你像人一般薄命无缘，随风飘走，
枉然有缠绵恩爱，空称道一往风流。

草木一样懂得哀愁？
大好年华，你早衰白头。
可叹今生零落，谁来把你拾起收留？
你卷进东风逝去，春君啊，竟不能相守！
任你长辞枝头，唯一知己忍心留连背后！

Willow Down
(To the Tune *Sugary Ditty*)

As pollen littered over the Flowery Island, [柳扬5]
So fragrance faded about the Swallow Villa.
All flying off as though in files and flocks,
O patches of willow-down being driven apart,
You're just like humans, homeless, roaming afar!
Now neither your sentiments will have you spared,
Nor such sublimity will get you anywhere.[1]

E'en bushes and trees from annoyance unsaved? [柳扬4]
Your hair turns hoary in youthful days!
"Alas, for my lifetime, be short as it may,[2]
Whoever is to have me kept and cared?
And Spring should have for me no regard —[3]
While he by himself is to linger in retard,
I'm to go with the wind, away to pass?"

〖评注〗

(1) 二行中 sentiment 与 anywhere 各有两个重读音节。

(2) be short as it may 相当于 Though my lifetime may be short, ... （柳絮自语）。

(3) 相当于：And should Spring have no regard for me, while ...?曹雪芹《红楼梦》写到第80回；后文残稿显示，宝玉在抄家时被拘走，经年不归，黛玉天天啼哭，悲痛致死。这柳絮词预示黛玉被风雨卷去，知己不在她身边。见330页评注 3。

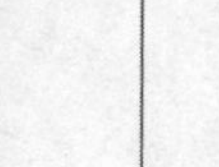

己亥杂诗（之五）

龚自珍（1792—1841）

浩荡离愁白日斜，吟鞭东指即天涯。
落红不是无情物，化作春泥犹护花。

〖评注〗

(1) 原诗说“东指”，但大方向是向南。鸦片战争前诗人从腐败清廷的京城辞官返江南故乡，出广渠门（东便门南）向东再转弯南行。the east then the South：后面 the South 指江南大地。

(2) 龚自珍词《减字木兰花》*To the Tune Magnolia*（Shortened）前有小序：偶检丛纸中，得花瓣一包，纸背细书辛幼安“更能消几番风雨”一阕，乃京师悯忠寺海棠花，戊辰暮春所戏为也，泫然得句。词云：“人天无据，被侬留得香魂住。如梦如烟，枝上花开又十年。十年千里，风痕雨点斑斓里。莫怪怜他，身世依然是落花！”

O destiny never has things the regular way.
By luck I've preserved your fragrant remains to this day.
A dream, so vaguely recalled as if by thin mists smeared,

Leaving the Capital

As the sun declines, my parting grief pours forth unbounded, [抑抑扬6]
With a whip now cracking, pointing to th' east then the South remotest.[1]
Yet fallen petals, bloody red, are never heartless —
Into vernal soil transmuted, they'll nurture flowers in earnest.

'Mong bushes blossoms bloomed and faded thro the years.[3]
A dozen years and a myriad miles beyond,
Still there such stains and spots from savage showers!
No wonder I feel for what you've undergone —
This lot of my own is the same as the fallen flowers'![4]

(3) 上面第三行的名词短语 A dream … recalled … 修饰本行的主语和谓语 blossoms bloomed… 。(Among) bushes blossoms bloomed，辅音头韵；下面有 Still … such stains … spots … savage showers 。

(4) This lot of my own 比 My own lot 更加强调自己这特殊的身世。正如 That (cruel) master of theirs 语气要比 Their (cruel) master 强烈得多。

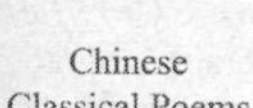

水调歌头

梁启超（1873—1929）

拍碎双玉斗，慷慨一何多？满腔都是血泪，无处著悲歌。三百年来王气，举目山河依旧，人事竟如何？百户尚牛酒，四塞已干戈！

千金剑，万言策，两蹉跎。醉中呵壁自语，醒后一滂沱。不恨年华去也，只恐少年心事，强半为销磨。愿替众生病，稽首礼维摩。

〖今译〗

忿然击碎，一双晶莹的酒杯；
慷慨激昂，心潮冲撞着心扉。
我满腔奔流着，热血和苦泪；
我要引吭哀歌，却无处可容我倾吐伤悲！
清王朝已延续三百余年，旧山河仿佛还满目依然，
但仔细看，今日人间：
权贵们仍沉湎于酒海肉山，
边疆已干戈四起、烽烟弥漫。

价逾千金的宝剑除奸御侮，铺述万言的大略救险扶危，
竟双双沉沦而销毁。
酒醉后，向墙头责地问天，妄吐狂言；
清醒时，任泪水涌流，如大雨连绵。
所恨的，不是大好年华虚度；
而是青春之理想，如今几尽摧残。
我仅能向佛陀顶礼膜拜，
祈求代替众生，来把苦难承担！

To the Tune *Prelude to the Waters*[1]

That pair of emerald tumblers I've smashed with a blow. [抑扬5]
O how is the fervent vehemence flaming high!
With blood-stained tears on swelling not to be choked,
To whom uncover my bitter grievance could I?
The dynasty's already hundreds of years of age;
Although the rivers and mountains are still the same,
Yet how affairs of the nation are found to stand?
Our bigwigs are giving banquets gorgeous and grand,
All borders being broken through by brutal bands.

In vain my thousand-tael-worth sword was gone;
No use that memorial on salvation strategies so long.[2]
Whatever painstaking efforts at length went wrong!
I rant and rave a-facing the wall when drunken,
But cooling off, I burst into tears like torrents.
'Tis not my waning youth effects the torment;
'Tis youthful aspirations wearing away
That sorely has me dejected, plagued and pained.
Devoutly I kneel, entreating 'fore Buddha's shrine:
O rather than the people's, let suff'rings be mine!

〖评注〗

(1) 这首诗写于1898年"戊戌维新"失败之后。

(2) memorial on …在这里指呈交皇帝的"奏章"，意见书，即原文"万言策"。下面隔行 a-facing：由 on 演化而来的 a-，在文学语言中可加于动名词使用，如词典例句 Set the bells a-ringing. 关于"呵壁"，见104页评注屈原向壁画问天故事。

挽刘道一

孙文（1866—1925）

半壁东南三楚雄，刘郎死去霸图空。
尚余遗业艰难甚，谁与斯人慷慨同？
塞上秋风悲战马，神州落日泣哀鸿。
几时痛饮黄龙酒，横揽江流一奠公！

〖今译〗

三楚雄据一方，控制东南半边；
刘郎为民捐躯，鸿图一时虚幻。
遗留未竟的任务呵，倍加艰难，
哪里再找你那慷慨激昂的呼唤？
塞北秋风里，疲于奔命的战马悲鸣；
神州夕照下，穷山旷野间哀鸿呜咽。
何时直捣满清老巢，到黄龙府举杯饮宴？
我们横揽大江清流，来把你的英灵祭奠！

Lamenting the Death of Liu Daoyi

The mightier half of the South-East, massive *Yangtze* shores![1] [6音步]
At Daoyi's decease, aborteth abrupt our noble cause.[2]
What onerous enormous tasks with us thou leavest behind?[3]
And where again will we hear that stirring calling of thine?

On frontiers, battle stallions neighing in autumn breeze,
O'er famished inland, wild geese cry at sunset bleak.[4]
A victory party being given at Tartars' den one day,
Let all of the river's waters be poured a libation to thee!

〖评注〗

(1) 孙文，字中山，号逸仙。其通用于英语中的名字是后者的译音 Sun Yat-sen。感叹句常有省略，这句相当于 The massive Yangtze shores (are really) the mightier half of the South-East! This poem was written either at the end of the 19th century or at the very beginning of the 20th century. The author of this poem, Sun Wen, has another name better known to westerners — Sun Yat-sen. He was the leader of the democratic revolution in China. It was through his relentless efforts, supported by his comrades and the broad masses of the people, that the *Manchu*(*Qing*) Dynasty was at last overthrown and the Republic of China was founded in 1911.

(2) departeth 和 aborteth 中的-eth 是旧时单数第三人称动词词尾，相当于现在的 -es/-s（如departs, aborts）。abrupt 相当于 abruptly。

(3) thou leavest 是旧时单数第二人称代词与其动词变位形式，相当于 you leave。thou 的宾格是thee（译诗末），相应物主代词是 thy(your), thine(yours)（下行末尾）。

(4) 成语“哀鸿遍野”喻流离民众在凄厉呼号。

对酒

秋瑾（1877—1907）

不惜千金买宝刀，貂裘换酒也堪豪。
一腔热血勤珍重，洒去犹能化碧涛！

With Wineglass in Hand

Ne'er grudging paying a thousand tael for a valuable sword,[1] [6音步]
I exchanged my marten coat for wine of my own accord.
O cherish to ourselves our ardent blood of highest worth —
By bloodshed a raging tide will be roused to refresh the world.

〖评注〗

(1) The author, young poet Qiu Jin, was a fervent democratic revolutionist. She had been to Japan to study, and there joined the Chinese Revolutionary League led by Sun Yat-sen. On returning to China, she founded the *Chinese Womens' Journal* in Shanghai. Then she worked as a college teacher, but was at the same time engaged in preparations of an armed uprising. Four years before the feudal *Qing* Regime was overthrown in 1911, she was raising an insurrection in *Shaoxing* City in response to actions in other provinces, when the *Qing* troops besieged their college. She fought alongside her students in an attempt to break through but failed. The *Qing* authorities put her on the rack trying in vain to make her reveal information about other revolutionists. She stood unyielding through all savage tortures. Unflinchingly, she died a heroine's holy death at the age of 30. A monument in her honor was put up in *Shaoxing* after the 1911 Revolution.

tael,（专指货币重量）两，银两。该词源出印度也按重量计算的货币单位。

“琴瑟友之，钟鼓乐之”（《关雎》），“红酥手，黄縢酒”（《钗头凤》），固然和美，但何以好景不常，又是风雨如晦？聆听中华诗章，何以欢歌少于哀唱？从《黄鸟》“彼苍者天，歼我良人”、《离骚》“虽九死其犹未悔”，到李白“我寄愁心与明月”、杜甫“环珮空归月夜魂”、苏轼“多情却被无情恼”、辛弃疾“料不啼清泪长啼血”，直到龚自珍“落红不是无情物”、秋瑾“一腔热血勤珍重”——为什么历代吟咏中这么多慷慨悲凉呢？

法雕塑家罗丹着力刻画的有：低头焦虑《思想者》的绞断肝肠，垂头失乐园《夏娃》的魄落魂销，埋头老歌女《欧米哀尔》的皮枯心死。罗丹说，比美更美的是“美的凋残”— “What is more beautiful than the beautiful is — the beautiful battered.” (A. Rodin) That is, to be sure, why some tragedies are more soul-stirring than comedies.

那就是悲剧的力量所在吧！鲁迅说，悲剧将人生有价值的东西毁灭给人看。草木零落，美人迟暮（屈原）；悲风动白茅，葬尽满城娇（李商隐）；风雨牢愁，寒蛩四壁（文天祥）；风刀霜剑严相逼（曹雪芹）。传统悲歌当代还在唱，是为寻求那比“美的凋残”还更美的吧？那是什么呢？如果不是植根尚半冻泥土中“美”的孕育和萌发？

What is more worth our further seeking after, if it’s not — BEAUTY evolving and a-budding, rooted in an icy soil a-thawing?

图书在版编目（CIP）数据

历代诗词曲英译赏析 / 刘国善等编译.
北京：外文出版社, 2005
ISBN 978-7-119-04261-9

I. 中… II. 刘 … III. 英语-对照读物，古典诗歌-汉、英 IV. H319.4: I

中国版本图书馆CIP数据核字（2005）第112472号

责任编辑：蔡莉莉
封面设计：邱特聪
内文制作：华审书装
印刷监制：张国祥

历代诗词曲英译赏析

刘国善 王治江 徐树娟 等 编译

出版发行：外文出版社
地　　址：中国北京西城区百万庄大街24号　邮政编码 100037
网　　址：http://www.flp.com.cn
电　　话：(010) 68320579/68996067（总编室）
(010) 68995844/68995852（发行部）
(010) 68327750/68996164（版权部）

印　　制：外文印刷厂
经　　销：新华书店 / 外文书店
开　　本：880mm × 1230mm 1/32
印　　张：11.625
字　　数：250 千字
装　　别：平
版　　次：2009年第1版　2009年第1版第1次印刷
书　　号：ISBN 978-7-119-04261-9
定　　价：25元　建议上架：翻译类